ISBN 978-0-282-97920-1
PIBN 10874464

1 MONTH OF
FREE
READING

at

www.ForgottenBooks.com

By purchasing this book you are eligible for one month membership to ForgottenBooks.com, giving you unlimited access to our entire collection of over 1,000,000 titles via our web site and mobile apps.

To claim your free month visit:

www.forgottenbooks.com/free874464

English
Français
Deutsche
Italiano
Español
Português

www.forgottenbooks.com

Mythology Photography **Fiction**
Fishing Christianity **Art** Cooking
Essays Buddhism Freemasonry
Medicine **Biology** Music **Ancient
Egypt** Evolution Carpentry Physics
Dance Geology **Mathematics** Fitness
Shakespeare **Folklore** Yoga Marketing
Confidence Immortality Biographies
Poetry **Psychology** Witchcraft
Electronics Chemistry History **Law**
Accounting **Philosophy** Anthropology
Alchemy Drama Quantum Mechanics
Atheism Sexual Health **Ancient History**
Entrepreneurship Languages Sport
Paleontology Needlework Islam
Metaphysics Investment Archaeology
Parenting Statistics Criminology
Motivational

MAN AT THIS EARTH

TO

THE MAN POSSIBLE

OF

AN ESSENTIAL BEING OF THE

UNIVERSE

———

BY

LEONIDAS SPRATT

JACKSONVILLE, FLORIDA

———

PRESS OF
THE H. & W. B. DREW COMPANY
JACKSONVILLE, FLA.
1902.

COPYRIGHTED, 1902.

ADVERTISEMENT.

This work is an effort to present by inductions of phenomena the hypothesis by deductions from which there are the phenomenal beings of the universe. And finding this in the being finite of beings infinite, of their affinities simply, in reciprocal limitations of each other, it further finds that this being finite at its every time and place about the axis of this universe is the product, and but the product, of such infinite factors. And such the star, sun, earth, plant and animal, from the universe to man, that such is man himself, but the being possible of that essential being of the universe.

INTRODUCTORY PREFACE.

This title, of "Man of this earth to the man possible of an essential being of the universe," intends a theory of nature and of man in nature; and of nature in the revolutions of a casual mode of finite being to be termed life, and of man, but the final term of that nature, at this earth.

It intends that there is being, and an universe of being, and but being in that universe, and that this is the being finite of beings infinite in reciprocal limitations of each other. That this is in spheroids and wheels of relatively static being in revolution on their axis of being dynamic. That dynamic being is life and static being the nature of that life. And such the universe of static being in revolution on its axis of being dynamic — that such is the star in revolution on its individual axis and in its eliptical orbit of revolution on the axis of the universe; and such the sun in its orbit of revolution on the axis of the star; and such the planet in its orbit on the axis of the sun; and such the matter of this earth in its orbit of revolution on the axis of the earth; and such the plant in its orbit of revolution on its axis of matter; and such the animal in revolution on the plant, and such the man in his revolution on the animal — each at its time and place, but the nature possible of life in resolution into it from the axis of the universe. And, intending that there is this being finite, and that this is the essential being of which are the beings of the universe, and that each being in its order is the being possible, and but the being possible, of that essential being; it intends that man himself is such. And that man, therefore, is not to the ends of his own invention, or to those of an anthropomorphic Theos in operation upon being otherwise existing and inert, but is simply to those of his finite being possible, and is — as is the animal and plant — to his most, therefore, and his best that he may be his most, of his means of subsistence on this earth; and to the man, therefore, possible of an essential being of the universe.

To man, in conscious being at this earth, there are two questions of capital importance. The *first* is whether there be an essential being of the universe? And the *second* is whether man, at this earth, is to the states and races of the most man possible, and the best man possible that he may be his most? And this title is affirmative of both.

It affirms that there is such being, and that this is the being finite and this the product of infinite factors in reciprocal limitations of each other. And that, of this, there are the universe and the beings of the universe to man at this earth, inclusive.

It intends that where there is now this universe of finite beings there was originally infinite being, merely. That this differentiated into infinites inversely to each other. That these were vacua and plena, reciprocally, and, as vacua, reciprocally, were reciprocally attractive, and as plena, reciprocally, were reciprocally repulsive, and of their reciprocal attractions were in coincidence on the axis of their neutral being intermediate; and, of their reciprocal repulsions, were in differentiations thence into spheroids and wheels of the most of the one infinite relatively static in revolutions on their axis of the most of the other, relatively dynamic. That every such spheroid was a being finite; and, — such the every infinitessimal unit finite — such was the universe of units finite, and such, of units finite reacting into each other, was the every being finite from the unit to this universe, inclusive.

It intends that the atomic infinities — but inversely of an integral being infinite — were, with respect to their neutral being intermediate, the one dynamic and the other static; and the one in eccentric radiations of its dynamic being to enlarge the other, and the other in concentric radiations of static being to constrict the one. And that thus, of their special radiations into each other oppositely, there was, and is, the spheroid and wheel of both; but each an orb, the one of being dynamic and the other of being static, the static of which is in revolution on its individual axis and in an elliptical orbit of revolution on the dynamic as its axis, the center of which is at one of the foci of such orbit. And intending that such is the unit of finite being and such the universe of units, it intends that the dynamic is heat and the static cold; and the one the minus and the other the plus of electricity; and the one the negative and the other the positive atom of the matter molecule; and the one the acid and the other the base of the matter compound; and the one the staminate and the other the pistillate principle of the plant; and one the male and the other the female of the animal; and the one the parent and the other the offspring of the human family; and the one the ruling family and the other the subject family of the human state; and dynamic being life, and static being the nature of that life — that the one is the life and the other the nature of the universe and of the every being of the universe, — but, at its time and place, the spheroid and wheel of static being in revolution on its axis of being dynamic.

But while such is the theory of nature and of man in nature intended by the title and confirmed by the existence and constitution of every being from the universe to man, which, without their being finite into the beings finite of it possible were the miracle of consequence without cause, or the work of an anthropomorphic Theos on being otherwise existing and inert — the neither of which is conceivable — I have not been fortunate in making it acceptable. This is the third of my efforts to present it, and so far I have had the response of no man of science ready to affirm the being finite as the exclusive source and cause of being in this universe. And the men of this, the foremost human state, are not only unwilling to admit that man at this earth is to the man ultimately possible of such being, but insist that he be to the man possible of parties of adult males, the major of which, for the time of its majority, is to be his government. And any failure to make it acceptable has been for the reason, I assume, that I have failed to make it intelligible.

The first of my efforts (assuming too inconsiderately the acceptance of the truth that there is an essential being of the universe in which is life, of which is nature, of which is man) was to the end that man, of this, was to the man possible of his means of subsistence possible. But finding this unconsidered, and, for the reason it seemed of an imperfect presentment of the nature intended, my next was to the end that there is nature in the static being of a dynamic being to be termed life in an essential being of the universe; and finding this unconsidered and for the reason, it seemed, of an imperfect presentment of that essential being, I now, in this, propose to show that there is such being. That there is being, and an universe of being, and but being in that universe. And that this is the being finite of the infinite will and word of God in space. That there is being finite of beings infinite in reciprocal limitations of each other; and the will and word of God — the causing cause — in such the finite of his beings infinite; and space the insensible substance of that word becoming sensible in finite beings, of which, at this earth, are plants, animals and man. And that the men could not exist without such being more than could the animals and plants. Nor more than the animals or plants can they live to other than the man possible.

And such the theory of man at this earth to the man possible of an essential being of this universe, it involves four, and but four, important propositions —

The *first*, that there is such essential being of the universe.

The *second*, that in this there is life and of that nature.

The *third*, that of this life in nature there is man.

And the *fourth*, that man of nature is not to the man of his own inventions, or to a man of the manipulations of an anthropomorphic Theos, but is simply to the most man possibly able to subsist upon the provisions available at his time and place in the course of life in nature from the axis of the universe.

And to the *first* it is contended that there is such being for the reasons —

First: That there is an universe of sensible beings which could not exist without their essential beings insensible.

Next: That there is being finite — possible, but of beings infinite in reciprocal limitations of each other, which is universal and exclusive of other being in that universe, and which, therefore, is the essential being of that universe.

Next: That there is the word, expressive of the will of God, which is universal, and exclusive of other being in that universe, and thus the essential being of that universe.

And next: That there is an essential being, of which are force, matter, and the mind of man, and all forces and matters man is able to perceive — the existence of which is established in the fact of their reactions.

It is intended that there is the reaction of beings, infinite or finite, but as they be of the same essential being inversely. That so, inversely, they are reciprocally vacua and reciprocally plena; and as vacua attractive, and as plena repulsive of each other, reciprocally.

And that, of their attractions, when adjacent, they meet upon an axis of the shortest line between their centers; and of their reciprocal repulsions are in radiations thence into a spheroid and wheel of both, in revolution on its axis of the one — dynamic, propelling the other, relatively static. That such beings of the same essential being inversely are so reciprocally intussusseptive of each other into the neutral being intermediate of both. That this is their reaction, whether physical, chemical or physiological; that this is possible but of beings so related, and that in that beings react there is conclusive proof that they are of the same essential being. And that for this reason all forces are of the same essential being, since every force reacts with every other; and all matters of the same essential being, since every matter reacts with every other; and all forces and all matters of the same essential being, since every force reacts with every matter; and force, matter and the human mind of the same essential being since force and matter react with the human mind. That every perception by the mind of an external object is a reaction between essential somethings in the mind and object. And that there is an essential being, therefore, not only of force, matter and the human mind, but of every being sensed by mind.

And that force and matter are of the same essential being for the further reason that any matter under force sufficient, whether of impact, pressure, or projection, even, is sublimed to force.

And it is intended that there is such being in the fact that there are in mind conceptions of the units of such being. In every human mind there are ideal spheres, in quadrants, each a cone, the apex of which is the center of the sphere, and its base the surface of the quadrant, and its axis the shortest line between its apex and the center of its base, the every section of which, by a plane at angle with its axis, is conic, and circular, elliptical, parabolic, or hyperbolic, as the plane be at right, acute, or obtuse angles with such axis. And such the sections of every cone, of every quadrant, of every ideal sphere, existing in the mind of every man as the condition of geometrical, or trigometrical truth, analogously such, are the elements of every such conic section. In the circle there are quadrants, complementary and supplementary, and in each sine and cosine; tangent and cotangent; secant and co-secant and in the ellipse parabola and hyperbola, there are elements of these beings about their centers, analogously such as are those of the circle, which can exist with the ideal spheres containing them, but as they be insensible reali- ties, and the products in the human mind of its reactions with a kindred being of the universe. And intended that these ideal spheres are real, and the originals of beings becoming sensible in spheres, and of the moments of force and the molecules of matter inorganic in stars, sun, and earth, and organic in plant, animal and man at this earth's surface, it is intended that a conspicuous and conclusive instance of such ideal spheroids becoming real, is this earth.

Intended that the earth is a being finite, and that at its time and place in the teleologic evo-involution of an universe of such being, it is a spheroid and wheel of atomic infinities, the one dynamic and the other static, and the one heat and the other cold, the one levitation and the other gravitation, reacting on its axis; it is intended that it is a hollow sphere of constrictive matter about its solid sphere of explosive space. And that its crust of matter is in concentric strata, the first metallic, and of metals the densest known; and the next of metallic oxides in granitic rocks; and the next of hydrogens, oxides in waters; and the next an atmosphere of gaseous mat- ters, in which, with oxygens and nitrogens, there are, rarely, the vapors of water, ammonia, and carbonic oxide; and this for the reason that these, its beings, reacting on its axis, would produce such center of space and such strata of matters in such order about it; and for the further reason that a rigid analysis of the phenomena of its mat- ters gives these strata of constrictive matters about its center of explosive space.

And, such the earth, it is intended that, analogously, such is the every finite being of the universe — a hollow sphere of relatively static being possible about a solid sphere of relatively dynamic being in eccentric radiations

to produce it. And, as such, that it is a conspicuous
instance in real being, the ideal of which exists in every
human mind.

And it is intended that there is such being, in that its
existence is the condition of philosophy and science. By
deductions from the hypothesis of such essential being of
the universe we have a philosophy of the phenomenal
beings of the universe, and by inductions of the phenomenal beings of the universe we have a science of such
beings in relation to each other and the universal being.

Second: And, such essential being, it is intended that
in this there is life and of life nature, in that there are life
and nature, the neither of which could exist but of that
exclusive being of the universe. And, in that, there are
teleologic processes of evo-involution and invo-evolution,
the one from the axis of the universe into its disk, and
the other from the disk of the universe into its axis; and
these also in every being of the universe, the one of which
is coincident with life, and the other with the nature of
that life. And the one of which is life, and the other the
nature of that life, the neither of which were possible but
of such essential being, itself, possible, but as it be in
such processes of evo-involution, and invo-evolution. And
that in this being there are life and nature for the further
reason that in this there is the word of God, the universal
cause, which, if not cause of life in nature, were the miracle of cause without consequence. And that there are
life and nature which, if not consequences of cause in that
word of God, were the miracles of consequences without
cause. And that there are not such miracles; that we
have not seen and cannot conceive such cause without
consequence, or consequence without cause; or reason,
or live but in acceptance of one unbroken continuity of
cause and consequence from the universe to man.

We accept God and the word of his infinites reacting
to express his will in beings of them generally, but, from
an extravagant estimate, possibly, of our own importance

we have misgivings as to the ability of this word to execute itself in man; or the plant, or animal, with him at this earth. We assume that, though God has vested infinite power and purpose in his word, he has reserved the power of interference at exigencies, in making it do what, of itself, it might not. That of these exigencies are plant, animal and man, to whose existences he has himself stooped from his throne, and by special creative act, or by anthropomorphic Theos, has caused their execution. Such act by himself, or Theos, were in breach of the uniformity of nature, and a miracle. And while we have not seen, or are able to conceive, the miracle, we yet assume the indefinite series of them necessary to the plant, animal, and man. But there is not only not a miracle seen, or conceivable, but there is not one consistent with the existence of this universe of beings from their one originating cause. To whom there is reason there is God: to whom there is God, there is the word of God. To whom there is the word of God there is the essential being of the universe, and to whom there is this being, to him there are life and nature — the only conceivable means by which, of that universe of insensible being, there can be the sensible beings of that universe. And, to rational man, therefore, the first and second of these propositions are true. And there is an essential. being of the universe, in which is life, of which is nature.

And so also is the *third:* "That of nature there is man." Intended that in the beings of this universe there is process, and that before there were the stars there was the universe; and before there was the sun, stars; and before this earth, the sun; and before the plant, the earth, and before the animal the plant, and before man the animal; it is intended that the cause, whether prime or efficient, of the first of these, is the cause of all. And that the cause of the earth, plant, and animal, is the cause of man. And intended that the efficient cause of earth, plant, and animal is nature; it is intended that nature also is the cause of man.

And that it is so, unless that providence in finite being of which is the nature of the earth, plant, and animal, be incapable of man, to whom, therefore, there is a special providence of God's word, uttered directly by God himself in man, or administered by man himself, or by an anthropomorphic Theos attendant upon man. And it is intended that the being finite of which is nature, capable of the earth, plant, and animal, is capable of man.

That with that in existence, that were no special providence to man. That there is no such providence uttered directly by God in man, and that there is no such providence administered by an anthropomorphic Theos attendant upon man. And that there is no such providence administered by man to himself. That such providence, not through being finite, and every act of its administration by God himself, or anthropomorph, or man, were the miracle of consequence without pre-existing cause, the one of which has not occurred in the course of this finite universe, whose factors do not vary, in even the remotest man, the one millionth of a moment, from their commissions delivered at the axis of the universe.

And it is intended that man is not of such special providence for the reason that, if so, the forces and matters of which is man were different from those of which are the animal and plant; while they are not different as is seen in the facts of their reactions. The forces and matters in man are the same in terms as are those in the animal and plant. And they are the same in fact—since every force in man reacts with every force in the animal, as it could not if not of the same essential being inversely. And every matter in man reacts with every matter in the plant, as it could not if not of the same esssential being inversely.

And intended that man is of the nature of the plant and animal for the reason that their elements of force

and matter are the same, it is intended that he is so, for
the further reason that his modes of being are the same.
Of the matter elements, oxygen, hydrogen, nitrogen and
carbon, reacting on the axis of their neutral beings intermediate, there are spheroids and wheels of life in nature
of which, by variations to the conditions of a larger and
better existence merely, there is the plant cryptogamic,
phonerogamic, endogenous and exogenous; and of these
elements with sulphur and phosphorous in addition, reacting on their axes intermediate, there are spheroids and
wheels of life in nature, of which, by variations to the
conditions of a larger and better existence merely, there
is the animal radiate, annulate, articulate, and vertebrate,
analogous to the four orders of the plant.

And of these elements of the animal, without the
addition of another, reacting on their axes in a sphere of
being beyond that of the animal, there are spheroids and
wheels of life in nature, of which, by variations to the
conditions of a larger and better existence merely, there
is man, agamic, polygamic and monogamic, analogous to
the radiate, annulate, and articulate orders of the animal,
with promise of yet another order in unions of unequal
human races in relations of inequality, analogous to the
vertebrate order of the animal.

It is intended that the first vertebrate animal, to its
food in Silurian seas, then continuously about the earth,
was the fish; which, to its food in marshes beginning to
appear, became the reptile; which, to its food in plants
rising from the soil, became the digitigrade quadruped;
which, to its food by capture, became the plantigrade
quadruped; which to its food in trees became the four-
handed animal; which to its more abundant food and
safety, to be had by methods of procurement, became the
two-footed and two-handed animal, with its organ of intelligence to co-ordinate the activities of its feet and hands.
And it is intended that, by variations to the conditions of
existence merely, this animal has became man.

And that man is of the animal two-footed and two-handed, is in that there was such animal after there was the animal four-handed, and before there was agamic, or polygamic, or monogamic man. And that there was such animal in that there is now such animal in man. And that there was such animal, in that nature were capable of such animal, and, capability cause, were cause of such animal; and that he is of that animal, and of the nature of the animal, therefore, in that man is but the solitary animal becoming social.

Every animal is solitary in that without co-operation or concert each procures by its individual efforts, from the chance products of the earth, the provisions to the continuation of its individual existence. And every man is social in that every one exists upon provisions procured and conserved by several acting in concert. The stock of unmarried mothers and their offspring exists but of these so helping each other. And so does the polygamic tribe and the monogamic state. And there is advancement from agamic to polygamic man, and from polygamic to monogamic man, but as the succeeding mode be better than the one before it to the means of human life possible.

Every such successive mode of association to a common life was as simply a variation of the two-footed and two-handed animal to the animal possible as was any one of those modes of organized activity by which the vertebrate fish became the animal two-footed and two-handed. Beyond the solitary animal two-footed and two-handed there were opportunities of food and safety obtainable by association, and, to obtain them, that animal became social, and is now, whether agamic, polygamic, or monogamic, but the solitary animal, two-footed and two-handed becoming social.

And that as man is without a special providence administered by God, or anthropomorphic Theos, as is the animal or plant; and as he is in continuation of the animal

into the man possible as each successive order of plant or
animal is in such continuation of the plant or animal.
And as the plant and animal are of nature, man is of nature.
Whence, of the three original propositions, there will
remain in question but the—

Fourth: That man of nature is in continuation of
nature to the man possible.

Such man possible were the most man possible, and
the best man possible that he may be his most of the possible products of this earth, cultivated as it can be. And
it is not more certain that man is of nature than that he
is of nature to such man. Such man were in states of
individuals differing in their capacities for duties in such
states. But so situated as that there is a place for each
and each in his place, no one will want the place of any
other, nor would any one strive to be head—not more
honorable than the foot. To such state, in fact, there
were no head, or foot, or artificial terminus, more than
there is to the human family, or other material being of
life, from within, propelling nature, and nature, from
without, regulating life. Each will have found his sphere,
and will have acquired the ability to discharge its duties.
There will be the production possible of provisions for
the support of man possible. These will be conserved to
the lives they are able to support. There will be super-
positions of industries, the ones utilizing the wastes of
others. There will be no wars or disorders, or strikes of
operatives, or oppressions by employers. And each state
will be a perfect exhibition of that ego-altruism of which
man alone is capable.

Egoism is the living for one's self. Altruism is the
living for another, and every being of the universe is
egoistic, in that it is charged with no other existence than
its own. And, charged with no other existence than its
own, no being is altruistic. But there is an ego-altruism
of which man alone is capable, consisting in his living for
others as parts of himself. The first of these ego-altru-

isms are families, the members of which are better as the family is better; and the next states, the families of which are better as the states are better. And under such ego-altruistic feeling the individual will suffer for his family as a part of himself as he will for himself. And the family for the state as for itself. The semblance of such ego-altruism does not appear in any plant or in any animal save in articulate or vertebrate parents for their infant offspring, to cease when the offspring is able to support itself.

And such the state of man possible, it is intended that there is to be such state at every point of the habitable globe. That this habitable surface will be extended; that seas and lands will be re-claimed; that there will be habitations on waters and in mines, and that, ultimately, in peace and plenty, and health and happiness, there will be thousands of men upon the earth to the ones there are upon it now. And that in these there will be the man possible of nature. As such he were the finite product possible of infinite factors reacting as in the animal and plant. And of his own motive, or of motive from any other than that infinite source, he can not stop short of that man possible, more than the animal can stop short of the animal possible, or the plant of the plant possible. And it is as certain, therefore, that man is in continuation of his nature and to the man possible, as that he is of nature, or that nature is of life in such being of the universe.

But, while this is so, there is not to be such man of any single human race alone.

And this for the reason that no single race could become the man possible, or would become the man possible if it could.

The present races are the Agamic, Polygamic and Monogamic. And the Agamic in stocks of unfathered children under the authority of unmarried mothers; and the Polygamic in tribes of wives and children under the authority of polygamic male parents; and the Monogamic in states of the families of monogamic male parents in such relations to each other as may be consistent with their well-being, to be determined by a government representing their respective interests. And such the races, while each were capable of the man possible of that particular race, and the agamic of the man possible of that race; and the polygamic of the man possible of that race; and the monogamic of the man possible of that race — neither were capable of the man possible of all the races combined in supplementary and harmonious relations to each other. Nor, if it were, would it accept of such conditions and be willing to forego its special nature in consideration of a better and more abundant nature of the whole. The whole would represent the course of cause through radiating natures from the axis of the finite universe; the particular race would represent the volitions of its individuals, merely, in assertion of their individual interests in the state. And while, therefore, of the volitional activities of the individuals of any particular race, there might be the man possible of that race, there could not be the man possible of all the races possible, each of which must assert itself in opposition to the every other.

And this, theoretically true, is consistent with the experiences of man. Agamic man, from want of the conditions of a longer human life, has yielded all contested territory to polygamic man. And polygamic man is yielding such territory, for the same reason, to monogamic man, the every state of whom divides into families, capable and incapable, the capables of which are lords, and the incapable commons, who, from their unequal capacities, become subject to a government in lords. But, of the same race, and naturally equal, the families of commons rise, and of the lords fall, until they come to the same plane of social and political equality, when the government becomes representative of both, and is exercised

2

through parties, major and minor, the major of which, for the time of the majority, is imperial in its power over both.

The monogamic states of Europe are now under governments of lords, upon whom their commons constantly encroach, while in those of America the encroachments have ended in recognition of the equality of individuals who exercise their governments through parties of adult males. Of these the foremost is this Republic — the present leader of the human world — and of which there is to be the man possible if of any single race there is to be such man. And of this there is not to be such man.

This Republic is now the leader of the Human world. The Agamic race in England had yielded to the Polygamic; and the Polygamic had yielded to the Monogamic; and the Monogamic in state had become divided into families of lords and commons — the lords possessing the government. But the commons — the natural equals of the lords — by prescriptions had encroached upon their lords until the real government of that state was in the majority of its House of Commons, though nominally exercised by king and lords. This nominal power in king and lords was repudiated by the colonists in their Revolution, who, when victorious, divided into parties of adult males, the major of which, for the time of .its majority, became the government. This ordered progress of the individuals of a state to the functions of self-government has not been made by the people of any other state. It is the condition of advancement in the way of man; and this is, therefore, now the foremost state of man. But while of these parties there may be the monogamic man possible of any monogamic state of man, there cannot be the man possible of all the states of the race of man.

These parties were first known as Tories and Whigs; and next as Whigs and Democrats; and next as Democrats and Republicans. And now, the one is known as Republican and the other is without a name, pending the preparation by prominent men (discontented with their fortunes in the Republican party) of an issue upon which they may defeat it. But that party formed and able to defeat the Republican party will but take its place in a government working, not to the advancement of man to the man possible, but only to the largest share it can take from the state to uses of its partisans. In this contest of parties for the properties of the state, the race of man becomes ignored. There comes indifference to marriage and repugnance to children by whom, only, becoming parents, can the race be continued. And while, therefore, this state — taking immigrants and properties from other states not so advanced — may become, for its time, the grandest state of the earth, it cannot exist perpetually or advance to the man possible through parties simply, warring on each other. Nor, for the term of its existence, can it have even the monogamic man possible. And the less can it have the man possible of its union with a lower race to an intermediate state of both.

In such intermediate state there were the patriarchal power of parents over offspring, and the proletariate power of offspring under parents. There is natural man— from first to last, and from the vertebrate animal two-footed and two-handed to the monogamic man in states of parties warring on each other for its government;— only in the union of parents and their offspring to the provisions for the subsistence and support of both. And such union there were in the intermediate state of unequal races concurring in provisions to a common life.

But, of the parties in this Republic contesting for its properties, there is no such union. Neither is concerned about the advancement of man in other races. Nor is either much concerned about the advancement of man in this Republic. Each would have the state the largest and strongest possible, but only in the hope of getting the control of it, to the enrichment of its individuals. And this state, therefore, while destined to become as much more populous and powerful than it now is—as was

Rome when from a republic it became an empire—it will not forego individual indulgence to produce the man possible.

But such man there will be, if from the center of this universe there be dynamic being into the static beings possible of infinite beings reacting on that center; such dynamic into static being there is if there be an essential being of the universe, which can be but the being finite of beings infinite reacting then in reciprocal limitations of each other. There is in question, therefore, but the existence of this essential being, and to that this work is now addressed. And who rejects the truth of its existence must be prepared to show of what else than beings infinite can there be being finite. And of what else than that finite word of God can there be the life in nature of this universe. And of what else than life in nature can there be man at this earth. And to what other end can there be man of life in nature at this earth than that of the most man possible and the best man possible that he may be his most.

But while quite assured that there is an essential being of the universe of which is man to the man possible, I am equally assured that individual man is not intellectually able to accept this truth; and this for the reason that individual man is not charged with this mandate of the cause of man. The individual, man or woman, is charged simply with the preservation of his or her individual existence—as is the individual animal or plant—and is not more able to produce himself, or herself, into the man—agamic, polygamic, or monogamic—possible than is the radiate animal, male or female, into the orders of animals, annulate, articulate and vertebrate, or the cryptogamic plant into the orders, phanerogamic, endogenus and exogenus. This power of self-production is not vested in the individual man, but is reserved and exercised by the originating and persistent cause of man. And individual man so situated, therefore, and unconscious of his cause, will not be able to accept it consciously. But its existence will be established, rationally, if rationally there appear such essential being of the universe. And to that estallishment is this further argument.

CONTENTS.

___

INTRODUCTORY PREFACE.

This title of man at the earth to the man possible of
an essential being of the universe intends a theory of
nature and of man in nature; and of nature in the resolutions of a finite being to be termed life, and of nature in
the resolutions of that life into the beings of it possible,
the last of which at this earth's surface is man, who, therefore, is to the man possible of that essential being and
him the most man possible and the best man possible to
be his most. To this it is intended that there is being
finite of beings infinite in reciprocal limitations of each
other; that this is original, universal and exclusive of other
being in that universe. And as such that it is being in
units originally insensible but capable of unions into the
beings sensible of which there are the beings in stars,
sun, earth, plant and animal from its universe to man and
the mind of man, inclusive; that to this the beings infinite
and different in products of the finite are fractions,
inversely, of integral infinites; that as such they are
vacua and plena of these infinites reciprocally; that so
they are reciprocally attractive and reciprocally repulsive,
and of their reciprocal attractions are in coincidence on the
axis of their mutual being intermediate, and of their reciprocal repulsions are in differentiations thence into spheroids
and wheels of the one infinite relatively static in revolution
on its axis relatively dynamic, that of these infinites the
ones are dynamic and the others static, relatively, and the
ones fast and the others slow, and the ones eccentric and
the others concentric in the every radiation of their common
being from their axis of reaction, that in this the static is

an orb of relative matter in its elliptical orbit about the
as its center at one of the foci of its ellipse, that such are
stars about the center of the universe, and suns about
stars, and planets about suns; and the crust of the earth
about its explosive center; and the plus about the minus
of electricity, and the positive about the negative atom of
the matter molecule, and the base about the acid of the
matter compounds; and the pistillate about the staminate principle of the plant, and the female about the male
principle of the animal; and the offspring about the parent in the family of man; and the weaker about the stronger
class of families in the state of man, and the weaker about
the stronger states in the races of man; and that thus at
his time and place in the evolution of the being finite—the
essential being of this universe—there is to be the man
possible of that essential being, who is thus destined not to
the ends of his own invention or to those of an anthropomorphic Theos in operation upon being otherwise existing
and inert, but simply to the man possible of his means
of subsistence possible.

But that there is not to be such man of any single
race. It intends that there is an union of infinites necessary to the finite being possible; that such infinites there
were in unions of unequal races; that without this every
state at its maturity in the theoretical equality of its individuals must come under the volition of those individuals
divided into parties major and minor, the major of which
for the term of its majority must be the government and
must exterminate the minor or be exterminated by it, in
either of which events there is the dissolution of the state.
And such the theory, it becomes important to consider
whether there be such essential being.

Chapter I.

And, such the theory of such essential being, it is
of little interest, but of much importance. And of little

interest. Few will consider, or care, whether there be
such being. And fewer still will take the imports of the
terms by which that being is expressed. But it is of much
importance to man himself, at least. If the theory be
true, and there be such being, it will be the only being of
the universe. And in this there will be the life of which
there is the nature of which is man, who, of such nature,
will be to the man possible, and but to the man possible on
earth, of his means of subsistence there available. This
man possible will be the most man possible, and the best
man possible, that he may be his most, at every habitable
place about the earth. In this there will be the most of
human life possible, and the best of human life possible.
There will be peace, order, industry, economy and progress
to a consistent and harmonious community of man, in
which there will be the most and the best of individuals
to the most and best of states, to the most and best of
races to that universal race, the most and best possible.
And it were important to the well-being of present and
prospective man that he consider and accept such theory,
if it be true. And it were more important for the further
reason that man is here on earth to the end, not only of
his individual enjoyments in his earthly life, but to the
end of an eternal providence beyond this life. This may
be in a moral being of the souls of man, who in their
earthly lives have contributed to it, and which, as a civilization, conserves to its existence the lives of man continually coming to exist on earth; or it may be in a heaven or
hell apart from this earth, into which the souls of individuals may go to take the rewards or punishments proper
for their conduct here. If there be such essential being of
life, nature and man in nature to the man possible the
end of that providence, of which is man, is such moral
being of the soul of bettered man to hover and brood the
race of man. But, if there be not such being, the end of
that providence, and of man himself, will be such state of
rewards and punishments, in which the souls of man dis-

charged from man on earth will not be further concerned
about such man. And while of his consideration man may
not alter these conditions, yet, if he is to a moral being
attendant on the race of man upon the condition that he
shall have contributed to the advancement of that race, it
is of much importance to him that he consider of the ways
by which he may advance it. And of importance is the
question, therefore, whether there be such essential being
of the universe.

Chapter II.

The only question that of its existence. If it exist it
is the being finite of the word of God in space, and as
either it is universal and exclusive of other being of the
universe. And is the universal being insensible of which
is the universe of beings sensible. And as such it is the
essential being of the universe.

Chapter III.

There is such space, if there be that which could not
be without it, in that there is cause to consequence; and
consequence to cause; and but cause to consequence, and
but to consequence; and but consequence to cause, and
but to cause; so that throughout the universe there is that
that can be, and that which can be is, or is to be; and
there is such being, therefore, if there be that which could
not be without it. And there is such being also if there
be but one being of which are all the beings of this
universe; and there is but one such being as is shown in
the fact that every being reacts with every other.

Chapter IV.

There were that which could not be without such
being, if there be being finite, or the word of God, or

space, in that each were not only universal and exclusive
of such being but as. that be of it, but were being physiological, as were such essential being, and as it were not if
not of the being finite or the word of God or space.

CHAPTER V.

Nor were there force or matter without such being.
Force were the action of one infinite on another in production of the being finite in such spheroid and wheel of
the one as axle to the other or its disk about the axis of
their neutral being intermediate. At every point in every
such wheel there were the reactions of its factors, the
resultants of which appear to us in the physical forces,
heat, cold, dark, light, electricity and magnetism. And as
there were not these resultants without the infinites in reaction, or these without an essential being of the universe,
there were not force without such being. And so there
were not matter, in that force and matter are the same.
And this, in that they react, as they could not if not of the
same essential being inversely. For this reason all forces
are essentially the same, and all matters the same. And
all forces and matters the same. And they are the same
for the further reason that all matters under force sufficient
are sublimed to the physical forces. And there not being
force, there were not matter without such being, that being
but the syntheses of force, as force is but the analysis of
matter.

CHAPTER VI.

Nor were there life or nature without such being.
Life and nature are the systemic forces of the being finite,
of whose intersections and production of the finite being
pysiological there are the physiological forces. And
regarding this as a spheroid and wheel of the one infinite
as dynamic axle evolving into its static disk and the

other as static disk involving the dynamic axle, the one
in that which in animals and plants are termed life, and
the other that which not only in animals and plants, but in
all other beings finite, we term nature. And as there were
not the disk without the axle or the axle without the disk
of such wheel, there were not life without nature or nature
without life in any being finite. Nor are there these, so
nothings but as they be of the same essential being
inversely; and but as there be such being. And there are
not life or nature, therefore, but as there be such being.

Chapter VII.

Nor were there the universe, star, sun or earth,
without such being. There were the universe, but as it
be the whole of the being finite of beings infinite, and this,
a being physiological of such infinites reacting on its axis
to produce it. Nor were there stars but as they be the
first beings finite possible about the axis of the universe.
And but as they be orbs physiological in orbits about that
axis. Nor were there suns but as they be such orbs in
orbits about the axis of the stars. Nor were there planets but as they be such orbs in orbits about the axes of
suns; or the earth, but as it be such orb in its orbit about
the axes of the sun and universe. Nor were there the
universe, star, sun or earth, but as it be the physiological
product of its systematic factors, the one energy and the
other inertia; and the one in eccentric radiations from the
axis of such spheroid, and the other in concentric radiations from its surface forming; and but as the matter of
such orb be from the reactions of these factors, the one as
levitation and the other as gravitation as they appear at
the surface of this earth and of which are the molecules of
matter in the earth's crust, the one atom of earth such
molecules being of levitation in specific heat and the other
of gravitation in atomic weight, which heat and weight in
every such elemental matter are inversely to each other.

And as there were not these, or the one of these, but on these conditions, there were not the universe, star, sun or earth without such essential being.

CHAPTER VIII.

Nor were there the plant or animal without such being. There are plant and animal at the earth's surface, and the plant in orders cryptogamic, phanerogamic, endogenous and oxogenous; and the animal in orders radiate, annulate, articulate and vertebrate. And the plant of the elemental matters oxygen, hydrogen, nitrogen and carbon; and the animal of these and surphur and phosphorus in addition. And of these matters simply are the plant and animal. There is no evidence of an intermediating agency to produce the plant or animal or to produce the plant or animal through other orders than those now existing. And, as these matters are of force, and force of an essential being of the universe, so are the plant and animal of such being, and were not without such being.

CHAPTER IX.

Nor were there man or mind in man without such being. There were not man, but as he be of the same elemental matters as the animal; nor were there these but as they be of force; nor were they of force but as that be of an essential being of the universe. Nor were there man but as he be of an animal two-footed and two-handed by variation to the means of a larger life from the animal four-footed or four-handed. Nor were there present man of such animal, but as there be unions for life between adults male and female; and between parents and their children. Such animals two-footed and two-handed with an organ of intelligence to co-ordinate the activity of feet or hands were but an animal so long as it were solitary. And it were solitary until there were such

unions, as is the animal four-footed and four-handed.
The adults male and female of these are together only
through the brief periods of their mating. And the
mother is with her offspring only through the brief period
of their helpless infancy. Each at other periods is dependent upon the chance products of the earth for its means of
subsistence, which without union it is unable to cultivate
or conserve, and so were the animal two-footed and two-
handed. But in such unions there were the production
and conservation of provisions for safety and subsistence
to a larger and better animal life than were possible of
the solitary animal. That larger and better life is to be
termed human and that more and better animal of such
life is man. But there were not such man without an
essential being of the universe. There were not the matter of the animal without this. Nor were the variation
of the animal of such matter into the animal two-footed
and two-handed without this. Nor were there the variation
of the solitary animal two-footed and two-handed into the
social animal in families, stocks, tribes and states of man
without such being. Nor were there mind in man without
such being. In every individual man there is a sensitive
being preceptive and reflective of the conditions incident
to the continuation of his individual existence under
them, which, perceptive, we term conscience and, reflective, mind. This is a finite being physiological of infinite
beings kindred and different in limitations of each other, as
is the individual man himself or other being physiological,
and is subject to the attractions, repulsions and inductions
of other such physiologies adjacent as in any other such.
And as there were not this without man, or man without
such being, there were not this mind in man without
such being.

CHAPTER X.

Nor were their law without such being. There is
law. In every being there is the rule that at the time and

place possible of the growing universe it be, and be the being possible at that time and place. This were its law, and this were deliverable to it only through antecedent beings of an one essential being of the universe. And there is thus, therefore, such being, and such intermediary and impersonal course of being in this universe if there be being infinite, or the word of God, or space, or force, or matter, or life, or nature, or the universe; star, sun, earth, plant, animal, man or mind in man, or law in this or other being, but upon the condition, only, that they be realities, and not conventionalities, merely. And real being and not conceptions, to which we give these names. They are such realities if they be of a finite word of God in space. And they are of that finite word.

CHAPTER XI.

In such realities there are the being finite, and the word of God and space. There is being finite, in that there is being not infinite. Being, simply, were being infinite, but being finite is in the limitation of one infinite by another infinite as itself. And as there is being not infinite, there is being finite. But this only of infinites in limitations of each other, and as such it is a reality. There is also the word expression of the will of God that there be the beings of this universe. There is an *anterior* and causing cause of such beings, and there is a consequential and mediating cause of such beings, and this mediating cause must be of the beings of that causing cause. As such it were the word expression of the will of that causing cause. And as such it were reality. And there is also space intervening matters and pervading and intermediating matters from which matters of static force sufficient come and into which matters of dynamic force sufficient go. This is where the finite word of God were. And it is as were the being finite of the word of God. And if it be not in fact the being finite of the word of such is a reality.

CHAPTER XII.

As realities also there are force and matter. There are forces thermal, photol, electric and magnetic. And these in the reactions, physical, chemical and physiological, of matters adjacent. And in the attractions, repulsions and inductions of matters at a distance, and in the levitations and gravitations of matters at this earth's surface. And these forces are the same in that they react with each other; and the same as matters, in that they react with matters; and in that the ultimate analysis of matter is force. And that, in every force, and every matter, and every reaction of forces, and of matters and of forces and matters, there is law; and the law that, of every such reaction at its time and place there be the being of force, or matter, or force and matter, the being possible, and this were possible but as both be of one essential being of the universe, and realities therefore.

CHAPTER XIII.

As realities also, there are life and nature. There is that we term life in plant, animal and man at this earth's surface as the cause of the beings at their times and places possible, the consequences of which cause in these we term nature, and all of these are of matters we term organic. But there is matter in metals, rocks and waters, which we term inorganic, which are the natures of a cause in force, as the plant; animal and man, are the natures of a cause in life. And the matters inorganic, and organic the sources force the casual principle of the one is the same as life, the casual principle of the other. And, their lives the same, their natures are the same. And force and matter realities, life and nature are realities, and realities from being of one essential being of the universe; they are realities also, from being physio-logical, as are force and matter, and as they were not without, they be of such essential being.

CHAPTER XIV.

As realities also, there are the universe, stars, sun and earth. And as such there is the universe. There is the universe. From its immensity we may not be able to perceive it, or conceive it, and we may not be able to perceive, or conceive it, for the further reason that it were inclusive of ourselves, and that the conscious being in man, however perceptive and conceptive, of the beings with which it has to do in continuing itself in man, and in continuing man in nature, may not be, and is not, in fact, perceptive, or conceptive of itself, and the less is it perceptive, or conceptive of an universal whole of that being of which it is. But rationally, if not consciously, there is, to that mind in man, an universe of that being of which there are the beings of the universe. And this by reason of deduction, and induction. By deduction from the hypothesis of such universe of being there is the every phenomenal being possible from the universe to man, and by induction of the every phenomenal being possible from the universe to man there is such universe.

CHAPTER XV.

And, as realities, also, there are the stars. As by reasons of deduction and induction there is the universe, a reality, for the same reasons, there are the stars, reali-ties. There were the universe of space in force and matter but as it be physiological of its systemic factors, the one energy and the other inertia, and the one in eccentric radiations of energy from its axis, and the other in concentric radiations of inertia from its disk. And of these revolving about the axis, there were beings physiological in orbs of matter, revolving on their axes of forces, and these in elliptical orbits and in a hollow sphere, about the axis of the universe, analogously such, and so, as there are molecules of elementive matters about the axis of the earth, from its systemic forces, reacting to produce them in a hollow sphere about that axis. Of these physiological bodies of force in matter, the most conspicuous were those we term stars. These were necessarily of the same being as the universe itself, and that reality, the stars were realities, by reason of deduction merely. But there is the star, a luminous orb of matter from force, with others in a hollow sphere about the axis of the universe, such as the systemic forces of an universal reality were able to produce, and this, if not of that reality, were the miracle or accident of consequence, without cause it is not, and, whether by reason of deduction or induction, as realities there are the stars.

Chapter XVI.

And as a reality also, there is the sun. The reasons of deduction and induction, through which it appears that the star is a reality, as is the universe, are equally efficient to show that the sun is a reality as is the star. By deduction from the star as a reality there were smaller orbs of matter about their centers of force, included, and these in their orbits about the centers of stars as those were about the centers of the universe. And about every such star there were mediately, or immediately, one such orb as is the sun, and about this there were orbs in elliptical orbits, such as are the planets. And the sun were in a crust of metallic matter about its center of space included. And about this there were its atmosphere of metallic and metallic oxide vapors and beyond this and in and near the plane of its equator, there were its planets, asteroids and comets, in their elliptical orbits about the center of the solar system. And by inductions of its phenomena, there is the sun, such orb of matter about space, and in its elliptical orbit about the axis of some star, or of some stellar system, and the crust of matter first about its center of space is metallic, and about this is its atmosphere of metallic and metallic oxide vapors forming into rocks to subside as spots upon the incandescent surface of the metallic crust. And beyond this on, in, or near, the planes of its equator, there are planets, asteroids and comets in elliptical orbits about the axis of the solar system of sun and planets. And as there were not the hypotheses without reality there were not the phenomena without it.

Chapter XVII.

And, as a reality, also, there is the earth. The earth is a reality if it be of being finite, or the word of God, or of space, and it is of this or the one of these, if it be physiological. And it is physiological if it have a crust of matter about a center of space. And if this crust be in strata, the first of metals, and the next of metallic oxides in rocks, and the next of hydrogens oxide, in water. And if about this there be a gaseous atmosphere of oxygen and nitrogen in the proportions of one to four, and if of these with water there be ammonias and carbonic oxides, and if of these there be the plant into the plant possible in the course of which there are produced the additional elements of matter, sulphur and phosphorus, and of these with those of the plant, there be the animal possible, including man. And it is of being finite or the word of God, or space, since either of these is universal and exclusive of other being in that universe. And if it be being physiological, as either of these is such.

And there is its space center in a solid sphere of dynamic and explosive force, and about this there is a hollow sphere of metallic and metallic oxide matter; and about this an envelope of hydrogen oxide matter in water liquid, and about this an elastic atmosphere of gaseous oxygens and nitrogens in the proportions of one to four, of whose reactions at or near the earth's surface there are gaseous waters, ammonias and carbonic oxides. of whose reactions on the earth there are matters termed organic, of whose reactions there are planets, of whose reactions there are animals, of whose reactions there is man.

CHAPTER XVIII.

There is a space center to the earth, in that, if there be a stratum of densest metallic matter in its crust, and this extending to its very center, it were many times heavier than it is. And, that there is such stratum, is in the fact that if there be not, the earth were then too light. The archaen rock of the oxides of lighter basic metals, seen in situ or in detrita at the earth's surface, is but two and one-half times the weight of water; and if this extended to the earth's center, as it would if there be not in it a stratum of metallic matter about the center of space, the earth would weigh but two and one-half times as much as an equal volume of water, while it is found to weigh five and one-half times as much. And there is such center for the reason that upon it, of whatever it might have consisted originally, there is the weight of its crust, thousands of miles in depth; and of its atmosphere, hundreds of miles in height; and of the ether beyond; and of its moon and meteorites, the aggregate of which were enough to sublime to primitive space the center of the earth, if that had been matter, and that matter platinum. And there is this center of space for the reason that there is no conceivable source of matter at the earth's center. And that there is the want of that space in force to sustain the matter of the earth's crust about it. And to propel that matter into the earth's atmosphere and through that into its plants, animals and men, and states of men. And that there is platinum within the earth, whose only office can be the holding of the earth's dynamic space, as the boiler holds its steam. And that such space within a belt of metallic matter is indicated by the movements of the magnet, which tends not about the earth, as an orb, but through it by its axis, as though about the equator of that axis there were a belt of metal, in which they were the current of electrical reaction, inspiring it. And that there is such space within the sun, a being physiological, analogous to the earth, and that it would exhibit in heat radiations that levitation resisting gravitation, which appears in all matters on the earth's surface, which can come of no other cause conceivable.

CHAPTER XIX.

There is also a metallic stratum to the earth's crust. Of the earth's systemic factors, the one energy and the other inertia, and the one in levitation and the other in gravitation; and the one in radiations eccentric, and the other in radiations concentric. There were the reactions, of which there were the elemental matters of the earth's crust, in each of which there were specific heat inversely to atomic weight. And of these the first to form about the earth's center of radiating energy were of the most atomic weight to the least specific heat such weight could seize and hold. These were the molecules of the metal platinum, the densest and most obstinate matter known. And there is such stratum, in that there is the metal platinum, which can have formed at no other place, and in no other way. And in that the platinum seen at the earth's surface is of vapors and from below the archaen rocks; and in that the magnet indicates the existence of such stratum in a belt about the axis of the earth, and in that there is such stratum now about the space center of the sun; and in that such boiler were necessary to the steam of the earth; and in that this in the earth were analogous to the limited membranes of organic cells, and in that without this there were not the earth's weight.

CHAPTER XX.

And about this a stratum of archaen rock. There is a rock of the oxides of potassium, sodium, magnesium, silicium, aluminum, calcium and iron, in quartz felspar and mica, embodied in the granite rock, seen yet in its original state and places; and in places where it is not so seen there are its detrita in geological formations to show that it was once the surface of the earth. And to the extent to which it has not been eroded it is now continuously about the earth, and is a stratum of the earth's crust next after the metallic stratum. And it is contended that there is this stratum, for the reason that, after the platanic stratum possible of the earth's systemic forces reacting into it there were these forces reacting into an atmosphere of gaseous matters, negative and positive, the negatives of which were oxygens, and the positives potassium, silicium, aluminum, and other metals possible of these forces; that, of these metals, as bases, and inertias, reacting with oxygens as acids, and energies, there were the rocky matters, quartz felspar and mica, appearing in the granite rock, of which there were such stratum; and for the reason that there is now that rock in places from which it has not been eroded, and that in places at which it does not appear there are detrita, which can have come from that rock disintegrated, and which are consistent with the supposition that, below the waters and the geological formations of the earth, there is still such rock continuously about its metallic stratum; and for the reason that there was an archaen stage of the earth at which were formed its metals other than platinum, with oxygen; and these with oxygen, into the rocks quartz felspar and mica, and these into the granite rock, as there is now an organic stage at which are formed acid oxygen with the relatively basic elements, hydrogen, carbon and nitrogen, and these into waters, ammonias and carbonic oxides; and these into plants; and these, with the elements, sulphur and phosphorus, into animals — the plants and the animals together forming an organic stratum about the earth, analogous to, and as continuous, as is that inorganic stratum in the rock. And that there is this archaen rock stratum for the reason that there are the rocks of metallic oxides, which can have come to exist in no other way — and that there is the granite rock not possible in any other way — and that there are geological formations not possible but of the detrita of this rock eroded, transported and deposited in such formations by water.

CHAPTER XXI.

And about this a stratum of water. As the earth's systemic forces at its archaen stage were capable of oxygen and metal in rocks, these at its organic stage were capable of oxygen and hydrogen in water. And there is evidence that this was once as continuously about the earth's surface as was the archaen rock — that at the beginning of the Silurian time there was water to a great depth about the surface of the earth; and at the surface of which did not appear the eroded or uneroded rock — and there is evidence, also, that the waters now seem to cover five-eighths of the earth's surface is by tradition of the Silurian seas.

It is not probable that any water existing at the Silurian time exists now. It will have resolved into metamorphic rocks, plants and animals, since existing. But the conditions of the Silurian waters will have continued. There will have been eccentric radiations of the earth's energy from its surface met by concentric radiations of its inertia. And though these radiations will have become less intense than they were at the Silurian time, and will have resulted in less water, they still will have continued

in the heat of 60° Fahrenheit and a presure of 15 pounds
to the inch from which there will have been the waters to
sustain the present seas and oceans. And that, actually,
at that time, and, potentially, since, there has been, and is,
a water stratum to the earth's crust. And this next about
its archaen rock stratum.

Chapter XXII.

And about this a gaseous atmosphere and about this
a moon. There is obviously a gaseous atmosphere about
the earth's surface, which will have been about its surface
when that was of water. And there is as obviously
beyond that atmosphere the moon. And though neither
of these is a stratum of the earth's crust, there is ground
for the belief that both are of the earth's systemic forces.
That of the radiations of these reacting on the surface of
water there is the earth's atmosphere of gaseous matters,
and that of these forces focussed and reacting on the center of the moon there is the moon. And that if they be not
such strata, their existences are as conclusive that the
earth is a being physiological of a physiological universe
in teledogic evo-involutions.

The atmosphere and moon are critical tests of the
theory of an universe of being, from an essential being
of the universe. Accepting that the earth's crust is in
strata metallic, rock and water, it is reasonably certain
that the rocks and metals were formed where they appear
and in succession, and the rocks after the metals. And
that the rocks ceased to form at a temperature of not less
than 6000° Fahrenheit, and under a pressure of not less
than 1200 pounds to the inch, and that under such conditions the external surface of the rock was incandescent,
and that beyond the rocks there was no one of the elements of non-metallic matter, now seen in waters, plants,
and animals, since no one of them, save oxygen, could
have existed under the conditions in the rocks. We must

3

suppose, therefore, that when the rocks ceased to form there was nothing beyond but an atmosphere of the earth's systemic forces in reaction; and that of these were the oxygens and hydrogens of which were the waters of the Silurian seas, and that these waters, represent, therefore, the earth's systemic forces from that temperature and pressure at which the rock ceased to form to those at which water became liquid at the surface of the rocks — and that then there was not other oxygen or hydrogen than that in water, or any nitrogen, carbon, hollogeno, sulphur or phosphorus, since neither of these was in the archaen rock, nor could have been formed through any conceivable means with water or before there were the waters of the seas. But after there was water, and of radiations from the surface of water, there was a gaseous atmosphere of oxygen and nitrogen in the proportions of one to four, in which there were, with the vapors of water ammonias and carbonic oxides, the additional non-metallic elements, nitrogen and carbon. And we are forced to assume, therefore, either that after the archaen rocks were formed there was a special creative agency to form oxygen and hydrogen and these into water, and after that another agency to form nitrogen and carbon and these into ammonias and carbonic oxides, or that of the systemic forces of the earth, of which were the metallic and rock strata of the earth's crust, there were its waters and the other non-metallic elements of which was its post archaen atmosphere, and the compounds of these of which are its plants and animals. It is not conceivable that there was such creative agency. It is conceivable that the earth's systemic forces, capable of the metals and the rocks, was capable of the waters, plants and animals — and the earth's post-archaen atmosphere is a critical test of the theory considered.

And so critical, also, is the moon. It is not obvious that the earth and moon are of a common cause. Both

are orbs of matter, and it is probable that the moon is of
a crust of matter about its center of space as is the earth,
with the differences that while the surface of the earth is
at a temperature of 60° Fahrenheit, that of the moon is
at a temperature lower than that of ice, and that while
the earth revolves on its own axis and in its orbit about
the sun, the moon does not revolve immediately on its
own axis, but is in its orbit about the earth, in its orbit
about the sun, and in such relation the question comes
whether the earth and moon are of separate creation acts
or are both of the systemic forces of which is the earth,
and as the separate creation acts were the miracle we may
not accept, we must accept if it be conceivably possible
that both are of the systemic forces of the earth. And it
is so possible. These infinite beings finite in limitations of
each other, and capable of the earth's crust of matter
about its center of space, were capable of transcending
that crust and its atmosphere, in eccentric radiations of
heat to be refracted and focussed at a distance from the
earth by concentric radiations of cold. From these foci
there were eccentric radiations of heat about which there
were concentric radiations of cold into elemental matters,
and these into a crust of matter about their centers of
space, as there was about the center of the earth, and
thus there were the moon of the same essential being as
the earth. It is probable that of these foci, there were
originally four, each the focus of rays from a quadrant
of the earth, and it is possible that there were four
moons, or more, originally about the earth; and that all
but the one have restored their heat to the earth in ceasing to exist; but that one remains, though without much
of its original heat, and in its existence presents a test as
crucial as does the earth's atmosphere, of the theory of
being in this universe. It is seen that there was a time
when neither existed and that after that time both came
into existence, and we are forced to accept either that
both came to exist of a special exercise of creative power,

in some genius apart from the universe, but attendant on it, and giving, instantly, to each being the being it exhibits, or that there is an essential being of the universe to which was originally committed the powers and purposes expressed in beings of the universe. And accepting this and that this is reality, we must accept that the earth of this is a reality as is the sun, star and universe.

Chapter XXIII.

As a reality, also, there is the plant. The plant cryptogamic, phonerogamic, endogenous and exoginous, at the earth's surface, is of the matter, elements, oxygen, hydrogen, nitrogen and carbon in waters, ammonias and carbonic oxides. And as these were in the earth's post-archaen atmosphere, of the earth's systemic forces in reaction, the question of whether the plant is of these forces, and a reality therefore, is but the question whether waters, ammonias and carbonic oxides under the conditions of the earth's atmosphere at that time could of their reciprocal affinities unite in the plant, or whether to such union and its evolution there was the intervention of a manipulating agent, and there was no such intervention. If there was such manipulation at the start of the plant then there is such now to its continuation. And there is not now such agent, nor is there place or occasion for such agent. Such unions as there are in the proximate elements of the plant, and of the affinities of these elements for each other. And, no' occasion, there was no place for such agent. He were as conspicuous producing the plant, as were the plant produced. And as he is not seen and nothing done by him, there is not, and there was not, such agent. And the every plant originally started, as the every individual plant now starts, of the earth's systemic forces in the waters, ammonias and carbonic oxides of its seed, and as these are realities the plant of these is a reality.

CHAPTER XXIV.

As a reality also there is the animal — Radiate, Annulate, Articulate and Vetebrate. This differs from the plant, in that, while the plant is of the elements oxygen, hydrogen, nitrogen and carbon, the animal is of these and sulphur and phosphorus in addition, and while the plant is sessile at the earth's surface, and mediating its systemic forces in heat from the earth and cold from the air, the animal is locomotive in procurement of these forces stored by the plant as food, to be further expressed in its beings and activities. And, as the special elements of the plant are from the earth's atmosphere of systemic forces, to the extent to which the animal is of them, it is a reality. And it is a reality also with respect to its additional elements, sulphur and phosphorus. For, though these were not found with the plant elements in the earth's post-archaen atmosphere, they were formed in the plant's forming of these elements, and sulphur, probably, of two oxygens, and phosphorus of four nitrogens, and thus existing at the earth's surface and of its systemic forces, and these realities, the animal is a reality.

CHAPTER XXV.

As a reality also man. There is man at this earth as there is the animal, and he is a reality as is the animal if he be but of the same elements as the animal; or be in continuation of the animal, or be of life in nature, or be to the race of man, or be *but* to the race of man. If he be of matter elements, and these be the same, and but the same as those of the animal, he is a reality from being of these elements, as is the animal. And so, also, if he be in continuation of the animal. The animal is of a process of the earth's systemic forces stored in plants, into the further beings of it possible, and if man be in continuation of that process of realities into the further

being of them possible, he is a reality as is the animal.
And he is a reality if he be of life in nature. There is
life but of the earth's systemic force in energy eccentric,
and nature but of its systemic force in inertia concentric,
accepting and administering life to its possibilities. And
these forces realities. Man is a reality if he be of these.
And he is a reality if he be to the race of man; and be
but to the race of man. The plant is a reality from being
to the race of the plant; and but to the race of the plant
possible. And the animal is a reality from being to the
race of the animal, and but to the race of the animal.
And so is man on the same conditions. And man is of
the same matter elements as the animal. That is of oxygen, hydrogen, nitrogen, carbon, phosphorus and sulphur essentially, and so essentially is man. And man of
the same matter elements, is, simply, in continuation of
the animal, to the animal possible in man. Thus is the
animal by gradations radiate, annulate and articulate to
the vertebrate, and the radiate animal by gradations from
the fish through reptile, digitigrate, plantigrade and four-
handed animal, to the animal two-footed and two-handed
which becomes man, first through unions of unmarried
female parents, representing the earth's eccentric force
of energy, with their offspring representing the earth's
concentric force of inertia. And next through the unions
of parents, married, with their offspring. Between the
solitary animal two-footed and two-handed, without these
unions, and the social man, agamic, polygamic or monogamic, with them, there is no other difference. And
these are but the variations, therefore, by which the animal, two-footed and two-handed, becomes in man the
animal possible, who, as man, is but the continuation of
the animal. And man is to the race of man the course of
human beings possible, and necessary from such unions
of his individuals. And he is but to the race of man, since
of his systemic beings he were capable of nothing else.
Of these there is a moral being in every race termed civili-

zation, consisting of the moral beings of the individuals who have lived in the race to its production — which moral being is to its race as is nature to its life, and to such senate of civilization the moral beings of the individuals of every race must come, where their physical beings shall have ended. But beyond this there is nothing else for man as a reality in after life. And if man be to more than this civilization to the man possible, or to another sphere of individual existence apart from and beyond this earth, he is not simply a reality of the earth's systemic beings, but is of some other source. But, not to such sphere of the earth's systemic beings, he is not to such sphere to any other word of God. There is no evidence of such special word, or occasion for such word, or evidences of such sphere, or occasion for such sphere, or place for such sphere, but in man's imagination of his want of it; and man is a reality, therefore, of the present word of God, in being of this universe.

CHAPTER XXVI.

And as a reality, also, there is mind in man. That sensitive being in the individual man, through which he is perceptive and reflective of the conditions incident to the continuation of his existence, and which, reflective, of these conditions we term mind, is a being physiological of its systemic beings in reaction, as is any ganglion of his nerves, or as is any one of its organs — the eye, for instance — or as is the germ of the plant, or embryo of the animal. And, existing but of the man, it is of the same matter elements as is the man. And these are through the same modes of reaction to their beings possible, in the being of them possible, as are the matters of the man. And such the mind of man, possessed of its systemic beings through man, as man is possessed of his through the animal, possessed of its through the plant, from the earth. As man is a reality from being of the earth's systemic beings, so, also, for the same reason, is the mind of man. The only ground for questioning this is in the assumption of a power in the mind not in man or in other beings of the universe, and this the power of originating its motives to activity. The man himself may originate his activities, of volitions, and his volitions of motives, but he cannot originate his motives; and is dependent for these upon his mind. But the mind cannot originate its motives more than can the man himself. · Of motives through plant and animal from the axis of the earth, the individual man exists in the family, stock, tribe or state; and is male or female, or white or black, or sage or simple. And, so, of the same motives is the mind of man at its time and place, but the mind possible, in the man possible, without the motive to be in any other mind, time or place, and without the power to perceive or reflect, other than the thing in incidence, as the mirror is without the power to reflect any other than the thing before it. Without this it is without the power to originate its motives. Without this it is as simply a reality in sequence of systemic forces, from the earth as is the earth, and is thus a reality as is man.

CHAPTER XXVII.

And as a reality also there is law. Accepting an universe of being into the beings of that universe, we must accept that there is a rule of that being into the beings of it possible. And that this rule is its law, and that being is itself the law administering itself, and that the word administering the itself is God. And there is this law in the being finite of beings infinite; and in the word of God imparting his will in power and purpose to the beings of it; and in space the substance of that finite word which in no other way could come to be the substances of it possible. And as there is such finite word of God in space, and as there is into the beings of it possible, there is law, not only as the substance of which are the substantive beings

of the universe, but law in the being of that substance
into the substances of it possible; and law in space; and
law of space into force; and of force into elemental matters; and of elemental into compound matters, inorganic
and organic, at the earth's surface, and of organic matters
into plants, animals and man, and the families, stocks,
tribes, and states of man. And of space through matters
into the earth, sun and stars. But there is this law only
as it be itself reality. And as a reality, therefore, there is
law. And as of this there are the realities from the universe to man there is in this that life, and of this that nature
of which at this earth there is man, who, under that law,
is in continuation of that nature to the man possible of
conditions existing at this earth. If not, he is here not of
law, in the being of the universe, as in my original work
I sought to show he was, but of some special exercise
of creative power not in the being of the universe. He is
not of such power, in that such power in contradiction of
law does not exist. If it did there were instances of it,
and there is not an instance of it seen. Nor in consistence
with the exact regularity of beings at this earth is it
possible that there can have been an instance of it from
the axis of the universe to man. And he is of law as
simply and completely as is any antecedent being of the
universe. So of law in nature he is in continuation of
nature to the man possible, and the best man possible that
he may be his most of the provisions available for his
subsistence. And such man in theory of his existence as
a being of an essential being of the universe, it will now
be shown that such in fact is his existence. That he of
an animal two-footed and two-handed, with an organ of
intelligence to co-ordinate the activities of his feet and
hands. That he has varied from this animal only in
unions of female parents and their offspring and of parents
male and female and their offspring, that the animal without these unions was solitary, that the man with them is
social; and that man, therefore, is but the solitary animal.

becoming social to the larger provisions for safety and subsistence possible of such association. That at present he
is "agamic," in stocks of children under orders of their
unmarried mothers; and "polygamic," in tribes and castes
of wives and children under the authority of polygamic
male parents; and "monogamic," in states of wives and
children under the authority of polygamic male parents, ·
theoretically, but actually, under that of adult males. That
these unions in variation of the solitary animal to the social
man has come in order and succession, and the polygamic
tribe by evolution of the agamic stock, and the monogamic
state by evolution of the polygamic tribe. But that of
neither is there now the man possible, and of neither,
alone, can there be the man possible. But that of unions
of these races, now unequal, in relations of inequality
there can be a race of the man possible. And, as of such
unions there can be such race, of such unions there will
be such race. And of that the man possible in reciprocal
and supplementary relations to each other at every point
upon the habitable globe. And such the theory of an
essential being of the universe in space, it will appear in
this that there are the three propositions —

First: That there is such essential being of the universe, in which is life, of which is nature:

And *second*, that man of nature, there is man.

And *third*, that man of nature is to the man possible.

And having thus shown that there is such essential
being, it will now be shown that man of this is to the man
possible; and but to the man possible of his means of
subsistence at this earth.

PART SECOND.

Chapter XXVIII

Man at this earth is to be the man possible. This were the most man possible, and the best man possible of his means of subsistence possible. And there is to be such man as well by deductions from the hypothesis of such essential being as by inductions of its phenomena. By inductions of its phenomena in force, matter, life and nature from the universe to man, we are led to the conclusion that each is the finite product of its infinite factors; and that, of these, each is the product possible. And that man such product is, or is to be, the man possible.

And by deduction from the hypothesis of such essential being of the word of God, we are equally led to the conclusion that of his infinite beings, as factors, man of such factors, as every other product, is to be the product possible; and, therefore, the man possible. And, by reason of analogy, man is to be the man possible, hence every finite being is to its being possible. Nor is there reason that man should be other than this man. He is not fitted to be more or less, or other than, at his time and place were the man possible. Nor is there reason that God should have intended him to be more, or less, or other. Nor is there evidence of such intention in his favor. And he is to be the man possible from the persistences of the sexual feelings in man, and the maternal instincts in woman. And to such man from the persistences of individuals in preservation of their existences. Nor will man be able to cheat himself of such achievement. The monogamic state of lords and commons, with what may be termed the patriarchal power in lords and its proletariate powers in commons, may become democratic in absorption by the commons of the patriarchal power in lords, who, thus possessed of its patriarchal and proletariate powers, may proceed to exercise them both in a government of popular volition, expressed through majorities of adult males in parties formed to dominate each other in direction of the state. And those parties may be inconsiderate of the state possible of its individuals, and of the race possible of the state, while intent only to sustain themselves, the one above the other. And thus the every monogamic state becoming adults in the possession by its commons of both its patriarchal and proletariat powers, may feel at liberty, as may the individual adult, to exercise its powers, not to its advancement as a state, but to the enjoyment of the situation, the modes to be determined by the party which at the time may be victorious. These parties, wearing each other out, may wear out the state, and thus defeat it of the man possible. But while this may be the fate of the monogamic states first becoming adult, it will not be the fate of adult states succeeding, the man of which will find, or make some way of continuing its existence beyond the point at which it becomes the subject of such partition. And there will be such man possible, not only for the reason that there can be such man, but for that such man is necessary to the complete acceptance of life in nature at this earth. And that there is no reason he should be to other end. And for that, no other being is to other end than its most and best.

Chapter XXIX.

But while man is to the man possible, he is not to be so of any single human race. And not of the agamic race from the want of its male element of manhood. And not of the polygamic race from its want of initiation and autonomy. And not of the monogamic race from its excess of initiation and autonomy. And while agamic man may become the agamic man possible; and the polygamic man, the polygamic man possible; and the monog-

amic man, the monogamic man possible, neither can
become the man of all possibly able to live upon the products of this earth.

Chapter XXX.

Yet there may be the man possible of unions of these
races in inequality; and there can be such. They can
unite in production of a race of their respective families
reciprocally dependent on each other for the means of
continuing their existences in common, as parents may
unite in production of a race of children male and female
reciprocally dependent on each other for the means of
continuing their existences in common.

These unions must be domestic — both families being
under the patriarchal power of one in *loco parentis* of both—
and for the lives of these respective families. And these
races can so unite.

They are unequal in ability to attain to the man possible; and can unite, therefore, only as unequals. But as
such they can unite, for such union were to the betterment
of both. And in families better, and in states better than
of any single race. And such union will be of strength
and stability to the superior race, and of existence to the
weaker, which, in contact with a stronger race, must be
absorbed or exterminated. And under favoring conditions, certain to occur, the superior race will accept
strength and stability and the inferior existence instead
of the horrors of extermination necessary without. And
that this will be so, not only for the reasons stated but
for that there was such union of monogamic whites and
agamic blacks in this Republic becoming adult.

Chapter XXXII.

And as there can be there will be such unions. This
follows from that there is to be the man possible; and

possible in this and in no other way. And from that there is to be that that can be. And that coexistence in relations of inequality will become the conditions of existences to unequal races in necessary contact. And from that both will be the better of such union.

CHAPTER XXXIII.

Nor averse to these conclusions are the experiences of this Republic in which at one time there was slavery and at another not. And in which it was seen that with slavery it was in progress to the man possible as he is not now without. They show that unequal races can unite indissolubly. There was no reason for the unions there not existing elsewhere, where races come in contact. In every such the weaker must be absorbed or exterminated. These unions in Africa will be colonizations; there then will be no scarcity of slaves; those coming will be taken, nor will there be opposition to the union by either race, nor, where formed, of any repugnance of either to this, will they be broken.

CHAPTER XXXIV.

And this is to the betterment of both. And, first, in their more abundance. So related to each other in a natural municipality assigning to the individuals of each race the office he was best fitted to fill, in procuring safety and subsistence to the whole, both races were in the way of being more abundant than either could have been without such union. And so also both were in the way of being fitted to become so more abundant. And this apparent from a comparison of the states and peoples north and south will more clearly appear in a state which at one time held slaves and at a later did not hold them. Such state was South Carolina, which, from holding slaves, and in larger proportions to whites than did any other state, is especially fitted to express these truths.

Chapter XXXV.

The whites were so better before emancipation than they are now. They were elevated, ordered, prosperous and progressive, and self respectful and honored as they are not now, with provisions for safety and subsistence they have not now.

Chapter XXXVI.

And the negroes then so better than they are now. They were better there than when they were in Africa. And they were better there then as slaves than they are now as freemen. They had their place and office in the foremost state of the foremost civilization of the world. They have now no place and office in any human state. They were there cherished and protected by their masters to the extent of their fortunes, now they are homeless outcasts, struggling for subsistence against their former masters, without the ability to leave or to say why they should stay in continuation of such unequal contest.

Chapter XXXVII.

And the state then better than the state now. It was then sovereign; it is now subject. It was then the equal and honored member of a confederacy of states, more potent than any history records, and that in condition to lead the human world to the human possible, now it is not such member of a confederacy of sovereign states but is the unconsidered constituent of a republic not in condition to lead the human world to the man possible. And then it was a state of monogamic and agamic races in harmonious union to the man possible of both, and now it is without such union, and but with these races antagonistic of each other, each grasping at its government, in a contest which cannot end until the one shall exclude the other.

Chapter XXXVIII.

But in other states such unions of unequal races. These will be caste or predal. And caste if a state of the monogamic race shall take imperial jurisdiction of a polygamic state as a subject province, and predal if the citizens of a monogamic state shall individually take proprietary jurisdiction over the individuals of a polygamic tribe or an agamic stock. And such unions will occur. The monogamic race, as I have said, is now at a point in the march of man to the man possible, from which it must roll back upon the antecedent agamic and polygamic races in occupation of other sections of the earth. There are monogamic states in Europe and America, and polygamic tribes and castes and agamic stocks in Asia, Africa and the Oceanic Islands. And in all the monogamic states of Europe, at least, there are contests of lords and commons for the patriarchal power. In these the commons encroach upon the lords. And ultimately, in every Teutonic state, at least, must become possessed of that power to the suppression of the lords. But pending this contest there will be migrations of higher races to lands of lower races of whom the higher will be lords.

Chapter XXXIX.

Such the theory, it raises questions as to the race of man and as to the races white and black in this republic. And as to the race of man, whether that be the better of its humanities or its inhumanities? And as to the races white and black in this republic, whether these can continually coexist? Or the one can long survive the other? To which the answers are: that the race of man is the better of its inhumanities. And as to the races white and black in this republic, that they can not perpetually coexist.

And as to the first: that man is the better of his

'inhumanities, in that of his inhumanities there is the state against the individual, and of his humanities, there is the individual against the state, and of the one despotism, and of the other anarchy. And of these despotism is the better, in that of this there can be, for a time, at least, the continued existence of the state, while of anarchy, there can not be such continuation.

And as to the second: That the races can not coexist continually, that they will not assimilate; that without this they can not coexist in the same state — each in assertion of itself; that the white civilization is the stronger and will live down the black, and that the whites can not long survive the blacks in a normal monogamic state, since this must end in anarchy or despotism, either of which is fatal.

Chapter XL.

And, another question, whether the republic shall end in a contest of parties of adult males for its patriarchal power? or shall survive that contest, and assert itself to a continued existence as a normal monogamic state? This as to the rights and liberties of its individuals is under a government by appointment of its male parents. And as to its appropriation of private property to public uses, under a legislation by appointment of proprietary parents, whether male or female, as the one or the other be the head of the family. Such is a real monogamic state underlying that of adult males existing now. This can survive in such assertion of itself if conscious of its existence. And the question of whether it shall so survive is of importance to the man of this republic. Of this there may be the assertion by this republic—the leading monogamic state — of its tutelary jurisdiction over lower races to the advancement of the human race. But if not, there may be postponement of the end of this republic, from whose existence there has been more of well-being than any people on this earth have yet enjoyed — in which postponement then will be advantage so long as it endure.

Chapter XLI.

Nor will such other unions be again dissolved.

There will be no contest of unequal races for the paramount patriarchal power, as there is not between parents and their offspring in the family. Both are better of their respective offices and so will be the races. And though before such unions shall become established the individuals might be averse to the restrictions they impose, when established they become the conditions of individual well-being, which were not without them. And for reason of this the individuals of the one race will be as conservative of their unions as will be those of the other.

Chapter XLII.

Conclusion. The completion of the work of an extended life. More than fifty years ago I proposed the reopening of the foreign slave trade. It seemed that with this closed, and immigration open, that the Northern section of the Republic would become more populous than the Southern. That so it could take the government, and would be forced to do so. That to this the Southern section would not submit, and that thus there would be a dissolution of the Union, or the subjugation of one section by the other. But that if slaves were allowed to come, the Northern sections would not become so more populous, and would not be forced to take the government. And I still believe that if this measure had been pressed it would have been adopted. But it was not. The war came on and the South was subjugated and her slaves liberated. And it then seemed that my dream of an union of unequal races to the man possible was ended.

But later it appeared that there might be such unions at other times and places. That these were apt to be facilitated by a statement of the truths involved, and I have undertaken such statement by deduction of them from the hypothesis of an essential being of the universe in a being finite of the word of God in space, the work of which I now submit, with the assurance that the fact will ultimately be accepted, and the sooner, possibly, from what may be said about it. And I present this argument to the special object of showing that the man who will ultimately continue nature to the man possible, is not the monogamic race alone, which is now beginning to overspread the earth in exclusion of all races not able to comply with the procrustean conditions of monogamic life, but it is the man of all the human races combined in an economy to the betterment and abundance of the whole. That in this inequality is not the slavery of the unequal in any objectionable sense, and that such inequality as existed between the whites and negroes at the South and now so generally reprobated, is not only not censurable but is, in fact, the sole condition upon which man on earth can advance to the achievement of his destiny on earth. And I yet indulge the hope that of this asserted and persisted in by those who come to realize the truth, an earlier age will come to its acceptance.

CHAPTER I.

THE QUESTION OF SUCH BEING IS OF LITTLE INTEREST, BUT OF MUCH IMPORTANCE.

It is of little interest. Of those who read this preface few will realize at once the meanings of its terms, and fewer still will accept their implications. The terms "essential," "being," "finite," "God," "force," "space," "matter," "life," "nature," "universe," "star," "sun," "earth," "plant," "animal," "man," and "mind," and "law," and "being physiological," are in common use as names of conventional conceptions. But few of us have a definite sense of the realities to which these names apply. And fewer will at once accept that there is being physiological; or that of this there is being insensible as real as that sensible, and in space as in force, and in force as in matter, and in matter as in life, and in life as in nature. Or that of this there is an universe; or that of this in teleologic evo-involution, there are the stars, sun and earth; or that these atomic beings are relatively static and dynamic with respect to the axes of their neutral beings intermediate; or that they are in coincidence and differentiation on and from their axes; or that these are in forms of wheels of which the axles are dynamic and the disks static; or that the dynamic axes are in evolution of the static disks, and the static disks in involution of the dynamic axles; or that in this the dynamic axles are casual and the static disks consequential, and the casual axles life, and the consequential disks the natures of that life in a being physiological of both; or that this is in teleologic evo-involution in production of offspring, such about the parent being; or that such are the matters of the sun's crust about its axis of space, and its nature

in matter about its axis of life; or that such are the sun
and planets, natures, about the axis of the solar system,
life; or the matters of the earth's crust, nature, about its
axis of life; or that the body of the plant is its nature
about its axis of life; or the body of the animal its
nature about the axis of its life; or the body of man his
nature about the axis of his life; or that the life of man
itself is such being physiological, as is that of the earth,
plant or animal, in teleologic evo-involution, of which
there is its nature in the man and his conceptions possible; or that the mind of the individual man is such being,
and his life to his nature in the individual activities necessary to his becoming the individual man under the conditions possible, or that the individual is life to his family
nature, or the family life to the state its nature.

All these propositions are implied in that of an essential being of the universe, and of the few who, reading
this preface, will take the meanings of these terms, there
are fewer still who will accept their implications — while
to the common man who reads it, or does not, it will be
as unconsidered as by passengers on shipboard were the
theory of the ship. They are there to have a pleasant pas-
sage to their place of destination, without perplexity as to
when or how, or of what, the ship is built. And so the
individuals taking these passages in their state of the
human race are not concerned as to when, or how, or of
what it started, or to what end it goes when they are
done with it.

They are not only not concerned that the state is of
man, and man of nature, and nature of life, and life of
such essential being, but none of them have realized, perhaps, or tried to realize such being, or the life of such
being, or the nature of such life, or the man of such
nature. Nor had he tried had he succeeded in consistence
with his acceptance of these terms, as descriptive, not of
real beings insensible, but of our conceptions of the phenomena of such beings, about which we have agreed and

recorded our agreements in such terms. The terms being, life, nature, space, force, matter, and the like, are not realities, or expressive of realities, but are conventionalities expressive of impressions made upon us by realities. And are as unlike the reality, as is the track the foot. And as of tracks we can not make the foot, so of conventionalities we can not make the reality — however, by inductions of them as phenomena, we may find that there are realities to cause them. But these inductions are not made. Tasked to the means of continuing their individual existences at this earth, the men of successive generations have neither time, inclination, nor immediate occasion, to inquire about a matter so remote from their ordinary and engrossing occupations. And so, as that they may individually procure such means, they are quite indifferent as to what may be the actual cause of beings in this universe, or as to whether there be an actually preexisting cause, or they be of it?

They would rather in fact that there were not such cause established. In that were the irrevocably vested will of God, and they would rather that will were not vested, but were ambulatory, so that it might be invoked to human exigencies. Nor were there, perhaps, a feeling so common as that of repugnance to the inexorable fate there were in such universe of cause to its universe of consequences, and such universe of the consequence of such inexorable cause. The individuals of families and the families of stocks, tribes or states, and the sects and parties of states, are not content with the share which, of their merits merely, they might take from the stores of a common providence, such as were that in an irrevocably vested will of God to the takers of it possible, but each would be favored by a special tutelary genius at the expense of others.

But in the way of man's acceptance of such cause is his inability to perceive it. That cause in its course of nature were as attenuated as it is in the mind of man

itself.   And he is not more perceptive of it in nature than
in himself, who is not more able to perceive his originating cause than is the plant its cause through the seed it
comes from, or the animal through the ovum of which it
started to exist as such animal.   The plant or animal, each
at every stage of its existence, has an intuitive sense of
the conditions under which it can continue and be more
and better, that it may be more, in consistence with such
external beings.   But with respect to its internal beings,
and especially with respect to the cause of its being,
immediate or remote, it is as without sense as if such
cause did not exist.

And so is man.   He has reason of his life in nature
as the plant or animal has not, and this in the ratios of
his subjective beings to the objective beings to produce
them.   The every human sense, and the object in incidence
producing such sense, are in ratios of an intermediate
being of them both.   And in comparison of such ratios,
there is reason, and of reason he has science, not only of
such objective being, but of his own subjective being in
relation to such objectives.   And thus, in reflection of his
recorded experiences to the exigencies of his current life
in nature, he comes to an imperfect sense of the cause of
his life in nature.   But of the actual cause of his life in
nature he is as insensible as is the animal or plant.   And
so insensible of its existence, and so insensible of the
want of such sensibility in continuing his existence in
consistence with beings at this earth, he is so unconcerned
as to whether there be an essential being of the universe
that not only are my arguments in assertion of its existence apt to be unconsidered, but I am liable to the imputa-
tion of simplicity in advancing a proposition so absurd,
or so inconsequential, if it be not.   And it had been impossible perhaps to have presented a proposition of so little
interest.

But, so uninteresting, it is not so unimportant.   If
there be this being finite of the word of God in space, of

this were that we term life, and of this that we term nature, and of this the natures from that universe to man, in whom there were a nature to the man possible, as in the plant or animal there is such nature.

He will have advanced from a two-footed and two-handed animal through agamic and polygamic to present monogamic man, yet destined perhaps to a further man possible, and him, perhaps, as much beyond the monogamic man now as the monogamic citizen is beyond the agamic savage. So by variations favorable to its existence the plant of its life in nature will have advanced from its cryptogamic stage through its phonerogamic, endogenous and exogenous stages to the plant possible. And the animal, by like favorable variations from the radiate polyp, through its annulate, articulate, and vertebrate stages to the animal possible, two-footed and two-handed.

But, while man of his life in nature were so advancing to the man possible, he were so in the assumption that he is not to the race of man possible, but that that race of man is to him. That, while the plant or animal of its life in nature is to the plant or animal possible, man, of his life in nature, is not to the man possible, but to himself; that human life, in human nature, is not to the race, but to the individual men and women of a ruling race who may come to exist of it. And, while it might not be important to the race of man what notions individual men may have of it, or of their relations to it, it were important to the individuals themselves, that their conceptions of their situation be correct.

If man be of the life in nature of such essential being of the universe, and so destined to the man possible, he were destined to be the most and best man possible, in the most and best families possible, in the most and best states possible, in the most and best race possible, of unions of unequal races. And, to his guidance and direction in that course, he were vested with a tutel-

ary moral being, such as is that in the state termed government, and that in the race termed civilization. This
moral being would consist of the moral beings of the
individuals through the ages, who will have lived rightly
into it. And it will have survived the individuals and
generations so producing it, and will continue the tutelary
genius of the human race to its most distant ages. These
so contributing will live in it, and it may be well that they
do so. Not so contributing they will not be in it, but will
have fallen out of, and off, from the human race to what
other home of refuge they may individually find. And it
may be well with their moral beings in their after lives
that they so live in that moral nature of the race to which
they will have so contributed.

But, without this, it were indisputably well with men
that in their earthly lives they comply with the requisitions of this moral nature of their race. It will require
of them, simply, that they individually live to their best
and most in families, to their best and most in states, to
their best and most in races, to their best and most in a
race of man the best possible and most possible of the
products of the cultured earth. And while it might be
questioned whether it were better that the souls of men
shall find their future homes in the moral nature of their
race than have to seek them in the wilds of their imagina-
tions, it can not be questioned that in these earthly lives
it were better that they live in consistence with its requisitions than without.

Important that they do this will of God, it is important they know it. And while, therefore, it had been hard
to have raised a question of so little interest, it had been
harder still to have raised a question of so much
importance.

For, though it may be doubted that man as a whole
by taking thought can add to his stature, or be different
ages hence from what we would be, as the individual by
taking thought can not add to his stature, or be other

than the man or woman, or grow to other than maturity as such, or not ultimately die, yet to the man as a whole, as to the individual, it is important that he live to the ends of his existence. This he can the better do by knowing what they are. If there be an essential being of the universe, and he be of it, his end will be to its continuation and enlargement; the end of the individual will be to the existence and enlargement of the family; that of the family to the existence and enlargement of the state; that of the state to the existence and enlargement of the race. Living to this end he will live the better. Knowing this end he will live to it the better. He will know this end if he know that there is an essential being of the universe of which he is. Without this he will consciously live, as he has lived, to no other end than that of his individual aspirations. It is impossible that, in such existences, he can be the larger and better man he would be of a conscious existence to the best individuals possible, to the best families possible, to the best states possible, to the best races possible. And important as it is that he be such man possible, so important is it that he know the conditions upon which he is permitted to become such man. These conditions are in his acceptance of an essential being of the universe in space. But to the wisest men, not accepting space as such essential being, this argument will be as unmeaning and ungrateful as are the utterances of insanity, while to the simplest, accepting space as such essential being, they will be grateful and familiar. To the ones, space will be a nothing from which the something seen can not come; to the others it will be a something from which the somethings seen can come. And that my labor be not vain, I must show that in reality there is such space, and that of this there are the forces and matters of the universe. And of these, the lives and natures of the universe, and the universe itself, and the stars, suns and planets about the axis of the universe, and this earth a planet, and the plants, animals and men, and states of men upon it.

But, apart from our conceptions of it, the capital importance of this theory to man is in the fact that it gives him the grounds, and only grounds, of science and philosophy. By inductions of the phenomena of this essential being, as I have said, there were the science of its being from the universe to man. And by deductions from the hypothesis of this essential being there were the philosophy of being from the universe to man. But without this there were neither science or philosophy in any proper sense of these terms. But empyrical conceptions, merely, as inadequate to truth as are these of augury or astrology. And important as it is that man have science and philosophy of himself and of the beings with him in this universe, so important is it that he consider whether there be this essential being of the universe in space.

And it is of even more importance still to man that it gives to him the end of man in after life. That providence of which is man intends that his moral being shall survive his present life on earth.

This we must suppose, in that we have not known, nor can we conceive of a moral being ending. Man's organic body may resolve into the inorganic matters of which it consists; and these into the forces of which they consist. But that moral being termed his soul may not so resolve into simpler forms of its own being, in that there are no such forms seen or conceivable, and it must go on, therefore, bettered and enlarged by its experiences in making man still more and better, to its end beyond man — either in a moral being to hover and brood the human race, still existing, to its most and best on earth, or it must pass off to another sphere of existence elsewhere. In the one case the souls of men who have bettered man in life will rise into that moral being which, as civilizations, rules individual races, and ultimately into a general civilization to rule the human race. In the other, transpiring man in life, they must take what fortunes they can find in a state of immaterial being elsewhere, which will have no office in man on earth, and in which each individual will have the task of continuing as it can its individual existence. If there be such essential being, man of it, will be, as is the animal and plant, to his most and best in life, to a civilization conserving him to the ends intended in that word of God. But if there be not such being, he will not be into such moral being of his race ; the beings of the universe will not be of the resolutions of such essential being into them, but will be of the manipulations of an anthropomorphic Theos in execution, of that will, on substances otherwise inert. These special agents of éternal purpose in man were not the souls of men who were, therefore, without such moral beings surviving them. And, accepting himself as but the subject of such moral ministrations, he accepts that he is but a body without a soul for after existence on this earth, or elsewhere. And if man of an essential being of the universe be vested with such moral being, as there is reason to believe he is, it is of much importance to him that he realize that fact and act upon it. And while, therefore, it be true that man now has little interest in this question, it is equally true that there is to him no other of so much importance.

But, without this, it is of practical importance to the race of man, and especially to the monogamic race, that it should realize the existence of such essential being. If there be this, man is of it, and to the man possible. But of the existing human races each is to its being possible in exclusion of the others, while neither alone is able to become such man. And of these so exclusive of each other the monogamic race is the stronger and can dominate the others. And does so dominate them wherever it comes in contact with them, and in declaring that they shall exist upon no lands of the earth but at its suffrance, and in this shall become monogamic, and so assimilate themselves to the monogamic peoples invading them as that there be no perceptible difference between them as individuals and their invaders.   This policy is avowed by all the leading monogamic states.   England avows it in the declaration that there be no slaves upon her lands.   In contact, races, as individuals, must exclude the one the other from the point of contact, however that be fatal to the weaker, or they must unite in occupation of it upon terms consistent with the' well-being of both.   These were in their acceptance of the respective offices of order and obedience in a common economy of both.   And these, however we may term them, to be efficient, must be those of lords and commons, and these the relations of masters and slaves.   And these, as slaves, monogamic England will not accept for reason, alleged, of its inhumanity, but really for the reason that it implies her sharing the earth with the races so conserved; while she would have it to herself.   In enslaving the lower races on the lands she would take from them, she conserves them to a life as extended and pleasurable as her own.   And this she would not from her imperial disposition as a monogamic state to dominate and absorb the whole of human life available.

Nor will this Republic, even more advanced, for the same reason accept such wardship of a lower race.   Having ended the contest of lords and commons for the patriarchal power by the establishment of her government in the volitions of her adult males, these males are conscious of their ability to run the government to the ends they desire without the complications of a subject race.   They acheived, as commons, their independence of their lords, still in the English Constitution, upon the plea that they were the natural equals of the lords in that they were men, and that all men are naturally equal. And, being so, the equals of the lords, that they were equally entitled to participation in the patriarchal power of government.,   And claiming equality and the government on this plea of natural equality, they, to be consistent, felt bound to admit the equality of lower races; and assume the wrong of subjecting them to slavery.

But while this was the plausible pretext, it was not the real reason for their exclusion of negro slaves. The state was under a government at the will of a popular majority; that majority had, by foreign immigration, become established in the tier of Northern States, in which there were no slaves; they could take the government with its emoluments and powers by repudiating slavery. This they did, and not for the reason that slavery was wrong in itself, but for the reason that such repudiation was the necessary pretext to their exclusive assumption of the government. As it has been in England and this Republic, so must it be in every monogamic state on its way to the liberation of its commons from the patriarchal power by inheritance in its lords. It will not accept of union with a lower race; without this it must exterminate that race when it comes in contact with it, though this be ruinous to both. But, accepting an essential being of the universe, man accepts that of this there is to be man, as of it there is the animal and plant. And man to the man possible, as is the animal or plant to the animal or plant possible, and by unions of the unequal orders of men as of unequal orders of animals or plants; without this the monogamic race is not the race it should be. And in every way, therefore, it is important that man should know, if it be true, that there is an essential being of the universe, however little the interest he may take in the discovery.

CHAPTER II.

If there be this, it were the being finite of the word of God in space. As such it were being physiological. And as such it were that being physiological in stars, suns, earth, plant, and animal, from the universe to man, inclusive. And in it, therefore, there were that life, of which there were that nature, of which there is man, and him in its continuation to the man possible of his means of subsistence at this earth; whence to the truth of the theory, there is but the question, whether such being does in fact exist.

And it were the being finite of the word of God in space. It were being finite in that it were being not infinite. There are beings infinite and finite, without other being in this universe, and the being finite is but in the limitation of one atomic infinite by another infinite as itself. This infinite being finite were therefore the essential being of the universe, in that there were no other of which there could be the beings of the universe. And it were such essential being, also, for the reason that it were being physiological, as are all the phenomenal beings of the universe; and as they were not without such essential being.

The being physiological is the being possible of kindred beings different, of their reciprocal affinities, simply in reciprocal limitations of each other. And such were infinite being finite. And such are the beings finite from the universe to man.

Such were the infinite being finite. Its infinite beings, self-differentiated, were kindred from being of the same integral infinite; and were different from being of that infinite inversely. So, inversely, they were reciprocally vacua and reciprocally plena, and reciprocally attractive and reciprocally repulsive; and of their affinities simply were in reciprocal limitations of each other into the spheroids and wheels of both, about the axes of their neutral beings intermediate. And these were beings physiological. That is, a being which has no finite existence until self-differentiated infinities shall have concurred in its production. And to such concurrence it were necessary that they react, and of their reciprocal affections of and for each other, merely, in production of a finite being intermediate. To this there were no being in force, *or extra*, but only that of the atomic infinities reciprocally intussusceptive of each other, in which there were the inherent forces necessary to the production of the intermediate being possible.

And such the hypothetical finite being physiological, such, in fact, is the every phenomenal finite from the universe to man, which can be, therefore, at its time and place about the axis of the finite universe, but the finite being possible of such finite being physiological.

And such, and so physiological, infinite being finite, such and so physiological were the finite word of God. That were of God's infinite beings in reciprocal limitations of each other to express his will in the finite beings of them possible. They were as reciprocally intussusceptive of each other, and as able to express the will of God in the intermediate beings of them possible as were the beings infinite becoming finite to produce the finite, since they were, in fact, but infinite beings finite. And such were space, the insensible substance of the finite word of God, of which there are the sensible beings finite from the universe to man. And, such the essential being of the universe, there is to its being that of which is the life, of which is the nature, of which is man to the man possible, but the single question—whether it exists.

And there are reasons why we should readily accept

the fact of its existence. It gives a sensible theory of the universe, and of available rules of philosophy and science with respect to it. There is philosophy in the will of God, as to the beings of this universe; there is science in the phenomena expressive of that will. And by deductions from that essential being of the word of God we become possessed of such philosophy. And by inductions of the phenomena of the word we become possessed of such science. Without these our philosophies are as vague as are the myths of lower races. And our sciences—of empyrical conceptions—as vague as are the deliverances of astrology. But, possessed of these clews to the labyrinths of life in nature, we can discard unnecessary speculation, and address ourselves to rational acceptance of the truths declared. But, without this motive to acceptance of an essential being of the universe, there is in issue but the question whether in fact there be such being. There is being, whether it be infinite being finite, or the word of God, or space. And of this there are the beings finite from its universe to man, in that, of this original being there are these beings finite since such original being were universal, and exclusive; and exclusive of such beings finite but as they be of it.

Thus, of it, they are of it either by the resolutions of such being, of its own motives, into them, or through the manipulations of it by attendant Theoi, who make it do what of its own motives it could not.

But there are not such Theoi. The every act of such Theos were the miracle of consequence without antecedent cause in such being, and there is not such miracle. And there is every finite being, therefore, simply of the resolutions of such essential being of the universe, contingent but upon that there be such being. But if it should appear, as it does not, that there are such anthropomorphic Theoi in administration of the will of God on earth, so amply able to administer itself, that fact were not conclusive that there is not that will in space; and this as real and substan-

tial as that in matter. And whether this be in administration of itself or be in the hands of such Theoi for administration, it were still the essential being in which is life, of
which is nature, of which is man to the man possible, with
but the question whether there be such being. We are
reluctant to accept this truth. There is in each of us a
sensitive being, perceptive and reflective of the conditions
incident to the continuations of our individual existences.
And while these sensitive beings are analogous to the sensitive beings in animals and plants, and all the beings of the
universe, in fact, through which they are acceptive of the
conditions incident to the continuations of their individual
existences, we are not conscious or perceptive of such
analogies, but assume, consciously or unconsciously, that
these sensitive beings in us are either original or self-
originated in us, or are the special endowments in us of
that general providence of which only are the other
beings of the universe without such special endowment.

And assuming this, and that we ourselves are the
products of our conscious minds, and not the resolutions
of a general providence of God in an essential being of
the universe, we are disposed to assume that so, also, are
not the other beings of the universe of such essential
being. And that, in fact, there is not such being. And
that God, administering his providence to man through
such special agencies, administers it so to other beings of
the universe. And that there is not, therefore, the being
of a general providence, and not, therefore, the essential
being of the universe. But the question of its existence, as
of every other fact, is one of evidence. And if evidences
show that there is such being we must accept the fact,
however averse we may be to its acceptance. And accepting that fact as cause, we must accept its consequences in
the beings of it possible. And in this accept that of this
not only are there life and nature from the universe to
man, but the every being possible, at its time and place

possible, of an universe of finite being possible, in teleologic evo-involutions from the axis of that universe.

I have suggested that of the finite beings of which is
the earth reacting on its axis, there were a spheroid of its
beings possible about that axis, and that of these there
were the molecular matters of the earth's crust, as they
became successively possible, and the strata of the earth's
crust as they became possible: And so the water stratum
and the atmospheric stratum, and in that the organic matters possible, and of these the plants cryptogamic and
phonerogamic, endogenous and exogenous, as they became
successively possible, and the animals, radiate, annulate,
articulate and vertebrate, as they became successively
possible. And the man agamic, polygamic and monogamic, as they became successively possible.

And affirming these as the facts of beings finite reacting on the axis of the earth, it is affirmed that analogously
such are the facts of such beings reacting on the axis of
the universe. That about this there are the beings at
their times and places possible, so that by a rigid analysis
of cause into the consequences, we would find at its time
and place about the axis of the universe the being possible, however we might be unable to find it otherwise.
And by an equally rigid synthesis of consequences into
their causes possible, we would find at their times and
places the every such being possible. So that, accepting
the existence of such essential being of the universe, we
accept the conditions, not only of life and nature from the
universe to man, but the conditions also upon which there
is the every being from the universe to man, and man
himself. We would accept that every being, from the
universe to man inclusive, is the finite product, at its time
and place, of infinite factors reacting into each other, on
and from the axis of the universe. That these infinite
factors are related, as in beings finite are these beings
opposite, the one of which we term energy and the other
inertia. That, as of these there is the every being from

the universe to man, of these is man himself. That his mind is energy and his body inertia, and his male energy and his female inertia, and his parents energy and their offspring inertia, of which the product is the family agamic, polygamic, or monogamic. Of which families self-differentiated there are stocks, tribes, and states, respectively, the monogamic states of which, being self-differentiated into classes, the ones of which owning the lands of which the others have only the use on terms, are possessed of the patriarchal power of the state, while the others have only the proletariate powers its individuals can acquire, subject to the patriarchal in the others. That of these classes the one is in representation of energy and the other inertia. And that of these powers the patriarchal is in representation of energy, and the proletariate of inertia. And that the holders of the patriarchal power are the lords and those holding the proletariate powers as commons.

And thus, accepting that every monogamic state at all the earlier periods of its history is of such classes, we accept also the truth of experience that the proletariate class in every such normal state advances upon the patriarchal, until they themselves become possessed of the patriarchal power, which they may exercise in consistence with tutelar lords as they do in England, or to the exclusion of them by name, even as they have done in this Republic.

And, accepting this, we must accept also that the commons can take the patriarchal power only by proscription or revolution, that either is achieved by the adult males of the state. That these obtaining the patriarchal power were bound to hold and exercise it. That this they could do only by majorities determined by vote to which there were parties advocating different policies, the major of which must hold the government. And that thus in accepting an essential being of the universe, we accept not only that there is the every being of energy and inertia from the universe to man, but man himself into constitutional kingdoms, such as is that of England or a democracy, such as is this Republic. In England there is the fiction of a constitution in the existence of the two orders of lords and commons, balanced against each other upon its stipulations. But in this Republic the illusion of a constitution has been rudely dispelled, in the subjugation of one section by the other. And who rightly accepts an essential being of the universe accepts that of this there is man agamic, polygamic and monogamic, and that of monogamic man there are constitutional kingdoms until their commons shall take the patriarchal powers from lords. And then republics under no other law than that consisting in the volitions of a victorious party of adult males — unless that law shall come from a monogamic state of unequal races united in relations of inequality, so as that to the higher race there be the patriarchal powers, and to the lower the proletariate power consistent with the patriarchal.

And thus it is that if there be such essential being it is the finite word of God in space; and as such is the self-executing cause of its consequences possible from the universe to man; and of man himself; and the families, stocks, tribes and states of man. And that with respect to this insensible being, as the cause of beings sensible, there is but the single question whether such being does in fact exist.

CHAPTER III.

This were that being insensible of which are the beings sensible: And that being of God, originating cause, through which there are the beings of that cause: And that being finite of beings infinite in reciprocal limitations of each other, of which, from the reciprocal activities of its infinite beings different upon center of their neutral beings intermediate, there are force, matter, life and nature in stars, sun, earth, plant and animal from the universe to man and that mind in man through which he is directed to become the man possible.

These infinites were different but as they be inversely to each other, and as such they were vacua and plena, and attractive and repulsive, reciprocally; and of their attractions were in coincidence upon a center of their neutral being intermediate and of their repulsions were in differentiations thence; and into two orbs in elliptical orbits about such center. And such the infinitessimal unit finite—a wheel of relatively static being about its axle of being relatively dynamic—analogously such were the compound of such units, and such the universe of compounds —a wheel of relatively static being in stars, suns and planets, in their orbits about dynamic centers and the whole about the dynamic center of the universe.

This being finite of beings infinite were such as is that in the physical forces, and such as is that in heat of the most of dynamic being to the least of the static; and as that in cold of the most of static being to the least of the dynamic; and such as is that in dark, of the most of heat to the least of cold, and that in light of the most of

cold to the least of heat; and that in electricity the minus
of which is dark and the plus light; and that in magnetism—but inverted electricity—in which the south of
magnetism is reacting with the plus of electricity and the
north of magnetism with the minus of electricity—in the
electro-magnetic spheroid of magnetic moments moving
about the conductor of electrical reactions producing
them.

It were also such as is that force of levitation from
the center of the earth through which beings dynamic
rise from the earth's surface; and as is that force of
gravitation through which beings static fall—levitation
being dynamic being from the center of the being finite
to project and sustain the static in its elliptical orbit about
that center; and gravitation that static being in its elliptical orbit of resistence to the radiations of that dynamic
being.

It were also the same as that force in impact pressure
friction, or projection, even, which when intense enough
sublimes the subject to heat and light, but which if not so
intense, produces at its opposite extremities the electricities plus and minus to meet of their reciprocal attractions
through an adequate and continuous conductor, in electro-
magnetic spheroids; but, if the conductor be not adequate
or continuous, to meet in sparks of heat and light; or, if
the conductor be a tube of glass from which the static
matters of this earth's atmosphere have been withdrawn,
to meet in the production of radiations lately discovered
by Roentgen, which cast the shadows of the more static
substances upon which they fall as does light.

It were also the same as that rythmical being at this
earth's surface the impressions of incident forces upon
which, at one point, are reported by telephone or telegraph
at another; and if the impressions be made upon it at the
focus of a parabolic reflector there is the report of them
by wireless telegraphy—discovered by Marconi—these
radiations are parallel from such reflector, as are those of

heat and light, and deliver to the sensitive being upon which they fall the impressions made upon that being without other medium of communication than the rays themselves.

These infinite beings, different in production of the being finite, were the Ions of Faraday and the dynamic being the anion and the static the kation; and the one were the cause and the other the consequence; and the one the force and the other the matter; and the one the life and the other the nature of every being finite from the universe to man.

And it were also the same as the mind of man itself — but the being finite of beings infinite in reciprocal limitations of each other — and this in units reacting within the units of external being to the continued existence of the individual man.

And there were thus the universe of beings, not of miracles, or of the manipulations of an anthropomorphic Theos, but simply of the resolutions of infinite beings different into the finite beings of them possible. And this creative cause were not discharged of its office in the creatures that now exist but were in them to sustain them as it was to create them.

And, such the essential being of the universe, there is this if there be that which could not be without it; there were that which could not be without it if there be being finite, or the word of God, or space, or force, or matter, or life, or nature, or the universe, star, sun, earth, plant, animal, or man, or mind in man, or the law that every being of the universe — essentially the same as every other — at its time and place be the being possible and but the being possible in consistence with the other beings of the universe. And there were not the one of these beings without such essential being of the universe. And there is such being therefore as there is the one of these.

CHAPTER IV.

There were not the being finite without such being, in that it, itself, were such essential being of the universe. There were not such finite, but as it be of beings infinite of their affection of and for each other merely in reciprocal limitations of each other into the finite being of them both. This of infinites were necessarily universal and exclusive of other being in that universe. And so original, universal and exclusive, it were, itself, the essential being of which are the beings of this universe, no one of which could exist but in consequence of that originating and exclusive cause.

It were, also, the essential being of which are the beings of this universe, for the further reason that it were being physiological, as are all the beings of this universe; which, if they could be without such being finite of beings infinite, could not be so physiological as they are without it.

It were being physiological. That, as I have said, were the being possible of kindred beings different of their reciprocal affinities simply in reciprocal limitations of each other into the one original, automatic, autonomic and exclusive being of them both, in which each were the fulcrum to the activities of the other, and each the cause of consequences in the other; while the being itself, as such, were without other cause than that of their reciprocal affections of and for each other.

And such were the being finite. Its infinite beings were kindred from being of the same infinite elements, and different from being of these elements inversely. So related, they were reciprocally vacua, and reciprocally plena — each wanting that not of itself in the other, and each not wanting that of itself in the other — and as vacua, reciprocally, they were reciprocally attractive; and as plena, reciprocally, they were reciprocally repulsive. And, of their reciprocal attractions, they were penultimately coincident on the axis of their neutral being intermediate. And of their reciprocal repulsions they were penultimately in differentiation, thence into an oblate spheroid and wheel of them both about such axis.

So different, they were relatively dynamic and static, and in coincidence oppositely, the dynamic were fast to the static slow. And the fast will have penetrated the slow, and projected it into an oblate spheroid of the slow about the axis in possession of the fast. And this were, in effect, a wheel of which the axis were the fast in eccentric radiations of its dynamic being into the slow to sustain it as disc in concentric radiations of its static being into the fast to sustain it as its axle.

This, however physical to other being such, in itself, were being physiological. And such, and so physiological, the every infinitesimal unit being finite, such and so were every medium of these; and such and so the universe of media. The units such were susceptive of reciprocal inductions into kindred beings different, capable of coincidence into such being physiological of both. And the units of every medium were so susceptive and so capable; and the medium of the universe itself were so capable of self differentiation, coincidence and differentiation, into the universal being physiological of all the units of the universe.

But while such were the wheel physiological of infinite being finite, of which the one were axle and the other disc, it must be observed that the axle of its own motion not more than that of any other wheel could

6

move its disc, or its disc revolve of its own motion on
its axle, or without the force of a crank upon the axle to
turn them both. Nor could the axle produce its disc
or the disc its axle without an intermediating force not
exclusively of either, but of both. Nor were there the
wheel of being finite, even of its beings infinite, without
an intermediary force not of either but of both. This
force were of the word of God, importing his will, without
which there were not of his infinites ever the finite being
physiological; which, though of infinite factors, is of
these only under the infinite force of such factors of their
own motions reacting with each other.

And, such and so, physiological the every sensible or
insensible being of this universe, such and so is the
human mind itself, through which man becomes consciously or rationally sensible of such beings. And there
were not the being finite so exclusive of other beings in
this universe, and so physiological as is the every being
of this universe, but as it be itself of the essential being
of this universe, and without there be such being.

Nor were the word of God without such being. There
were God but as the supreme originating cause of being
in this universe personified. But even that God, so
supreme in power and purpose, and so unconditioned in
their exercises, were unable to accomplish ends, such, at
least, as are those of beings in this universe, without means,
and these of his own infinite beings, and these the means
appearing in these beings. Nor of his own infinite beings,
so far as we can see, could he cause these beings finite to
us but as he causes his infinites themselves to become
finite in their reciprocal limitations of each other. Nor
were they in such reciprocal limitations of each other but
from such their reciprocal affections of and for each other
merely. And this only conceivable word of God, therefore, simply were being finite. And it were also being
physiological, since its every word and letter were the
possible of kindred beings different of their affinities sim-

ply in such relation to each other. It were as universal as were being finite, and as exclusive as were being finite, and as physiological as were being finite, and as teleogical as were finite being physiological. And so, but being finite, the essential being of the universe, there were not the word of God without such being.

It were not the being finite simply, as I have said, which were inert, as is every other being finite without that word. But were finite power importing its infinite purpose, and cause its consequence, and force its matter, and life its nature. And while, therefore, there were not the being physiological, of which is life in nature of this universe, of the word of God even, without being infinite, or this of being finite without the word of God, yet there were not such finite word but as it be physiological, or such being physiological without it be that essential and exclusive being, of which are the physiological beings of this universe.

In every such physiology it were purpose in execution of its power and life in production of its nature, and it were a physiological instead of a theological agent in production of this sensible universe. And as such, it were itself the essential being of the universe, as were being finite. And it were the being finite with the difference only that in this there were purpose, not necessarily implied in the powers of being finite simply.

Nor were there space without such being. There is that we term space in a seeming void of force and matter. And if there be such void there were this without its being the essential being of the universe, and without such being therefore. But if there be being infinite, and the more certainly if this be the word of God, importing his will into the sensible beings of this universe, and yet the more certainly if this be the source of that force of which there is matter, there were not such void. But, in that seeming vacuum which we term space, there were the finite word of God, insensible to us, but as real and substantial as it is in its beings sensible. That were real space, and if there be this, not as a conventionality but as a reality, it were itself the essential being of the universe, and there were not this without such being.

It were so universal and exclusive as were the being finite, or the word of God. And it were so original, universal and exclusive as were the being finite, or the word of God. And it were so physiological as were the being finite, or the word of God. And so original, universal, exclusive and physiological, there were not this but as it be that universal but insensible being physiological of the universe, in which and of which, there are stars, suns and planets in their orbits and systems. And that physiological atmosphere of the earth in and of which are its gaseous matters in their orbits and systems, and which transmits with absolute accuracy to one point the impressions made by force upon it at another.

In acceptance of its existence as such insensible being physiological about the earth only is there the reason for sight, or sound, or the telegraphic or telephonic message, or for the physical forces, or the reactions of matters at a distance, or the attractions, repulsions, inductions, levitations or gravitations of matters, or the gaseous matters of the earth's atmosphere, or these into water, ammonias, and carbonic oxides, or these into the matters of which are plants and animals. Not only were there no sight or sound, or telegraphic or telephonic message of the reactions of matters at a distance, or the sense of matters at a distance, or the attractions, repulsions, inductions, levitations or gravitations of matters at the earth's surface, but there were not the gaseous matters of the earth's atmosphere but as that atmosphere be a being physiological of its systemic factors in reaction; and but as these matters be the products of such physiological atmosphere. And, as there were not these matters without these forces, or these without this atmosphere, or this without space, or this without it be being finite, or this without it be the

word of God, there were not space without it be the essential being of the universe. But if it be not being finite,
or the word of God, and so universal and exclusive, and so
the essential being of the universe, and the prime cause of
such being, it were yet such in being itself the prime cause
of every being of the universe.

In ultimate analysis of every sensibly substantive
being of the universe there is matter; and in ultimate
analysis of matter there is space — an omnipresent but
invisible being physiological, automatic and autonomic,
and cause and consequence of its own beings. And this
such resultant of all the beings of the universe, were the
prime cause of all the beings of the universe. And as
such were the essential being of the universe. And there
were such space not only from analysis of matter, but as
the originating cause of the beings of this universe, from
its being the source of electric force.

If there be moderate force on matter there is the
battery at the poles of which appear the electricities,
minus and plus, of whose meeting in the gaseous medium
there is the electric spark of heat and light, and of whose
meeting in the adequate conductor there is the electro-
magnetic spheroid; and of whose meeting in the vacuum
tube there are what have been termed radiant matters which,
transpiring the tube, are termed X or Roentgen rays.
This insensible fluid, expressed by any kind of force from
any kind of matter, or by any body of matter in motion
upon another at rest, is termed, becoming sensible, electric force, which therefore can be but the abstract of rest
and motion in a medium of both, of which motion is minus
and rest plus. And these, in their reactions obviously
originating under different conditions, the spark spheroid
and Roentgen ray as certainly originate the beings possible
of these; and these the beings the ultimate source and
substance of which is space, the electricities of space in
their reactions immediate or remote, originate. And space,
of which is the electricity originating these, were the essen-

tial being of which are these. And these the beings of the universe, this electric space were the essential being of the universe. It were the same as that force in heat, cold, dark and light and magnetism from reacting with it; and the same as that in matter from reacting with it. And the same as that of which there are the inductions, deductions, attractions, repulsions, levitations and gravitations of matters, themselves but the syntheses of electric forces.

And space, the essential being of the universe from being the finite word of God, were such essential being also from being the originating cause of all being in this universe.

And there were not, therefore, the being finite, or the word of God, or space, but as there be an essential being of the universe. And if there be these, or either one of these, there is such being.

CHAPTER V.

NOR WERE THERE FORCE OR MATTER WITHOUT SUCH BEING.

There were not force. That or that we term force is a being which, from its effects in incidences upon a sensitive being in ourselves, we term heat, cold, dark, light, electricity or magnetism; and which in its interventions of matters causes their attractions, repulsions, inductions, levitations and gravitations. There are reasons to be given later that this is a finite being physiological of beings infinite reacting with each other. And that this is the same as that of which are the other finite beings of the universe, in that it exhibits force in changing the states of our feelings, and of the matters upon which it is incident, simply from reacting with them. That in the infinite beings energy and inertia, of which are all the beings of the universe and that sensitive being in our-selves, heat is of more of energy to less of inertia, and cold of more of inertia to less of energy. And that so are dark electricity and levitation of more of energy to less of inertia; and light, magnetism and gravitation of more of inertia to less of energy. And that this being, of the same elements as the sensitive being in us and in matters, is able to react with them, and in this produce the changes in them we perceive. That in this the energy of the one is in want of the inertia in the other, but not of its energy; and so is attractive of its inertia and repulsive of its energy; and so the inertia of the one is attractive of the energy of the other but repulsive of its inertia; and that thus in every such case of contact of this force with other being of the universe there is that reciprocal intussusception of each other which we term reaction, of which are the changes in these subjects we observe.

And such force it were possible of an essential being of the universe. And so possible it were true of such being. It were possible of such being in that, that of the finite word of God in space were universal and exclusive of other being of the universe and of force, therefore, but as this be of it. And force existing but of such being, were possible of such being. And possible of such being it were of such being, so exclusive of all being not of it. And as there were not such being without force, there were not force without such being. It were the most attenuated form of that being of which are the sensible beings of the universe, and were to this as is gaseous matter to the liquid and solid matters from which under successive increments of heat it is sublimed. And as there were not these solid and liquid matters without the gaseous matters into which of heat they are sublimed, there were not that gaseous matter without such solid and liquid matters, or without that being of which there are these solid or liquid and gaseous matters. And so there were not force without such essential being of the universe. But if we may not see that there is such force, and can see the forces but as the aspects of distinct beings of whose real beings we know nothing, still we must accept them as modes of a being finite of the word of God in space, which, universal and exclusive of other being of the universe, and itself the essential being of the universe, were exclusive of forces but as they be of it. And as there were not this essential being of the universe without these forces, whatever they may be, there were not these forces whatever they may be without such being. They were then themselves the anthropomorphic agencies through which God, the cause of being in this universe, will have carried it into the actual beings of the universe. And however these energetic agencies be different from the inert being of that word, they are yet of the same essential being of that word. And as there were not that word without these agencies to its execution, there were not these agencies to its execution without that word. And there were not, therefore, force or the forces of an essential being without such being.

Nor were there matter without such being. That, universal and exclusive of force but as that be of it, were exclusive also of matter for the same reason. And it were also exclusive of matter for the further reason that force and matter are essentially the same as is seen in the facts that all forces and matters react. And that all matters under force sufficient are sublimed or reduced to force. It is, or may be, seen that all forces react with each other as they could not but as they be of the same essential being inversely; and that all matters react with each other, as they could not but as they be of the same essential being inversely. And that all forces and all matters react as they could not but as they be of the same essential being inversely; and that all matters under dynamic force sufficient are sublimed to force, and all forces under static force sufficient are reduced to matter.

All forces react with each other in that of the incidence of any one force upon another their states are changed respectively into a being intermediate of both; as if there be heat on cold or cold on heat; or dark on light or light on dark; or the minus on the plus or the plus on the minus of electricity; or the south on the north or the north on the south of magnetism; or electricity on magnetism or magnetism on electricity, or any one of these on any other. In any such case there is the being intermediate of both of which the constituents are exactly proportioned to the forces coincident.

And all matters react with each other in that of the incidence of one fluid or gaseous matter on another they are changed respectively into matter intermediate of both. As if there be the coincidences, in such conditions, of oxygen and a metal, there is the metallic oxide, or of oxygen and hydrogen there is water, or of chlorine and sodium there is salt. Or if there be the incidence of one solid matter on another not with the explosive violence to fuse or sublime it there is the force intermediate of both, which, though not as sensible as matter, is as real and substantial and as consistent, and as proportioned to the forces in the matters coincident as is the salt, water or metallic oxide to the matters coincident in them.

And all forces and all matters react with each other in that of any force on any matter there is the disappearance of the force but in a change of the state of the matter proportioned to the force absorbed.

These reactions were rationally possible, but as the forces be reciprocally attractive and repulsive, and the matters reciprocally attractive and repulsive, and the forces and matters reciprocally attractive and repulsive; and there were these attractions and repulsions but as the forces be of the same essential being inversely, and the matters of the same essential being inversely, and the forces and matters be of the same essential being inversely.

There were not force or matter, therefore, without such being.

At least, there were not force or matter as realities without such being. We are directly sensible of some things termed heat, cold, dark, light, electricity and magnetism, and we are rationally sensible of some things muscular or mechanical—moving matters to and from each other; and of some things chemical—dissolving or composing matter which we term forces. We are also sensible of some things termed hydrogen, oxygen, carbon, nitrogen, sulphur, phosphorus, the halogens, and others, in compounds inorganic and organic, which we term matters; and if these be realities, or more than the terms by which we express the impressions made upon us by external beings different from each other, of which we can know

know nothing more, there were not force or matter without that essential being of which are these, and without an essential being of the universe, since that being of which there were force and matter were itself that essential being.

This were apparent in the fact that this being, whether of force or matter, were of elements; and that these elements of both were the same; and that these elements of their reciprocal attractions and repulsions were in reactions resulting in central beings intermediate, about which, relatively dynamic, the elements themselves, relatively static, were in elliptical orbits with these central beings at one of the foci of each ellipse.

This true of any two kindred elements adjacent — that in their reaction they produce the spheroid and wheel of relatively static beings about an axis of relatively dynamic being — were true of any two spheroids and wheels of these adjacent; and true also of any duplicates of these, and so on to any spheroid and wheel such as is this earth in its crust of constrictive matter about its center of explosive space. This being of force and matter were thus the essential being of this earth; that of this earth were the same as that of any other planet, sun or star, and the same as that of the universe itself. And thus of the being of space and matter there were the essential being of the universe. And as there were not this without that of force and matter, there were not that of force and matter without this — if, only, force and matter be of elements and these be the same, and these be capable of spheroids and wheels of relatively static being in revolutions on their axes of beings dynamic. And they are of elements and these the same and capable.

They are of elements. The sensible beings of force are heat, cold, dark, light, electricity and magnetism; and heat of elements, heat and cold — the heat prepotent — and cold of elements, cold and heat — the cold prepotent; and dark of elements, dark and light — the dark prepotent; and electricity of elements, minus and plus — the minus prepotent; and the magnetism.of elements, north and south—the north prepotent.

The sensible beings of matter are oxygen, hydrogen, nitrogen, carbon, sulphur and phosphorus, with others incidental to the beings possible of these combined; and oxygen is of elements dynamic and static, the dynamic prepotent; and hydrogen is of elements, static and dynamic, the static prepotent; and nitrogen is of elements, oxygenic and hydrogenic, the oxygenic prepotent; and carbon of elements, hydrogenic and oxygenic, the hydrogenic prepotent; and sulphur of elements, oxygenic and nitrogenic, the oxygenic prepotent; and phosphorus of elements, nitrogenic.and oxygenic, the nitrogenic prepotent.

And such the elements of force and matter, those of force are the same, in that they react with each other; and those of matter the same, for the same reason; and those of force the same as those of matter, for the same reason, and for the further reason that force under static being sufficient becomes matter, and matter under dynamic being sufficient becomes force.

If there be cold enough upon the insensible vapors of platinum, the densest metal, they become first liquid and then solid, and if there be heat enough on solid platinum, it becomes first liquid, then vapor in heat and light, to show that matter is but the static state of force, and force but the dynamic state of matter.

And this being of force and matter were capable of the spheroids and wheels of static about dynamic being, as may be seen in the fact that from every incidence of force on matter such dynamo-static being is produced.

If there be immoderate .force on matter, that matter is sublimed to force; but if there be moderate force upon a body of matter, irregular in-outline and insulated, at its extremities the most distant from each other appear the electricities, minus and plus, which, since the matter is unaltered, can be, of course, but transformations of the forces incident. These electricities (as are all finite beings) are reciprocally attractive and repulsive, and of their reciprocal attractions tend to react upon the center of their being intermediate in a spheroidal spark of heat and light if there be no intermediate conductor, but if there be such conductor and this be much too small, it is instantly sublimed to heat and light; or if it be but slightly insufficient, there are in it only heat and light, and if it be quite sufficient for the current of electrical reactions there are in it electric currents oppositely, and about it circles of magnetic moments moving oppositely. These magnetic circles were vertical to the electric currents in the conductor, and every magnetic circle were a section of this electro-magnetic system, and each section were an oblate spheroid of static being about its axis of being dynamic. In the electric elements there were dynamic beings, and in the magnetic circles static beings, and of the whole there were a prol-oblate spheroid of static beings in revolutions on their axes of beings dynamic analogous to that of the planets about the sun, and to that of this earth in its crust of matter about its center of explosive space. This force producing electricities at the extremities of matter may be either of heat, cold, dark, light, electricity, magnetism, percussion, friction, pressure, or projection even, from which it is apparent that not only were these incident forces the same, but that they are of elements the same as is electricity—able to produce, under suitable conditions, the spark of heat and light and the electro-magnetic spheroid of static being about its axis of being dynamic; and thus the moments of force; and the molecules and compounds of matter; and the planets, suns, stars and universe. This were the essential being of the universe, and there were not force or matter without this. The ideal figure of electro-magnetic force and matter is represented by the agaric mushroom in its magnetic pileus on its electric stem and by the palm in its magnetic whorl of leaves upon its electric trunk, and, generally, by the exogenus plant in its magnetic foliage on its electric stalk.

Force and matter are in fact the two departments of the being finite. And to us, intermediate, there are two aspects of that automatic and autonomic being; and the one the causal and the other the consequential, and the one the parental and the other the progenital; and the one of force and the other of matter. And these departments are in spheroids and wheels of static beings in revolutions on their axes of beings dynamic. And in each there is an ideal wheel; and this of constituents, each a functionary; and these in every way analogous; so that heat in force is as oxygen in matter, and cold in force as hydrogen in matter; and dark in force as is nitrogen in matter, and light in force as is carbon in matter; and electricity in force as is sulphur in matter, and magnetism in force as is phosphorus in matter. And the incidental forces of impact, percussion, friction, pressure and the like, are as are the incidental elements chlorine, sodium, selenium, tellurium and the like, which are not of the vital constituents of organic matter, but are necessary to the efficiencies of such constituents. Such to us were force and matter in relation to each other; and to us, at least, there were not force or matter without such being of the universe.

CHAPTER VI.

We may not agree as to what are life and nature. And a definition of either, given by any one person, were apt to be unsatisfactory to others. And this for the reason, it is to be presumed, that we have not the hypothesis of any one noumenal being of which these are the phenomena. But adopting the hypothesis of a finite word of God in space as the noumenal being of the universe, of which is life, of which is nature, we must accept that there were not the phenomena of life or nature without such being.

We must accept this whatever be this thing of life or nature, for such being were universal and exclusive of other being in the universe; and of life and nature, therefore, but as these be of it, whatever they may be. And whether there could be that being, such as it is, without life or nature, such as they are, it is at least certain that there could not be life or nature without such being. Since, while there might be a noumenal being without such phenomena, there could not be the phenomena of the noumenal being without the being noumenal. It might be argued with equal force that there could not be such being without life and nature, supposing that there be life and nature, since it were so universal and exclusive, as I have said. But it is enough for my present proposition thus to show that there were not life or nature without such essential being.

But, while logically clear that there were not life or nature without such being, it were clearer to common apprehension if it should appear that of such noumenal being there were beings such as are these to which we give the names of life and nature, and it does so appear.

To one intelligently accepting such space it is in units, each an infinitesimal being finite of beings infinite, in reciprocal limitations of each other into a spheroid and wheel of the one infinite, as axis, to the other as its disk. And it were such for the reason that the infinites to so react must be different and, both infinite, they can differ but as they be of one integral infinite inversely. But so differing they must of their reciprocal affinities react on the axis of their neutral being intermediate into the spheroid and wheel of both, of which one is axle in eccentric radiations of its special being into its disk of the other, and the other is disk in concentric radiations of its special being into the axle to sustain the disk about it in composition of such automatic and autonomic being physiological, whose elements were expressed to another such being adjacent, in terms of the physical forces, heat, cold, dark, light, electricity and magnetism involved in its production.

To such being as the conscious being in man, for instance, the axle were heat and the disk cold. And the eccentric radiations from the axis to the axis itself, or to our intelligence in the place of such axis, were dark, and the concentric radiations from the disk to such sensitive being in the place of the axis were light. And the whole were an electro-magnetic being physiological, such as results from the meeting of the self-differentiated and atomic electricities, minus and plus.

Attentive observations of phenomena show that if these electricities meet in a medium of gaseous matters there is the spark of heat and light in a spheroid and wheel of which the axle is heat and the disk cold; and the eccentric radiations of heat dark and the concentric radiations of cold light. And that if they meet, not in a medium of gaseous matters, but in an adequate conductor, there is not the spheroid of heat and light, but instead an electro-magnetic spheroid of magnetic moments moving in a disk about the axis of electrical reactions producing them.

And that if they meet, not in the gaseous medium or adequate conductor, but in a tube from which the gaseous matters of the earth's atmosphere have been withdrawn, there is not the spark of heat and light, or the electro-magnetic spheroid of electricity and magnetism, but the Kotode X, or Roentgen rays of electricity in search of responsive magnetisms, which are but minus electrics in search of the plus they did not find in the tube, but which they do find in the more static matters obstructing them without, whose shadows they thus cast.

It is thus seen that electricity is the axle of a wheel physiological, of which magnetism is the disk. And that electricity is minus to magnetism plus, and electricity heat to magnetism cold; and the one dark to the other light; and the one force to the other matter; and it may be further seen that in every such electro-magnetic spheroid and wheel there is a cause and course of its being from axle to disk, and this met by a cause and course of its being from disk to axle. That these spheroids and wheels of force are analogous to like wheels in matter in which there are these courses eccentric and concentric; that of these there are the stars, sun and earth, and the plants and animals at the earth's surface. That of these in the plant and animal the one from the axle is life and the other from the disk nature. That this, so in the animal and plant, is analogously so in all matters organic or inorganic, and are but the opposite modes of that infinite being finite of which are all forces and matters. And life from the axis of every such being to distend its disk. And nature from the disk to constrict and place the radiating axle. And such the relations of life and nature to each other in all the beings of the universe, they can be but of that being of which there are the beings of the universe. These were not into these beings of the universe without life and nature. And there were not life or nature but as a mode of such being, or either life or nature without such being. But, if we may not accept these axial and peripherential modes of the being finite as the originals of life and nature, we must see that at this earth's surface there are beings opposite, and from the seed into the stem and foliage of the plant and from the ovum to the body and limbs of the animal; and that however the plant may start from its seed, with its roots up and its bud down, it will right itself and send its roots down and its bud up; and that any amorphous section of the polyp will develop its head from its upper surface and tail its from its under. This neither can do but of beings in it, the one of which tends to the center of the earth and the other to its surface; and but as the one tending to the center of the earth draws the substance from the center that being of which it consists and injects it into that tending from it, to be administered by it to the plant or animal possible. Of these tendings the one were the life and the other the nature of the plant or animal. There were not the one of these beings but as it be of an essential being of the earth, and this of the essential being of the universe. And there were not the life or nature of the plant or animal, at least, without such being. And if there be not the life or nature of the plant or animal without such being, there were not the life or nature of any other being of the universe.

And there were not the universe.   From its immensity
we may not be able to conceive an universe.   And we may
not be able to conceive it for the further reason that it·
were inclusive of ourselves and of that sensitive being in
ourselves, through which, only, could we have perception
of this, or other objective being, and which perceptive of
such objective being were not perceptive, or conceptive,
of it, as inclusive of itself.

But, hypothecating an universe of being, we hypothecate · a being infinitely large, of beings infinitesimally
small.   And hypothecating it as the whole of the being
finite of the word of God, we hypothecate it as an illimitable spheroid finite of infinitesimally attenuated spheroids
finite, each a wheel of what may be termed inertia revolving on its axis of energy, producing its disk, producing its
axle.   And such the infinitesimal unit, such were the universe of units, which not possible without its units, its
unit were not possible without such universe.   Such units
were the essential beings of that universe; and as there
were not these beings without the universe, there were
not the universe without these beings, which together
were its essential being.   And there were not, therefore,
an universe, whether of the finite word of God or of being
simply, without an essential being of that universe. ·

Nor were there stars without such being.   There are
luminous objects in the celestial sphere to which we give
the name of stars.   And these are probably orbs of matter, in themselves inert, but revolving, each on its axis
of included force propelling it: And it is probable that

these are in elliptical orbits, mediately or immediately, about the axis of the universe. That they are of different magnitudes. And that while some, and these the largest, are in such orbits immediately about the axis of the universe, others, smaller, are in such orbits about these; and others, yet smaller, in such orbits about these; and others, yet smaller, in such orbits about these; and so on to those of the size of the sun of this solar system, about which are planets in their orbits such; and about which are there moons, in their orbits such. And regarding these, however unequally related to the axis of the universe, as stars, there were not these or the one of these but as it be of an essential being; and that the essential being of the universe; and as there were not the universe without its essential being, there were not the stars without such being.

And this, the logical deduction from the hypothesis of an essential being of the word of God in space, were equally the induction of the phenomena of such beings.

And if it shall appear that the universe of such essential being were capable of the stars, or that the stars, as we see them, were possible of such universe, it will conclusively appear that the stars are of the same essential being as the universe. And that, as there were not the universe without such being, there were not the star without its being; and that the being of the universe.

And it does, or may, appear that the universe of its essential being were capable of the stars, and that the stars were possible of this being of the universe. The universe, as I have said, were an illimitable finite spheroid physiological, of inertia in revolutions, as matter, on its axis of energy, as force. And energy were in eccentric radiations of its special being into inertia; and inertia were in concentric radiations of its special being into energy. These radiations, meeting oppositely about that axis, were reciprocally intussusceptive of each other; and in this were reciprocally refractive of each other, so that, upon points in a hollow sphere about that axis, and at graduated distances from it and from each other, there were foci of the reciprocal refractions, about each of which there were a disk of inertia revolving on its axis of energy.

This were a spheroid physiological in every way, but in size the same as the universe. And from the axes of these there were eccentric energies met by concentric inertias reciprocally refracting each other to foci about these axes. About these there were others, such, and so on, from the universal spheroid, the largest possible, through continually lessening spheroids, to the smallest possible in molecules of matter and moments of force at this earth.

The larger of these and the nearer to the axis of the universe, at least we term stars. And of these the universe of finite being physiological were capable. And that capable of these, these were possible of that.

And that were capable of these. If, of infinite being finite, simply, the universe were a spheroid finite of infinite beings in reciprocal limitations of each other. And thus were in effect a wheel of inertia revolving on its axis of energy. And in this inertia were as matter to energy as force. And of its energy and inertia, eccentric and concentric, there were their reciprocal intussusceptions and reactions into smaller spheroids finite at graduating distances from each other and the axis of the universe, each of which were of inertia as matter about its axis of energy as force, such as would seem to be the stars, each of which is, as far as we can see, an orb of matter about its center of included force. And if the universe be of infinite being finite, simply, there were beings about its axis in likeness of the stars. But if it be also of the finite word expression of the will of God—the universal cause of all being in this universe personified—these beings in likeness of the stars were in fact the stars we see as such. And their central energies were in fact forces. And their peripherential inertias were in fact matters, since that one only cause of beings in this universe will have caused the stars we see, and causing these will not have caused others in likenesses of these, but different from them. Nor causing forces and matters such as seem to be the centers and crusts of stars, it will not have caused other beings in likenesses of force and matter, but different from them, which do not elsewhere or otherwise appear. There were not, therefore, this essential being of the universe hypothecated, whether as the being finite or the word of God, without the stars. And as there were not this being without the stars, there were not the stars without this being.

Nor were there, for the same reason, the sun without such being. There are reasons to be given later that the sun is the central figure of a system of finite being extending from its axis to the orbit of its most distant planets; that these extremes, the one in radiations of energy eccentric and the other in radiations of inertia concentric, react upon the intermediate points possible; and that of these reactions there have been, first, the surface of the sun in a crust of the densest metallic matter possible. And, next, the atmosphere of the sun in vapors of less obstinate metals and metallic oxides. And, next, the four inner planets; and, next, the asteroids; and, next, the four outer planets; and, lastly, the comets and nebulæ from which they come.

There are reasons also to be given that this system, from whose reactions have come these constituents of the solar system, is still in operation. And that from the sun's atmosphere of metallic oxide vapors there are forming archaen rocks to fall in spots upon the incandescent surface of the sun to sustain it in its radiations of energy into its most distant region of inertia, in which are forming comets to form into planets, to march successively, from loss of heat, into the sun; and that the sun's crust and its planets, asteroids and comets are in elliptical orbits about the radiating center of the solar system, and this from the alternate prepotencies of the energies and inertias reacting in them.

And such the sun, the likeness of its system were possible of an essential being finite. And that system itself were the product of an essential being finite of the word of God, without which it were not, since without this it were the accident or miracle, the neither of which exists, and as there were not this without the sun, there were not the sun without this.

Nor were there the earth without such essential being. There are reasons to be given later that the earth, also, is the central figure of a system of being finite extending from its center of energy to a region of inertia beyond the orbit of the moon.   And that of these, eccentric and concentric in reaction, there has been, first, the earth's crust of matters in strata, the first stratum of the densest metallic matter known; and the next of the matters of metallic oxides in rocks; and the next of hydrogen oxide matters in waters; and that of these extremes further reacting there has been, next, the earth's atmosphere of gaseous matters reacting into waters, ammonias and carbonic oxides, reacting into plants; and, next, the moon, the last, perhaps, of others, on its way to absorption by the earth, as is the planet to absorption by the sun.   These were possible of a medium of infinite being finite.   They were certainly of that finite word of God of which are the earth and its crust, atmosphere and moon.   Nor were there that word of God in earth without the earth.   And as there were not that essential being in the earth without the earth, there was not the earth without that essential being.

And there were not, therefore, either the universe, star, sun or earth, without such being of the universe.

CHAPTER VIII.

NOR WERE THERE THE PLANT OR ANIMAL WITHOUT SUCH BEING.

There are two orders of being at this earth's surface, the one termed plant and the other animal; and while it is admitted that these are beings apart from and independent of our conceptions of them, and as realities, therefore, so far as that they have existences of their own, it is not admitted that they are realities in the sense of their being physiological in teleologic evo-involution merely of an essential being of the universe. In each there is a causal mode of its being termed its life, and a consequential mode of its being termed its nature; and it is not admitted that each at its time and place is the self-existent automatic and autonomic being of its modes simply; or that of these, at any one stage of its existence, it can vary to the next under the conditions possible. But it has been, and is yet, assumed by many that it is started to exist and is put in motion by an external power in purpose attendant on it. And that of this it is made to vary to the conditions of its existence changing. And, as each is in classes, orders, genera and species, it is assumed that not only is its existence in classes, orders, genera and species determined by this attendant genius, but that no one of its species can depart from its genius without the order of such attendant. And if this be true it must be admitted that the plant and animal are not of the evolutions of an essential being of the universe. And that there may be the plant or animal without such being.

But if it be not true, and the plant or animal be not of the manipulations of such attendant genius of eternal purpose, but are of eternal purpose itself, expressed in terms of the being finite of beings infinite, the plant or animal were then not without such space; and whether either is of such space will depend on whether space be capable of the plant or animal, or the plant or animal be possible of space. If either be possible of space, space were capable of either, and to show, therefore, that this plant or animal is of space, it is only necessary to show that space were capable of the plant or animal, or that the plant or animal were possible of space. And either may be shown.

If there be beings finite of infinite beings different in such spheroids and wheels of matter about their axis of forces included, and of these there be the universe, star, sun and earth, there were, of the earth's surface of matter, eccentrically radiating forces in heat perceptible as levitation into concentrically radiating forces in cold, perceptible as gravitation.

These would react in every such eccentric and concentric radiation, and into infinitesimal spheroids different, some energetic and some inert. And some as oxygen containing more of heat and levitation than the others as hydrogen, containing more of cold and gravitation. These were gaseous matters such as are now in this earth's atmosphere, termed oxygen, hydrogen, nitrogen and carbon. These so different from each other will have been of the same essential being inversely. And so inversely of the same essential being will have reacted. And into ammonias, of more of gravitations to less of levitations; and into carbonic oxides of more of levitation to less of gravitation; and into water neutral; but from its consistence of both oxygen and hydrogen, intermediating these and forming with them ammonias compound, both acid and base, and thus an organic matter, which, by successive variations to the conditions of its existence, becomes successively, the cryptogamic, phonerogamic, endogenous and exogenous plant.

It is thus that of a medium of an essential being of

the universe, where now is the earth's system within the orbit of the moon there were the earth's plants at least, of which that being were capable, and which, therefore, were possible of that essential being. And as that being at this earth's surface capable of the plant were not with- out the plant, the plant were not without that being.

Nor were the animal. That being in the plant at this earth's surface were capable of the animal and the animal were possible of that.

That being of the earth capable of the plant at its surface were capable of the animal. It consists, in the plant, of the matter elements oxygen, hydrogen, nitrogen, and carbon, in waters, ammonias and carbonic oxides, reacting into ammonias compound acid and base ; react- ing into the cryptogamic plant of its occluded stamen and its conspicuous pistil; reacting into the phonerogamic plant of its stamen and pistil, both conspicuous ; reacting into the endogenous plant of its stamen and pistil ; reacting into the exogenous plant, sessile at the earth's surface, and drawing its energy in acid oxides by its roots from the earth, and its inertia in basic ammonias com- pound by its foliage from the air, under the inspirations and directions of a moral being of the word of God attendant on all beings physical. And of these beings moral and physical in the sessile plant still reacting, the one as the male and the other as the female, there were the locomotive animals in acceptance of the earth's phy- siological energies stored in and tendered by the plant.

Of these animals the first was the radiate in which the male element was occluded, as in the cryptogamic plant. And the next was the annulate of radiates, in which both male and female elements began to appear. And the next the articulate in which three sections of the annulate were united, as cephalon, thorax and abdomen, in the insect. And the next the vertebrate of the two articulates united upon a cerebro-spinal axis intermediate. And the radiate animal capable of the annulate, the annulate were capable of the articulate and the articulate of the vertebrate. But not more capable than was the sessile plant of the locomotive animal. And that essential being of which there is the earth, capable of the earth, were capable of the plant and animal at its surface, which were then possible of that essential being, whether as infinite being finite or the word of God. And as without that being there were not the plant and animal, there were not the plant or animal without that essential being.

Nor is it argued now that the plant and animal are in fact of such essential being as realities, or that there are the plant and animal. But only that, to the existence of such being, there were not the plant or animal without it. And this will appear in that this were capable of the plant and animal, and that the plant or animal were possible of this, and that if that be capable of the plant or animal at their times and places it were capable of nothing else at these times and places; and that if the plant or animal at its time or place be possible of this, it were possible of nothing else, and that they were not either, therefore, without such being.

CHAPTER IX.

NOR WERE THERE MAN, OR MIND IN MAN WITHOUT SUCH BEING.

There were man, but of the vetebrate animal two-footed and two-handed. Such animal were solitary as is the animal four-footed or four-handed. Each of those is solitary from its being without unions for life between parents and parents and offspring, and from each being dependent for safety and subsistence upon its instant use of the chance products of the earth. And so solitary were the first becoming two-footed and two-handed. These with their two feet and two hands, under the direction of an intelligence to co-ordinate the activities of their feet and hands, were capable of a more abundant safety and subsistence, and of a larger life in a larger nature, therefore, than were any antecedent animals four-footed or four-handed. But they were not so capable of the life in nature possible of such animals associated for life, in the relations of husband and wife and parents and off-spring. Such animals could so unite. Adults, male and female, could unite for life in production of families of offspring with whom they were united for the lives in common. And they have so united. Adult females with-out marriage have given birth to families of offspring, between whom there have been unions — loose, perhaps, but still unions — in joint efforts to their common support, from which there have been stocks of agamic men. And adults, male and female, have united in families of one male to several females, to the offspring of which they were united, and of which there have been polygamic tribes and castes of tribes. And adults, male and female, have united in families of one male and one female, to the offspring of which they were united in families, and of which there have been monogamic states. And of these unions there have been more and better animals two-footed and two-handed than could have been without them. And these animals so existing have been men. And there is man, therefore, but of the vertebrate animal two-footed and two-handed. And as there were not such animal without an essential being of the universe, there were not man without such being. But besides this there were not man without such being, if such being be capable of man, or if man be possible of such being. And it were capable of man, and man were possible of it. And without this there were not man without such being, since such being were the finite word of God in space, which, universal, were exclusive of man without man be of it, who could not be of it without there be such being.

And such being were capable of man. The universe of this in teleologic evo-involution capable of the earth, were capable of the plant at its surface, and of the animal beyond the plant; and of the radiate into the annulate animal; and of the annulate into the articulate; and of the articulate into the vertebrate; and of the vertebrate fish, originating in Silurian seas, then continuously about the earth; and of the reptiles to food in marshes beginning to appear; and of digitigrade quadrupeds to take foliage and fruits from rising plants; and of plantigrade quadrupeds to chase and capture food; and of four-handed animals to take food and safety by climbing; and capable of these it were capable of the animal two-footed and two-handed, with its organ of intelligence coordinating the activities of its feet and hands. There will have been the animal from the radiate polyp to the vertebrate animal two-footed and two-handed, by variation simply of that being in the polyp to the conditions of its being more and better that it might be more. And that power in this being of varying to the conditions of its further existence will have been the same as that through which there is the union for life of unmarried human mothers and their offspring in procurement of the means to their lives in common. And this will have been the same as that through which there are the unions for life between one husband and his several wives; and between the husbands and wives and their children in families. And this will have been the same as that through which there are the unions for life between the single husband and wife and between these and their children. The animal two-footed and two-handed varies simply to its being more and better in becoming, first, agamic man, and next, polygamic man, and next; monogamic man. And, possessed of such power of variation, that being in the radiate animal were capable of man. And capable of man were cause of man; and man were possible of such being, and possible, were consequence of such being and were not without that being of which it were the consequence.

But without this, as I have said, there were not man, to man himself, without an essential being finite of the word of God in space, since to whom there is being finite, or the word of God, or space in any rational sense of either term, there is to him of these, an universe, and this exclusive of other being in that universe, and of man himself but as he be of it.

Nor were there mind in man without such space. That were a being in him, individually, perceptive and reflective of the conditions incident to the continuation of its own existence in the man, to the continuation of the existence of the man himself in consistence with the existences of other men and other beings under the same conditions with him. This were a being to the man as a whole as is the nerve, afferent and efferent, to its special cell. There are ultimate anatomical elements in every man and every animal, in force, about each of which there is a limiting membrane of relatively insensible substances, to and from the center of which, itself an intensely sensitive substance, there are lines of the same substance

through which it receives impressions of external beings;
and by which it reflects the action proper to its continued
existence in relation to such beings; and to its sensitive
and insensitive beings in relation to each other. These
lines of sensation and reflection are termed nerves, and
the cell a ganglion of nervous beings physiological in
reaction of their reciprocal affinities simply in production
and preservation of the spheroid and wheel of both as
are real infinite beings different in production and preservation of their spheroid finite.

And such the ultimate anatomical elements of man,
analogously such is the man of such elements—his body
being the insensitive substance about its sensitive center,
and his brain the sensitive substance within that substance
insensitive, and his sight, touch, taste, smell, and hearing
the lines of sensation through which he becomes sensible
of conditions incident to inspire the reflections necessary
to their acceptance. In this acceptance and reflection of
conditions, incident to the continuation of his existence,
there is what may be termed the mind of every individual
man. And whether we regard this mind as substance, or
function, or as the brain, or a function of the brain, it is
equally of that being of which is man, and as there were
not man without such essential being of the universe
there were not mind in man without such being. And
this for the reason that such being, capable of man, were
capable of mind in man. And for that mind in man possible of such being were possible of nothing else. And
for that, if it do not so appear that the mind of man is of
that being of which is man, it will so appear in that man
is of the being finite of the word of God in space. And
that this is universal and exclusive of other being and of
mind in man but as that be of it.

We are apt to assume each for himself that, originating his activities of motives incident of which he is unconscious, he originates his motives to the activities he
exhibits. And that thus in his mind there is an originat-

ing power not in the cell or in that being of which there is the cell. That this to him is not in the general endow-ment of infinite being finite from the cause of man, but is of special endowment from that or some other cause. That this ability to originate its motives is the cardinal constituent of the human mind, and that to this extent, at least, it is of other than that being finite, simply, of which is man. But for reasons not necessary now to be more attentively considered, it will appear that these assump-tions are illusive. That the mind of man, not more than the mirror, can accept or reflect the object that is not, or has not been, before it, or incident upon it; or respond in action to promptings it has not felt or does not feel.

Nor is there reason that man should have a mind to other end than the continuation of its existence in man to the continuation of man's existence in nature. Nor is there reason why man to this end should be of other being than that of which is man, Nor does it appear that God, the cause of man, could not have caused his mind to be what it is, and do what it does of that being of which is man, or that sufficient, that he would have used other agency to the man possible, or that he was in want of, or had use for other than the man possible of his finite beings at this earth. And the less does it appear that he was in want of man to instruct him what to do with man. And to elect themselves to be his chosen people. And to grasp his power, to the punishment of people differing from them. And there were not man or mind in man therefore without such being.

CHAPTER X.

NOR WERE THERE LAW WITHOUT SUCH BEING.

Law were the rule of parts in relation to their whole. And it were the rule therefore of consequences to their central causes and of weights to their central power; and of workmen to their central work; and of citizens to their central state in ordering their activities to its preservation and enlargement. And in this universe of beings finite it were the rule of beings finite in relation to the center of that universe; and of the parts of every being finite in relation to the reaction of their infinites producing them. And there were this law of parts to the whole and of the whole to the parts of this universe, and of the parts to the whole and of the whole to the parts of every being finite of this universe, but as of the finite universe and of every finite of that universe there be a central being in cause of its perepherential beings consequent. And in power of its weight, to order its parts as workmen to their works, and as the state orders its citizens to its preservation and enlargement. This were the essential being of the universe. And it were not only the cause of law but were itself the embodiment and source of the law it causes. And if there be this there is law, and if there be law there is this. And there were not law without such essential being. And it may be successfully contended that there is law, and this a being and this under rule. And this the rule that at its time and place in universal being it be its possible, and this its most and its best that it be its most. And that this its being under rule were a being antecedent to and independent of the beings of it. And it were the instant inherent and creative cause of the beings of it, and the present and persistent will of God— the prime creative cause—that there be such being. And as such abstract being under rule, it were that for which we have no other name than law. But it were as real and substantial as is space, force, or matter of it; and as natural and therefore as physiological as were either one of these.

And, such law, there were not this without it be itself the essential being of an universe of the will of God. And there were not this but as it be that essential being of which are the beings of the universe. And there were not this, therefore, without such essential being.

We may doubt that there is law, or that this is being or being under rule, or that this is real and physical and antecedent to space and the cause of space. Or that it is the concrete will of God and this present and persistent in the every being of the universe, and the universe itself. Or that of this there are the stars possible about the axis of the universe, or the suns possible about stars, or the planets possible about suns, or that of this there is the earth a planet, or of this the plant at the earth's surface, or of this the animal, or of this the man, or of this the mind of man. And may accept the alternative that these are accidents, or miracles, or of the instant manipulations of genii, and come and go as these be tutelary or destructive. But if there be such law of being under rule, there were not this without an essential being of the universe.

We may not be able to conceive this as an independent being anterior to space, and of substance, as is space, force or matter. But if we rationally realize that of this there is space and space into force and force into matter we must realize and accept as the truth that there is such law. But whatever our conclusions as to the existence, or attributes of law, we must admit that there were not such law without an essential being of the universe to give it currency.

The first of the beings to carry law were space and

the next force and the next matter, and we may regard the first of these becoming sensible as the essential being of the universe. But this, whether as space, force or matter, were not without law, which therefore were not without such being of the universe.

And as there were not the being finite or the word of God, or space, or force, or matter, or life, or nature, or universe, or star, sun, earth, plant, animal, or man, or mind in man, without such being, so there were not law resolving into one consistent whole these beings without it be, itself, or the first sensible taker of it, be such being, and without there be, therefore, such essential being.

And it remains but to show that as realities, and not as conventionalities, merely, or as names which may or may not express a real being in existence, there are these beings or the one of these. If there be the one there is the every one of these — since there were not the one of these without an essential being of the universe, or such essential being without it be universal and exclusive of all beings else and to the establishment of such essential being — therefore it remains but to show that as a reality there is infinite being finite, or the word expressive of the will of God, or space or force, or matter, or life, or nature, or the universe, star, sun, or earth, or the plant, animal, man, or mind in man, or law in these or the one of these.

CHAPTER XI.

As to whether as realities there be being finite and
the word of God and space, there is but the question
whether there be being finite or the word of God or space.
If there be being finite it is the word of God. And if
there be the word of God, it is space. And if there be
space of the finite word it is the essential being of the
universe of God. And that reality, as realities there are
the being finite and the word of God and space, if there
be the being finite, or the word of God or space.

The being finite of beings infinite, in reciprocal limitations of each other, were universal and exclusive of the
word of God, but as this be being finite. And the word
of God, the universal cause, were universal and exclusive
of space but as this be the word of God. And as to
whether as realities there be these, there is but the question whether the one of these exists.

And there is the being finite, as I have said, if there
be being not infinite. Being simply were being infinite,
and there were, therefore, the being finite only in the
limitation of one infinite being by another infinite as
itself. And as to whether there be being finite there is
but the question whether there be being not infinite. And
there is that in the universe, stars, sun, earth, plant and
animal from the universe to man and mind in man
inclusive.

The universe, though without conceivable limits
either in time or place, were not infinite in that, however
inconceivable its dimensions, it were yet within the term
universe as is not the being infinite. Nor are the stars.

Of these there may be myriads as there are atoms of gaseous matter in this earth's atmosphere. But they were in relation to the dynamic center of the universe as are the gaseous matters of this earth's atmosphere to the dynamic center of the earth producing them. And though of these stars there be inconceivable myriads, the whole is not more infinite than is the individual star whose limits we perceive. Nor is the sun infinite, or the earth, plant, animal, man, or mind in man. Each of these is obviously finite. And there is, therefore, the being finite. There is also the word of God. There is, as I have said, the word of God, if there be God. There were God, but as cause personified. And he were cause, but through means but of his own infinite beings in limitations of each other to express his will. This were his word. And there is this word as there is God. And to whom there is God there is the word of God.

And there is space. There were of the finite word of God, insensible, as the cause of beings sensible, an original universe of beings insensible which were not distinguishable from that insensible being between matters and in matters which we term space.

And there is in fact an immeasurable region of being insensible, in and from which stars, suns and planets emerge and move, as there is a region of being insensible about this earth's surface in and from which its gaseous matters emerge and move. And this is that for which we have no other name than space. And this is the source of the sensible forces and matters appearing in it. And it is as real and substantial as are these forces and matters. And there is a being, therefore, where there were the word of God, and where there is that we term space, which, however we refuse to realize it as substantive space, is in fact such space. And which exists as certainly as does the being finite, or the word of God going into it, or force of matter coming from it.

There are thus the being finite and the word of God

and space. And each of these the essential being of the universe, and that reality; as realities there are being finite, and the word of God and space. And rationally, therefore, there are, by deduction from the hypothesis of the finite word of God as cause of being in this universe as well as by induction of its phenomena as realities, the being finite and the word of God and space, however we be unable to perceive them otherwise.

We may not see how being finite can cause beings finite, as we do not see how electricity produces the spark, or the seed the plant, or the egg the animal. But we may and must see, in seeing the being finite, that it is being physiological of beings infinite. That its infinite beings are atomic and complementary from being in parts of one integral infinite. That so they are kindred and different from being of that infinite inversely. And seeing this we may see that they are reciprocally vacua and reciprocally plena, and reciprocally attractive and reciprocally repulsive, and of their attractions are coincident on the axis of their mutual being intermediate, and of their repulsions are in differentiations thence into a being physiological of both. And we may see also that such, and so physiological, is the every being of the universe, and the universe inself. And that every such being physiological from the axis of the universe is subject to a process of teleologic evo-involutions through which every antecedent being is forced into the next succeeding being possible; and thus see the way by which the finite being of the universe can cause the finite beings of this universe. But, whether we do or do not see this, we see enough to show us that there is infinite being finite. And that this, by whatever way, is not only universal and exclusive being of infinities, but is cause of beings finite existing only of it. And so is a reality.

And so, also, as to the word of God. God, in the proper sense of that term, is cause personified. We are so constituted as to be obliged to assume a cause for every consequence, and a consequence of every cause, and causes, therefore, of the impressions made upon a sensitive being in ourselves; and of these in external beings incident; and a causing cause of such external beings; and of that sensitive being in us to accept the impressions of such external beings. This causing cause we personify and term that person God, who, therefore, to conscious man, is the prime, or originating cause of all beings in this universe.

But while it is true that to conscious man there is such God, it is not true that all conscious men concur in their conceptions of such God. So constituted as to conceive consequences but of cause, and the beings of the universe and themselves and their own conscious beings included as consequences of cause and of God, therefore they do not concur in their conceptions of such God.

The human races of the least intelligence are apt to conceive him as a being considerate only of themselves, and as capricious as themselves; and a genius, tutelary or destructive of them, as they may please or displease him; and without conception or thought of his relation to other beings of the universe. And races, even of the most intelligence, accepting that by one dispensation of his providence he has caused the other beings, by another and special dispensation he now causes man. And not to the ends to which he causes such other beings. It is, or is coming to be, admitted that other beings are to their most and their best, that they be their most under the conditions of their existences. But that man is not to his most and best, that he be his most simply in the state of his earthly existence, but to an earthly existence of his own invention, and to a state of moral being in some other sphere, where he will receive rewards or punishments for the way in which he has conducted himself while here.

It is not seen that this is his permanent abiding place, as it is of the plant or animal; and that the moral being of one generation, enlarged and bettered by its experiences, goes into the next, there to be enlarged and bettered for the next, and so on to the most and best man possible, as does the vital principle and moral being of the plant or animal. And without seeing that this is the only sphere of his existence, and that in this he is to the man possible as the animal to the animal possible, or the plant to the plant possible of its means of existence from the earth, or as is the earth to the earth possible of its means of existence from the sun, he is without a rule for the observance or transgression of which he is to be rewarded or punished. And, without such rule of moral being in this earth, he sets himself to devise such rule, which, examined, is found to be what were the will of a tutelary but capricious genius attendant on the race or state of man devising it.

This is the God of every human race of the intelligence to formulate a God, who in turn chooses that people from all others, and who commands, not that they be their most and best to the uses of the God of this universe, or even that they continue their existences on earth as it may be possible, but only that they rule all other peoples and bear their God aloft above the gods of others. There are thus not one, but as many Gods as there are human races.

But man may not make his God, more than he may make his cause. And despite his misconceptions, there is an one only God of this universe, as there is an one only cause of this universe. And this God—but cause personified—if not himself the essential being of which are all beings, and the reality of which are all real beings, is the cause of that essential being and of that reality, and so is the causing cause of the beings of this universe. And of beings inanimate as of beings animate. And of man and of individual men, but only as they be tributary to the man possible, and to the man possible at this earth.

And, such God, of him there is his word expressive of his will in the beings of it possible. It may be, for aught we know, that God is himself his word; that with his infinite beings he has entered wholly into the finite beings of this universe, and is himself the essential being of which are its beings; and the reality of which are its realities.   Or it may be that of but an inconsiderable part of his infinite being he has caused the being finite into the beings finite.   But in either case that being finite is his word expressive of his will in the finite beings of it possible.   And it is his entire and fully-uttered word to this universe at least; without this there were not cause to every consequence and consequence to every cause, and these so perfectly adjusted that there is not the abnormal variation in the orbit of a planet of the one-thousandth of an inch in one thousand years.

This finite, therefore, whether the God himself or but of the infinite beings of God, is his word, and his fully-uttered word, to this universe at least.   And to this and to man in this and to mind in man it is reality in that it is the real being of which are the beings real of this universe, inclusive of man and the mind of man.   And it is so inclusive of the mind of man for the reason that it is universal and exclusive of other being in this universe, and of the mind of man but as this be of it.   And it is so universal and exclusive for the reason that it is the word of God, the universal cause, which admits no other.   And for the reason that it is being finite of beings infinite, which is universal and exclusive.   And to the mind of man, of the word of God, that word is a reality—as real as is the mind of man itself.   And as to man, his mind, through which only he is sensible of his existence, is real to man, the word of God, through which is his mind, is as real as is that mind.

And as such reality, also, there is space.   Space, as I have said, were being finite and the word of God.   And as universal and exclusive as is that word, and as physiological and automatic and autonomic as is that word.   And it were as real, therefore, as is that word, with the difference only that space were the finite consequence of that infinite cause. And, as the first finite expressive of that infinite cause, it were the medium of that infinite cause to its finite consequences in force and matter; which, however insensible and seemingly unsubstantial, were yet the source of sensible and substantial beings in force and matter.

And there is such space. There are intervals of nothings sensible between matters at rest relatively. And there are places of nothing sensible left, from which matters are withdrawn. These seeming vacua we term spaces. And if they were in fact without real or potential beings there were not space as a reality. But they are not such vacua. As the medium of the infinite word of God as cause into its finite consequences there are in space the real beings of that word. And as the source of force the source of matter, there are in it the potencies of force and matter. As such permeable septa between the infinite and its finites it is replete with infinite beings finite, each an infinitesimal being physiological, capable with others of resolutions into the physical forces, capable of resolutions into matters. And space, therefore, is as real as is being finite of the word of God composing it; and as real as are forces and matters coming from it.

The only question as to whether space be reality, will be from our not seeing that in it there are the beings physiological capable of resolutions into forces and matters; or, seeing this, from our not seeing that these beings are the finite words of God. But the evidences are conclusive that in space there are these beings. And there are reasons equally conclusive that these beings are such words of God.

There are spaces between matters stationary or moving with respect to each other; and spaces occupied by such matters. And prolate spheroids of space between the planets and the sun; and elliptical spaces circumscribed by planets in their orbits about the sun. And there are oblate spheroids of space occupied by the sun and planets at the successive instants of their existences. And in all these spaces there are beings without which there were not the movements of these matters, and beings without which these matters themselves could not exist. The matters are themselves inert. The sun and planets, as matters simply, could not so affect each other as to cause the sun to revolve upon its axis, and the planets to revolve upon their axes and in their elliptical orbits about the sun. But between them, and in their intermediate spaces, there must be the forces of attraction and repulsion to keep them in their respective movements, at their respective distances. If between them there were elastic beings, however attenuated and insensible, connecting them, as there were if the intermediate spaces were of infinite beings physiological from beings different in reciprocal limitations of each other, the elliptical movements of the planets about the sun were reasonable. And so, also, if within the sun and planets there be centers of such elastic beings, compressed intensely by their crusts, there were transpiring their crust concentric forces analogous to the heat from the surfaces of the sun, earth and more distant planets. And if these elastic beings had been captured by the matters of the sun and planets, from a physiological medium of such being within that sphere of space circumscribed by the orbs of the outer planets and comets, not only were the elliptical movements of the planets reasonable, but so also were their movements on their axes about their respective spaces included.

And from such original media of space, therefore, there will have come, not only the movements of the sun and planets on their axes and in their orbits, respectively, but the spaces and matters of the sun and planets. But, without this, the every movement of the sun or planet, and the every sun or planet, were the miracle of consequence without cause. And that original medium itself, were such miracle, without it shall have consisted of such beings physiological.

And so, also, there is no space between matters through which there are not the forces of attraction and repulsion; and no space about either matter through which there are not the forces of levitation and gravitation, the one as heat and the other as cold. Nor is there a matter that is not under force sufficient, resolved to force the same as that in space, and which did not, therefore, originate from force originating from space. And such space the source of force, the source of matter, cannot be without those beings, however insensible of which are forces and matters. And, with and of such beings, it were the reality of which are the real beings in force and matter of this universe, if there were not reason, that is the physical expression of the finite word of God.

But there is reason, and that conclusive, that it is such word. It is where there were that word; it is such as were that word. It is as physiological as is that word. And 'in being the source of force and matter in this universe, it is as universal and exclusive as is that word. And space, if it be not that word, were the miracle of consequence without cause. And the word, if not the cause of space, were the miracle of cause without consequence. And, as there is not such miracle, and as the word is reality, space is reality. And as realities, therefore, there are being finite and the word of God and space.

And this truth that the finite word of God is a reality is more apparent in the facts that it can exist only as a reality, and that it does exist. We have the same reason for believing that there is this as the insensible cause of sensible beings in this universe we have for believing that in an animal and plant at an earlier period of this earth there was an insensible cause of the animals and plants now sensible. In coal and lignite we find the remains of cryptogamic and phenerogamic plants, and in silicic and carbonic rocks, and in the jurassic or triassic sands and clays we have the exervae and tracks of radiate, annulate, articulate and vertebrate animals, and it were just as reasonable to suppose that the animals and plants existing now are without the animals and plants existing then as that the sensible beings existing now are without an insensible being existing now. And as no sane or intelligent man is so unreasonable, to us at least, as realities there are the being finite and the word of God and space.

CHAPTER XII.

In a previous chapter I have shown that there were not force or matter without an essential being of the finite word of God in space, and that reality, without reality. And it remains but to show that of such space there are force and matter. And whether by deduction or induction there are force and matter of such space. And there is force. There were such word, but as it be the finite of atomic infinities in reciprocal limitations of each other, into the spheroid and wheel of both, from and to the axis of which there were its eccentric and concentric radiations of energy and inertia. On the every point, in the every ray, of which, there were the reactions of energy and of inertia into the spheroids and wheels, actual or potential, possible, each in actual or potential revolution on its axis and in its orbit of revolution on the axis of the parent wheel. And these were forces — the power in one being to change the state of another on which it falls — in the coincidence of these infinites on the axis of their mutual being intermediate, and forces in the systemic radiations, eccentric and concentric thence; and forces in the reactions of these into their spheroids and wheels, and in the revolutions of these on their axis and in their orbits of revolution on the axis of the parent wheel. And, taking this earth as an instance of such infinite being finite, there were its infinite factors, the one from its south and the other from its north. And these of their inherent forces consisting in their reciprocal affections of and for each other, were coincident upon its axis. And in forces eccentric and concentric were in radiations thence. And of forces of these there were their reactions into the molecules of solid and liquid matter of which is the earth's crust; and into those of gaseous matter of which is its atmosphere of one oxygen to four nitrogens; and of their reciprocal forces, these were in such physiological groups of one to four, in relation to each other and the earth. And of these elements reacting of their forces there were the additional elements, hydrogen and carbon. And of all these elements reacting of their forces there were waters, ammonias and carbonic oxides. And of these reacting of their forces there were ammonias compound, acid and base. And of these reacting of their forces there were the spore of the cryptogamic plant, reacting of its forces into the phenerogamic plant, reacting of its forces into the endogenous plant, reacting of its forces into the exogenous plant.

And of the elements of the plant reacting of these forces there were the additional elements phosphorus and sulphur. And of these reacting with the elements of the plant, there were the radiate animal. And this into the annulate. And this into the articulate. And this into the vertebrate fish. And this into the reptile. And this into the animals four-footed and four-handed. And this into the animal two-footed and two-handed in unions of whose sexes and of whose parents and their offspring there were man, agamic, polygamic and monogamic, in stocks, tribes and states. And thus by deduction from the hypothesis of such essential being of the universe there were force, and of this the every being of the universe, the most conspicuous of which, to us at least, were the earth with the plant, animal and man upon it. And by reason of deduction, therefore, there were force as simply as there were the one of these beings from the universe to man. No one of which were possible without it.

And by induction of phenomena also there is force.

Accepting the earth as one of the phenomenal beings of an universe of phenomena without noumenon, and of consequences therefore without cause, we must accept that there is not this without force. There were not the earth of its beings, whatever they be, the one from its south and the other from its north, without their meeting on its axis. Nor were there this meeting but of forces in their reciprocal attractions. Nor were there radiations eccentric and concentric thence but of forces in their reciprocal repulsions. Nor were there reactions at all points in every such ray into actual or potential spheroids and wheels without their attractions and repulsions. Nor were there the actual revolution of every such wheel upon its axle without such forces. Nor were there the revolution of every such actual wheel in its orbit about the axis of the earth without such forces. Nor were there the molecule of matter in the earth's crust without such forces. Nor were there the gaseous matters in the earth's atmosphere without these forces — the one as levitation and the other as gravitation, and the one as specific heat and the other as atomic weight. Nor were there the physiological units of one oxygen to four nitrogens in the earth's atmosphere without these forces. Nor of these were there hydrogens and carbons without these forces. Nor of all these were there waters, ammonias and carbonic oxides, or these into ammonias compound, acid and base, and these into plants, or the plant into the animal, or the animal into man, without these forces. And so, of the inductions of phenomena and without the deductions of hypotheses, there is force.

And by deduction and induction, also, there is matter.

Matter is but solid force, while force is but fluid matter, as is seen in the fact that both are of the same essential being, and matter that in which there is more of cold to less of heat, and force that in which there is more of heat to less of cold, as is seen in the facts that they react as they could not but as they be of the same essential being inversely; and that matter under dynamic force sufficient is sublimed to force in heat and light, and under static force sufficient is reduced to force in cold and dark.

And, such matter, it exists as well by induction as deduction.

The matter of which we have any experience is that in the crust and atmosphere of this earth. And, taking this earth as a being finite of the word of God, there were at the forming surface of its systemic forces levitation and gravitation reacting, spheroids and wheels of dynamic and static beings inversely to each other, such as are its molecules of elemental matter. And these into compounds, and these into forms of matter such as are seen in plants and animals. And by reason of deduction therefore there were matter.

And by reason of induction also there is matter, in that there is that which could not be without it; and without which it, itself, could not be.

There are matters, or sensible and obstinate beings resistive of force which we term matters, metallic and non-metallic, in compounds acid and base, and these in bodies inorganic so called as are the earth and the rocks and waters of the earth's crust, and organic as are the substances of which are plants and animals at the earth's surface. And, accepting matters as the finite products of infinite factors in force, there are these matters not only by deduction of such matters from the hypotheses of force, but by inductions of their phenomena, no one of which could exist without force.

There is force but in infinite beings finite reacting between foci, the one of which is in representation of the infinite, and the other of the finite. And there is matter but in the spheroid physiological of such forces in reaction. And there is no one of the things we term matters but as it be the spheroid of the forces producing it. And as there were not force without this matter, there were not matter without force. And there is matter, therefore, as surely as there is force. And as there were neither but as it be of such essential being of the universe, and as there

9

is reality, there were not force or matter but as they be realities.   And as realities there are force and matter as surely as there are force and matter.

And there are force and matter.   There is something from whose incidences we have our senses of heat and cold and dark and light.   And there is also a something exhibiting the phenomena of electricity and magnetism. And also a something which, intervening matters, causes them to exhibit the phenomena of attraction, repulsion, levitation, gravitation and induction.   And these some-things we term forces.   And this for the reason that in their incidences they change the states of our feelings and of the matters upon which they fall.

There is also a something of which is matter, and somethings of which are the different kinds of matter. And which in matters causes them to exhibit their specific features, and to change their states.   But these some-things of which are matters, and which in matters cause them to change their states, we do not term forces.   We do not commonly admit, in fact, that there is a something anterior to matter, of which is matter.   Or that there is anything in matter, apart from the matter itself, to cause its changes.   Or that what we term force and what we term matter are related.   And the less do we admit that they are of the same essential being, and still less that they are the sensible modes and aspects of that insensible being, or that that is space and that these are but the suc-cessive stages of space into the matters of it possible; and that force is but liquid space, and matter but solid force.   And we assume, therefore, that these are two dis-tinct orders of beings — each from its own originating cause, and that the cause of one is different from that of the other.   And that they exist and operate upon each other but to the extent to which we are able to perceive their existencies and operations.

But while our conceptions of force and matter are so vague and inadequate, it is at least certain that they thus really exist apart from our conceptions of them and are of the same essential being and but the successive beings of space, that essential being into the beings of it possible, they exist—and as realities as real as is space itself, the real substance of the finite word of God.

And it is certain that each exists apart from our conceptions of it, from the fact that of each we have impressions as we could not if it did not exist to make them, more than could the mirror reflect the object not existing, or not before it.

It is certain also that they are of the same essential being from the facts that they react as they could not if not of the same essential being inversely. And that matter under force sufficient is sublimed, or reduced to force.

And that they react. Of any incidence of force on matter there is a change in its state proportioned to the severity of force; and in every such change there is reaction, and this were possible but as force and matter be of the same essential being inversely. So inversely of the same essential being, they were reciprocally vacua and reciprocally plena, and reciprocally attractive and reciprocally repulsive, and in coincidence and differentiation into the being physiological of both. But, not so inversely of the same essential being, they were not vacua and plena, and attractive and repulsive, and in coincidence and differentiation into the physiology of both. And, in that they do react, they are inversely of the same essential being. By parity of reason we will also find that all forces are of the same essential being. And all matters of the same essential being. And that there is, therefore, but one essential being. But it is enough for my present purpose to show that the essential being of force and matter is the same; and this is further shown in the fact that of force enough on matter it is sublimed to force.

If, as I have said, there be heat or other dynamic force enough on any solid matter—be it even platinum— it becomes liquid. And if upon this there be further such force enough it becomes vapor. And if upon this there be further such force enough it becomes heat and light. And if upon this there be further such force enough it ceases to be sensible. And, as we may not suppose it ceases to exist in ceasing to be sensible, we must suppose that it then becomes merged into space, or is absorbed by that dynamic force insensible by which it is sublimed.

And if upon the vapor of even platinum there be cold, or other static force enough, it becomes liquid. And if upon this there be further such force enough it becomes solid. And if upon this there be further such force enough it becomes impalpable dust. And if upon this there be yet further such force enough it ceases to be sensible. And as we may not suppose that it then ceases to exist we must suppose that it is then merged into space, or is absorbed by that static force by which it is reduced. This were so but as these matters react with these dynamic and static forces. And this were so but as the essential being of matter be the same as that in dynamic or static force. And this were so but as these dynamic and static forces be essentially the same. And this were so but as the resultant of matter under dynamic or static force be the same as that of an essential being of which the matter originally consisted. And but as forces and matters and force and matter be the same and but different modes and aspects of the same essential being. And but as force and matter so differ in appearances only to us from their being successive stages of the word of God through space into the being of it possible. And the one stage of space into force, and the other the stage of force into the matter. And finding thus that force and matter are essentially the same, we also find that both are real and substantial beings apart from our conceptions of them. We see that matter at least is such. It is in so many ways obstructive of our senses and activities that no rational man can doubt that it has an existence of its own. And seeing matter so real and substantial we must see also that so is force the same as matter.

And seeing thus that force and matter are real beings apart from our conceptions of them, we will also find that these are of space.

Space, the finite word of God, were the original, real, universal and exclusive being of the universe, and were exclusive of force or matter but as this be of it. And force and matter, such real beings, were of space or they were themselves self-existent, original and the miracles of consequences without cause if they be not. And as they are not such miracles, and as space were exclusive of these but as these be of it, and as in space, the being finite of the word of God, there is the cause of force, the cause of matter, it is logically clear that force and matter were of space if it did not appear in other ways that they are of space. And in other ways it does so appear.

It appears that force is not original or self-existent, but exists of being antecedent. And it appears that matter is not original or self-existent, but exists of being antecedent, and that being force. And it is not rationally possible that matter can be of force and force of being antecedent without that antecedent being be space — the insensible substance of the word of God. We may doubt that there is space or that space is substance, or that it is the substance of the word of God, or that there is the word of God, or the God of whom there is such word. But to whom there is God to him there is the word of God, and in this substance; and that substance that for which we have no other name than space. And if force and matter be not original and self-existent to him accepting space as the word of God, there are force and matter of that space.

And they are not original and self-existent. And so is not force. In every sensible phenomenon of force there are insensible beings reacting to produce it. To every sensible being of electricity there are its insensible beings minus and plus. And to every sensible being of magnetism there are its insensible beings south and north. And so, also, of every heat, cold, dark, light and every attraction, repulsion, levitation, gravitation or induction of matters sensible there are its insensible factors. And each is a being physiological of such physes; and, however, each may be original at its time and place as such force and be self-existent of its factors, supposing them its own. But they are not its own, and the sensible force is as simply the product of its factors as the sensible offspring is the product of insensible paternal and maternal principles concurring in it.

And this so of forces is more obviously so of matters. The molecule of elemental matter is of its atomic factors negative and positive. And the compound of its factors acid and base. And so of its factors in every other matter inorganic or organic. It accepts existence of its factors but does not give existence to them. And not doing so there is not matter original or self-existent. And as such there is not either force or matter.. And to whom there is God to him there is, consciously or unconsciously, the word of God in space. And to whom there is such space there are forces and matters of that space. And as there is God and the word of God in space, and this reality, and force and matter of this, as realities there are force and matter.

And this becomes the more apparent when we consider the different grades of force and their sources. These grades are electricity and galvanism, and the source of electric force is in the relation of the molar matters at this earth's surface to each other in composition of the earth. And that of galvanic force is in the relation of the atoms of these molar matters to each other in composition of the molar matter.

Between any two molar matters at this earth's surface there are reciprocal attractions, repulsions and induc-

tions, from which they tend to opposite electrical states
respectively, and thence of their reciprocal attractions tend
to meet, and do meet, potentially, at every point in the
shortest lines between the centers of the matters, and of
their reciprocal repulsions tend to part, and do part, potentially, in production at every such point of a spheroid and
wheel of plus electricity in revolution on its axis of the
minus in eccentric radiations to produce the plus in concentric radiations to produce the minus. At every such
point there is an oblate spheroid of the plus potential
about the minus, but of the whole there is a prolate spheroid of which the matters reacting on the poles respectively. Such spheroid there is between every two matters
adjacent at this earth's surface, and by these they are
placed in relation to each other and the center of the earth.

But the molar matters themselves are of molecules,
and these of atoms, and between the atoms of every molecule there is such spheroid, and between the molecules
such spheroids, by which they are placed about the center
of the molar being, as the molar being is about the center
of the earth. Of these spheroids between molar matters
there is that force we term electric. Of those between
molecular matters there is that force we term galvanic.
The one is from the surfaces merely of the molar matters
involved in natural relations to each other, and, until surcharged with other force, it is not sensed by any instrument of observation, but when surcharged it appears as
electricity. The other is not simply from the surface of
the molar matters involved, but is from the surfaces of
all the molecules composing the molar matters. It is in
expression, therefore, of an electric force as much more
intense than that between molar matters about the earth,
as that of molecular matters is, than that between molar
matters merely. And, such the relation of frictional and
galvanic electricity, neither of these could be without force
and matter, nor were there either without the real word of
God in space, and without they be realities.

CHAPTER XIII.

In a previous chapter it is shown that there were not life or nature as real beings without an essential being of which they are. And that if there be life or nature, therefore, there is such being. But in this it was assumed that the essential being of which are life and nature is the being finite of the word of God in space; that this is in spheroids and wheels physiological of infinite beings in reciprocal limitations of each other, and from the axis of their neutral beings intermediate; that of this there are radiations eccentric and concentric, of the one as energy and the other its inertia; that these radiations are systemic and in reciprocal activities to the production of an intermediate whole of both, in which energy expands inertia, and inertia accepts and places energy in the spheroids of energy and inertia possible about the axis of the parent spheroid. And, such the systemic factors of every spheroid finite in this universe, and of the universe itself, it will be found that the one systemic factor is in representation of life and the other of the nature of such life. And it will be true that as realities there are life and nature, if it be true that as systemic factors there are the lives and natures of the universe. And it is true that they are such factors. Life is that of which there is nature in the plant. There were not the plant without its life; nor were the life of the plant into the plant possible without its nature to accept and place it, and to accept and place it in spheroids physiological about the axis of the parent life. This so of the plant is so of the animal and analogously so of every nature of the universe. The every nature, whether of the animal, plant, matter, or force, is a consequential being in administration to its possibilities of a causal being, which, however we may term it, is the analogue of that being in plant or animal which we term life. And such the life and nature of the plant and animal, and of every being finite from the universe to man, inclusive, they are such systemic factors of every such being, as are energy and inertia in eccentric and concentric radiations of the finite being physiological they concur in forming.

And they are the factors, in fact, of every such being, and realities therefore, unless the cause of being in this universe, discarding the infinite being finite capable of the every being of the universe, shall have seen fit to enter in person, or by personal agency, upon this universe of such being, and, by special creative acts, caused it to be and do what it was abundantly able to be and do of itself, or have caused it to be and do what of itself it could not. And we can not accept that the cause of being in this universe, so ordered and methodical, can have discarded its original endowments for special creative acts. Nor can we conceive that, by such acts, God has caused the being finite to be and do what of itself it could not, when we must admit that this being finite of the word of God was capable of the every being of it possible, and of the every being that there is, and of the every being that there can be. This he must have done, or life and nature are systemic beings finite and, as such, realities.

The question, therefore, of whether life and nature be realities is but the question whether they be systemic factors of the being finite. And this is but the question whether they be incidents merely of infinite being finite, or be the several products of successive creative acts without the being finite of beings infinite. And it is rationally clear that they are not such several products of such creative acts, and that they are the incidents merely of infinite being finite, into the beings in which, as life and nature, they appear.

And this is so clear, as well by reason of induction as

deduction. By reason of induction of the phenomena of nature it is clear that it exists but of cause as life. And by induction of the phenomena of life, that it exists but of cause in matters reacting. And by induction of the phenomena of matter, that it exists but of forces reacting. And by induction of the phenomena of force, that it exists but of the reaction of atomic infinities, whence it becomes clear that not only force and matter, but life and nature, are simply the successive phases and factors of infinite being finite into the finite beings of it possible.

And such the induction of phenomena, such is the deduction from the hypothesis of such infinite being finite. There were not this but of atomic infinities in reaction, or this but of their forces of attraction and repulsion in production of the spheroid and wheel of both, or this but as it be the matter of these forces, or this but as from and on its axis there be beings eccentric and concentric, or these but as the ones be such, analogously, as that we term life in the plant or animal; and the other such, analogously, as that we term nature in the plant or animal. And thus, by induction of the phenomena of life and nature in plant and animal, we come to infinite being finite. And by deduction from the hypothesis of infinite being finite we come to life and nature in the plant and animal, and necessarily to life and nature in every being intermediate, the universe and man. And in consistence with these reasons of induction and deduction it were rationally certain that life and nature are but modes of the reality into realities possible; that as such they are the incidents simply of infinite being finite, and are not the products of current creative acts, if it were not clear that in the course of life in nature there is not a being without its necessary sequent beings, or a sequent being without its antecedent causes. This invariable correspondence of cause and consequence were inconsistent with life and nature of arbitrary creation acts; and they are, therefore, but the incidents, phases, and factors of infinite being finite. And as such realities.

they exist, as surely as that they do exist. And the question, therefore, of whether as realities there be life or nature is but the question whether there be life or nature as real beings, independent of and apart from our conceptions of them. And they are such beings.

Life is a real being. Or it is a being as real as the plant or animal, which could not be, as it is, without it. And nature is a real being, and as real as the plant or animal, which, even of its life, could not be the being it is without it. And if the plant or animal be a real being, so is life or nature. And the question, therefore, of whether as realities there be life or nature is but the question whether, as such, there be the plant or animal. And as it will not be questioned that the plant and animal are such, it can not be questioned that life and nature are such.

The plant and animal are beings physiological. They are such and so but as they be the finites of atomic infinites in reciprocal limitations of each other. And such and so must be the life and nature of which there are the plant and animal.

And life and nature to the plant or animal are, analogously, such as are force and matter to the compound matter, inorganic or organic, they concur in forming. And there are the plant and animal and their realities as surely as there are beings physiological, or force and matter, or space, or the word of God, or being finite; and so, as realities, there are life and nature.

CHAPTER XIV.

AND AS REALITIES, ALSO, THERE ARE THE UNIVERSE, STARS, SUN AND EARTH.

There are phenomena to which we apply these terms respectively and if of these phenomena there be noumena — the real causes of such apparent consequences — these are realities. And there are these realities, from their not being conventionalities, existing only in the terms which for convenience we apply to them. And these are realities and not conventionalities, for the reason that they exist, and existed before there was man to apply such terms; and they would have existed if there never had been man, and will exist when man is gone. And they are realities also from being of the finite word of God in space, the one only real being of this universe. And from being of force and matter, and life and nature, realities. And from being physiological — the only mode of such insensible reality into the sensible realities of it possible.

And as such there is the universe. There is an universe. However from its immensity and its inclusion of ourselves we be unable to perceive it, or conceive it — in that there is the being finite of beings infinite, of which there were an universe; and the word of God the universal cause of which there is an universe; and space the substance of that finite word, and as universal as is that word; and being physiological, which were possible only of such universe. And this is a reality in that it consists of its own inherent being, and not in our conventional expressions of it; and in that it is of being finite, reality; and the word of God, reality; and of space, reality; and of force, matter, life and nature, realities. And in that it is of being physiological a reality, in its existence simply of its own essential beings.

Not seeing the universe we may not see that it is of atomic infinities inversely in coincidence and differentiation on, and from, the axis of their neutral being intermediate. Or that to and from this there are eccentric and concentric radiations of beings dynamic and static into spheroids and wheels of static beings as disks in revolutions on dynamic beings as their axes. But rationally we must see that there is such universal being physiological in seeing that which could not be without it. And that were seen in being finite; and the word of God; and space; and force; and matter; and life; and nature; and the stars, suns and planets, as a disk of matter static about the dynamic axis of the universe.

We may not see that there are stars, suns and planets in a disk about the axis of the universe, or about any axis intermediate. But if there be the being finite or the word of God or space, there were such universe. And this were being physiological in a disk of matters about its center of space included. And these matters were in orbs, such as are the stars, suns and planets; and these were in elliptical orbits mediately or immediately about an axis intermediate. And in a disk of such matters so moving about that axis. And as there are stars, suns and planets moving, possibly, in such orbits in such disk about such axis, in these there is that which could not be without such universe.

The star, sun or planet were that which could not be without such universe. We rationally know, or may so know, that the every star, sun or planet is an orb of matter about its center of included space. And that each moves in such orbit about a center of intermediate space. And we may so know that they were not such orbs in such orbits without of them all there were a disk about its center intermediate; or this without they be beings physiological of an universal being such. And that there is the star, sun or planet possible of such universe, but possible of nothing else conceivable, is proof conclusive that there is such universe, if it were not that there is being finite of the word of God in space, of which there were an universe — to us, at least, whether we see that it is such being physiological or not — and that this is a reality.

There are luminous objects in the celestial sphere to which we apply the term stars. We may not be able to see or conceive the illimitable numbers of the stars or the extent of space they occupy or traverse; or that all move or that any specific stars move in elliptical orbits about central spaces intermediate. But we may see that there are these objects, and see rationally that they are as to their exteriors orbs of matter about their centers of included spaces. And that these are reacting with each other into one continuous system of the whole.

. And these are realities in that they exist without dependence on our perceptions or conceptions of them for their existences. And that they are of the universe a reality. And of the finite word of God in space a reality; and of force or matter a reality; and of life in nature a reality; and of being physiological a reality, inclusive of all other modes of an universal reality. And these are conclusive that there is such universal reality and that the stars, themselves such beings physiological, are of it.

And to know that the stars are realities it is only necessary to know that they are beings physiological. And to know that they are such it is enough to know that they exist in independence of our conceptions of them, or as constituents of a self-existent universe of the being finite of the word of God in space.

And to know that they so exist of such space it is enough to know that they are in orbs of matter about centers of space included. There were not their crusts of matter without there be solid spaces, or centers of space, but as these be liquid matters. And there were not their

crusts of matters without they be constrictive of their
included spaces or their centers of included spaces, but as
they be explosive of their crusts of matter. Nor were
there their crusts of matter but as they be the products of
the dynamic and static spaces included. Nor were there
their centers of space, but as these be the products of
these matters static and dynamic about them, both under
mandate of a creative and causal reality in force and matter at and from the axis of that universe of stars.

And to know that they are such orbs of matters about
spaces it is enough to know that their exterior surfaces
are of matter. And to know that their surfaces are of
matter it is enough to know that they affect our senses of
them, as they could not but as they be of matter.

Accepting mind in man as the object glass of an
elongating telescope of life in nature from the axis of
universe, in observation of the ways and means to its
extension further, we must accept that the deliverances of
that mental glass to man of that life in nature are the truths
of that external world before it. And that if the stars are
incident upon it as orbs of matter they are such orbs, and
if, therefore, it rationally appear that the stars are orbs of
matters about spaces in elliptical orbits, mediately or
immediately about the axis of the universe; or if it appear
only that they are orbs of matter about spaces; or if it
only appear that they are orbs of matters merely, we were
bound to accept that, as there were not orbs of space and
matter but as they be in elliptical orbits about intermediate centers of space. Or if it appear only that they are
orbs of matter merely about spaces, without that they are
in such orbits, we were bound to accept that they are in
such orbits. Or if it merely appear that they are orbs of
matter, we were bound to accept that of each there is its
included space. And that of such orb of matter about its
included space it is in its elliptical orbit about an exterior
center of space within such orbit.

And this not only for the reason that we have no experience of matter without space, or without space included; or without it be an orb of matter about its space included; or such orb of matter about space without it be actually or potentially in its elliptical orbits about a center in space circumscribed by that orbit.

The every molecule or compound of matter in every such stellar crust may not be about a space sufficiently large to be sensible, or, as an orb of matter about space, be in an actual orbit about an exterior center of space included, as is the molecule of gaseous or nebulous matters. Yet every such molecule or compound, if unable to move actually from being in such crust, has the potence and tendency to so move and in this give cohesion and consistency to the mass of matter within which it is involved.

And such the star there is this and this a reality. It may be that the essential stellar beings are as invisible to us as is the universe. And that these are visible and invisible. And that as many are invisible as are visible. That there is a spheroidal universe of being originally invisible. And that this is in quadrants, each such spheroid and wheel; and this in quadrants, each such, but becoming continually more consistent of its beings denser and larger until they become dense and large enough to affect our senses of them, when they come to be named stars. And that there are stars, therefore, of every degree of density, consistency, sensibility and life from the universe of finite being in space to the stars included in the celestial sphere. But these at the every stage and phase of their existences, for the reasons stated, are realities.

And that these are realities to us, at least, is for the further reason that we cannot accept them as the accidents of consequences without cause, or the miracles of purpose executed without means. And must accept, therefore, that they are of the manipulations of an intermediary

10

anthropomorphic Theos in instant administration of infinite power and purpose to finite exigencies or of the resolutions of infinite power and purpose committed to the infinite beings themselves, of which there is the being finite, of which there are these beings finite. Of these causes, that one were the Theos and the other the Physis, and the beings of this universe into the beings of it, were theological of physiological.

But it is not theological. To be this there must have been the intermediary Theos in every moment of force, and in every molecule and compound of matter inorganic, and in every plant at every instant, and in every act of its existence; and in every plant and every animal and man, and family, stock, tribe or state of man, and in the earth, sun and stars. And in these or in any one of these the intermediary Theos does not appear. To its appearance it were necessary that if it be not sensible, it shall at least cause these beings, or the one of them, to be or do what of its own beings it could not. And the moment of electric force to be other than it would be of its plus and minus; and the spark other than it would of its heat and light; and the molecule of matter to be other than it would be of its atoms positive and negative; and the compound other than it would be of its acid and base; and the plant seed to be other than it would be of its staminate and pistillate principles; and the plant other than it would be of its seed; and the animal ovum, so other than of its male and female principles, and the animal other than of its ovum; and the man other than of his parents; and the family other than of its parents; and their children, and the stock, tribe or state other than of its families; and the earth, sun, star and universe, other than they would be of their respective elements. In neither of these does such Theos so appear. Not so appearing it does not exist. And in every finite being, therefore, from the first sensible appearance of such being to us at this earth as force to its resolutions into the inconceivable universe of force in matters, there is but the product of its physical factors of their reciprocal affinities, simply in reciprocal limitations of each other. This were being physiological possible of but a reality of infinite beings finite in space. And such the universe it were a reality; and such the star it were a reality; and as a reality there is an universe and stars as certainly as that there are the universe and stars, however it may be with the sun and earth.

CHAPTER XVI.

AND AS A REALITY ALSO, THERE IS THE SUN.

There is the sun, an orb of luminous matter with stars in the celestial sphere, and with but the question whether it be a reality — such physiological being finite of beings infinite — and it is such reality if it be a star. Or if within its orb of luminous matter there be its center of explosive space; or if its surface of luminous matter be metallic; or if from that surface there be eccentric radiations of dynamic being in heat, and to it there be concentric radiations of static being in cold, reciprocally intussuscepting each other into an atmosphere of gaseous matters about such surface. Or if these matters be oxygenic and metallic. Or if these — acids and bases, respectively — react with each other into metallic oxides. And these acids and bases, respectively, react with each other into the rocky matters mica, quartz and felspar; and these unite in a granitic rock so dense and obstinate as, in a liquid form, to withstand the heat of such atmosphere; and to fall and lie for a time in spots upon the incandescent surface of the sun.

Or, without this, it is such physiological reality if transpiring that atmosphere there be eccentric radiations of its dynamic being in heat, refracted by concentric radiations of its static being in cold to the plane of the sun's equator, and to foci in that plane; and these in a spiral of such foci at graduated distances from each other; and this winding from the sun through gradually widening distances to the limits of such equatorial plane. And if about every such focus in its order there comes to be a crust of constrictive matter inclusive of its center of explosive space. And if there be orbs of matter revolving on their axes and in elliptical orbits about the axis of this solar system, at or near the surface of the sun, as are the planets in order of such spiral of such successive and widening distances in the plane of the sun's equator.

And without this, even, the sun were such a reality if it be the sensible consequence of an insensible cause, and that be a moral being to order and exact its beings physical.

And such physiological reality in its physical being of its moral cause inherent is the sun. It is a consequence sensible of a cause insensible. And its cause insensible is a moral being in the sun to order and direct its beings physical. And transpiring its atmosphere there are such radiations refracting each other to such foci. And there are such matters oxygenic and metallic to form in rocks upon the sun. And there is its atmosphere of metal and metallic oxide vapors. And within this its metallic crust. And within this its center of explosive space.

In and of the sun there is such moral cause. There are physical activities and features of the sun which could not originate themselves, and which are not accidents. It revolves on its axis, and moves with its planets among the stars, and without collisions with them, as it could not without the order of a regulative cause, and that a moral being to give the order. And from it there are radiations of its beings which affect us at this earth as heat and light; and which attract and repel its planets to their elliptical orbits about the axis of its system. And there is its crust of constrictive matter about its center of explosive force.

There is its exterior surface, and this is of matter, and that metallic; and that the densest possible; and that intensely heated, as it were if it were about a center of explosive space.

And there is such center to the sun for the reason that without it it were of greater weight than that observed.

There is reason that the surface of the sun is of the densest and most obstinate metallic matter. That matter at this earth is in a group of metals termed platanic; this is twenty-one times the weight of water, and if that matter were extended from the surface to the center of the sun the weight of the sun were twenty-one times that of an equal volume of water, while its observed weight is but a fraction more than that of water; from which we must infer that within the sun's crust of such matter there is that imponderable substance for which in its insensible state we have no other name than space.

And there is such center for the further reason that upon it is the weight of the sun's metallic crust, thousands of miles in depth; and of its atmosphere of metallic and metallic oxide vapors as many miles in height; and of its planets, asteroids and comets, with moons about the planets, which press upon the sun's centers with forces equal to their combined weights, under which it were sublimed to force in space, if it were originally metal, and that metal platinum.

And such center also for the reason that such space under the conditions were force, and that force heat, whose eccentric radiations were necessary to counteract the concentric radiations in weight of such crust, atmosphere and planetary bodies, as the steam in the boiler is necessary to sustain in activities this engine and machinery of dependent functionaries.

And such center, also, as the electricities in reaction to produce and sustain in their places and activities the sun's magnetic matters forming on them in the sun's crust and about them in its atmosphere, and in its planets, asteroids and comets. And that space in heat were able to sustain the weight of these members of the solar system is apparent in the fact that it is practically resistless. It expands the densest matters into which it enters. Of enough of this on solid platinum it becomes liquid, and of more on liquid platinum it becomes vapor

in insensible molecules of the metal about the infinitesimal centers of heat producing them. And these reacting
with each other analogously, in relation to the source of
such heat, as the sun, atmosphere and planets do in relation to the sun's central heat.

And there is such center of space, also, to the sun for the
reason that there were not cause of matter at such center.
If the center of the sun be not of such space it is of matter, and of matter from some exterior and unilateral cause.
And while there were a cause of matter in the sun's crust
from the reaction of its dynamic and static forces, the one
eccentric from within, and the other concentric from without, counteracting each other into the molecules of a hol-
low-sphere of matters about a radiating center of dynamic
forces as space, there were no conceivable cause of matter
at the center of the sun. And if there be not space but
matter at the center of the sun it were the miracle of
consequence without cause, the existence of which we
can not accept. And about the sun's center of space
there is its crust of matter, and this for the reason that
without it the weight of the sun were not as great as
were an equal volume of water. Nor were there a limiting membrane of sensible substance about the sun. Nor
were this in the form of an orb, or this in revolution on
its axis.

And there is a surface of matter about the sun, in
that from it there are rays of heat which could not come
to us at such distance but from a heated body of matter.
And this metallic and of density and obstinacy sufficient
to withstand in a liquid or solid state the heat of which
there are such radiations.

And there is a membrane of matter about the space
center of the sun for the reason that the sun's eccentric
and concentric forces of levitation and gravitation, meeting about the radiating center of the sun, would produce
such membrane. And this, cohesive and metallic, to contain the explosive force, through which the sun propels

its atmosphere and planets; as does the boiler the steam through which the engine propels its machinery.

And there is this as the floor upon which the metals and metallic oxides form to rise in vapors and fall in rocks.

And about this is a gaseous atmosphere of metals and metallic oxides, in that of the sun's forces of levitation transpiring its crust, and of gravitation meeting them, there were the gaseous molecules of such matters in an atmosphere of metallic and metallic oxide vapors, analogously such as there is reason to believe there was about the metallic stratum of the earth's crust when that had formed about the space center of 'the earth, and which is now forming into a granitic rock stratum upon the metallic stratum of the sun's crust as that did upon the metallic stratum of the earth's crust.

The solar spectra show that in the atmosphere of the sun there are oxygen with the basic metals, potassium, sodium, magnesium, calcium and iron; if it does not show that there are also silicium and aluminum, of which in micas, felspars on quartz, there is the granitic rock about the earth's metallic stratum. There are spots upon the metallic surface of the sun such as would appear from the subsidences of such rock upon it; these spots form and fade, as will have formed and faded the first formations such upon the incandescent surface of the earth. There is reason for believing that these spots can have come of such subsidences. There is no reason for believing that they can have come in any other way. And in that of the sun's radiations of dynamic being, which even at this distance we feel as heat, met near the sun's surface by its complementary static being cold, there could have been such atmosphere of metals and metallic oxides; and that there is an atmosphere of oxygen and metallic vapors, such as could have come of such meeting, and that there are the rocks which can have come of such elemental matters in reaction, and which can not have come of any beings else conceivable — we must conclude that there is such atmosphere of essential being from the sun's metallic stratum, itself, of radiations from. the sun's center of included space, itself the being finite of the word of God. And that reality, that the sun of that is also a reality if there were nothing more.

But at graduated distances from the sun, and in or near the plane of its equator, there are smaller orbs of matter termed planets, each in its elliptical orbit about the center of the solar system near the surface of the sun, about which in its elliptical orbit also is the sun itself, while each is in revolution on its individual axis, and in a correspondence so perfect as that there is not seen to be the variation of either from its normal of the one-thousandth of an inch in one thousand years. Of these planetary orbs four are at successive planetary periods from the solar center, after which, in occupation of the next period, come the asteroids. And after these come four other planets at successive periods. And after these, but at no definitely established periods, come nebulous bodies of matter termed comets.

Of the four inner planets, all, as to their matter surfaces at least, are solid, and the two nearest the sun — Mercury and Venus — are without atmospheres and moons, and are probably so intensely cold that their atmospheres, if they have them, are in water and that in ice, while the two more remote — Earth and Mars — have atmospheres, and the one of them one moon and the other two, and the nearer one a temperature consistent with organic life of the highest order, while the further one has a temperature too high for any but the very lowest of such orders. It is not seen that the asteroids have atmospheres or moons, or that their temperatures are higher than that of Mars. But it is probable that they are higher, and that about these orbs, there are atmospheres and the equivalents of moons.

Of the four outer planets, Jupiter, the nearest, has probably a surface of matter as solid as that of the sun, and about this an atmosphere of metallic and metallic oxide vapors, such as is that about the sun. And that this is forming into rocks, as is that of the sun. It is probable that Saturn, the next, has not quite completed its metallic stratum; that Uranus, the next, has but started its metallic stratum; and that Neptune, the last, is but about to start it, while the comets are but nebulous media, capable of ultimate resolution into planetary bodies about the sun, but which have not yet started to take form as orbs, or to establish available orbits about the sun.

And such the probable states and conditions of sun and planets. It is further probable that all are in the same process of space through force into matters possible; that to this there is in each a center of explosive space within a cordon of constrictive matter; that through this the impatient space works continually into the matters possible; that of these the first are these of metallic oxides into rocks, and the next those of hydrogens oxide through waters into plants and animals. That these workings are at successive periods, the first termed archean and the next organic; that of these the organic period is that about which are the inner planets, Mercury, Venus, Earth and Mars, the more advanced; and the archean period that about which are the sun and outer planets, Jupiter, Saturn, Uranus and Neptune.

And probable that such is the solar system, it is just so probable that of an original medium of the finite word of God in that space where there are the sun and planets, there was the resolution of its dynamic being upon the center of the sun, and the resolution of its static being about that center, and that in this there was the incipient sun. And terming its dynamic being energy and its static being inertia, it is just so probable that this energy transpiring, its cordon of inertia formed into its atmosphere of metals and metallic oxides, and transpiring this that its

radiating energies were focused by its inertias at successive distances in or near the plane of the sun's equator,
about which foci of energies there were cordons of inertia,
as there were about the center of the sun; that each of
these foci thus became an orb of matter, with inertia about
its center of space as energy; that the energy of each
transpiring, its first cordon of inertia formed into an
atmosphere of energies and inertias, forming into strata
of such liquids or solids upon the preceding stratum, while
each, revolving on its axis, was in its orbit of revolution
about the sun, itself in revolution on its axis and in its
orbit about the center of this system of sun and planets.
That in the course of its formation into its orb of matter
possible, there were in each two stages, the one the
archaen and the other the organic, and the one that on
which were formed, or to be formed, its granitic rocks,
and the other that on which were formed, or to be formed,
its waters and organic matters. That of these planets
starting in succession, the inner first to start are the most
advanced, and are now in or about the organic stage; and
that the outer planets, starting later, are in or about the
archaen stage; and that the sun is in its archean stage,
though starting to form before its planets, for reason of
its greater magnitude, requiring it to proceed more slowly.
And that the movements of the sun and planets in correspondence is from their being in parts of the same common being, and their movements in elliptical orbits about
the axis of the system from its being physiological.
That not only is the system such being physiological
from its consistence of center and crust as energy and
inertia in reaction upon an axis intermediate, but that the
sun and any one of its planets is such — the sun energy
and the planet inertia — and the one the minus and the
other the plus of electricity — and the one the current of
electrical reactions in the adequate conductor and the
other the magnet revolving around it. That the sun and
any one of its planets being so physiological, so also is

there the being physiological of the sun and all its planets, which requires, to their harmonious coexistence, that there be their correspondence in such orbits.

And so probable that such has been the genesis of the solar system, and such that of the sun, its central figure, it is possible that the sun is of such medium of the finite word of God. And possible, it is certain that it was of such medium, in that of such medium the possible is true. Such word were capable of the being possible, and the being possible were possible of this. And possible of this, were possible of nothing else. So that the sun, possible of this and possible of nothing else, were certainly of this. And this reality, the sun is a reality, as certainly as that there is a sun.

CHAPTER XVII.

AS A REALITY ALSO, THERE IS THE EARTH.

It is not questioned that there is the earth, but only that it is a reality. And it is a reality if it be of an essential being of the universe. And it is of such being if it be of being finite, or the word of God, or space; or if it be of force or matter, or if it be physiological. And it is physiological if in it there be a center of space in force, or about this there be a crust of matter, or about this an atmosphere of gaseous matters, or beyond this a moon, or if, with its moon, it be in an elliptical orbit about the sun.

The being finite of the word of God in space were the essential being of the universe, and as such it were universal and exclusive of other being in that universe. And as such it were the reality. And if the earth be of this, it is itself a reality. So also is it a reality if it be of force — of transfiguration of space — or of matter, but transfiguration of force.

And so also is it a reality if it be being physiological, which can consist but of realities in reciprocal limitations of each other into the spheroid and wheel physiological of both, in which the one reality is static in revolution as disk on the other dynamic, as its axis.

And it is so physiological if as an orb of matter, liquid or solid, there be within it a center of space in force. There were such center of force but of eccentric radiations of dynamic force, or of static force becoming dynamic, from the crust of matter, or such crust of matter but of concentric radiations of static force, or of dynamic force becoming static from the center of that space included.

And it is so physiological, also, if about its crust, liquid or solid, of matters there be an atmosphere of gaseous matters, which can have come to exist as such but of eccentric radiations of the earth's forces physiological transpiring its crust.

And it is so physiological, also, if beyond its gaseous atmosphere there be its moon, which can have come to so exist as it does in relation to the earth but of the earth's forces physiological transpiring its crust and atmosphere to become focused into such being physiological as is the moon.

And it is so physiological, also, if it be in its elliptical orbit about the sun at one of its foci. This were possible if the sun and earth be beings physiological, reacting on the axis of their neutral being intermediate near the surface of the sun. But without this it were the miracle of purpose, without means, as were the moon itself, and the earth's atmosphere, and its crust of matter, and its center of space, which miracle we cannot either consciously or rationally accept. And we must accept, instead, that if there be the earth in a center of space, with its crust of matter and its atmosphere and moon in its elliptical orbit, that earth is a being physiological; and, as such, that its matters are physiological of its forces physiological, and its forces physiological of an original medium of space physiological in that segment of being about the sun, where now is the orbit of the earth; that this space was, and is, its essential being. And that the word of God, and that infinite being finite and that reality, that the earth is a reality contingent but upon its being of the being finite, or the word of God, or space, or force, or matter, or its being physiological.

And it is of being finite, if there be being finite, since that were universal and exclusive of the earth but as the earth be of it. And it were of the word of God, if there be the word, since that were so universal and exclusive of the earth. And it were of space, if there be space, since that were so universal and exclusive. And it were of force, if there be force, since that were of space so universal and exclusive. And it were of matter, if there be matter, since that were of force existing but of space. And it were of being physiological, if there be such being, since there were that but of force, or force but of space, or space but of the finite word of God.

And it is as clear that the earth is a reality as that there is the being finite, or the word of God, or space, or force, or matter, or as that it is being physiological. And it is as clear that it is physiological as that it is of a center of space within a crust of matter within an atmosphere of gaseous matters, beyond which is its moon, with which it is in elliptical orbit about the sun.

And as it will not be questioned that it is of the being finite and the word of God and space, or that about it there is a moon, whatever its significance, or that with its moon it is in an elliptical orbit about the sun, it will not be questioned that it is a reality, however it be questioned that it is a being physiological in its center of space, within its crust of matter in strata of different densities, expressive of the conditions existing at the successive periods of these formations about the earth. Or that there is an atmosphere of gaseous matters now forming about the earth's surface of solid or liquid matter.

But if it shall appear that there is such crust to the earth in strata expressive of the conditions of their successive formations into it, and if there be now an atmosphere of gaseous matters forming in expression of the conditions now existing at the earth's surface, it will appear that the earth is not only a reality as being of the essential being of the universe, but is a physiological reality, in its ability of its own essential being, to produce itself. And that in looking into the earth as such we have before us the actual process of infinite being into being finite.

And in illustration of this truth it will be shown that there is a space center and a matter crust to the earth. And that this crust is in strata, the first and nearest to its center of space of metallic matter, the densest and most resistive of incident forces possible. That about this there is a stratum of metallic oxide matter in rocks; and about this a stratum of hydrogens oxide matter in water and the resolutions of water; and that about this there is another stratum of gaseous matters forming in an atmosphere about the earth. That these are forming now of the earth's systemic forces, the one dynamic and the other static, and the one eccentric and the other concentric, meeting in such atmosphere. That as these non-metallic elements of matter are now forming in its present atmosphere, so of the same forces, but more intense, were formed in a previous atmosphere the metallic elements of matter, of which are the metallic oxides in rocks. That of these elements, whether metallic or non-metallic, there are molecules each of atoms, the one levitation and the other gravitation, and the one specific heat and the other atomic weight, inversely to each other. That in earlier atmospheres there were the conditions which required to the existence and integrity of every element the most of atomic weight to the least of specific heat, That in later atmospheres there are the conditions which require to the existence of the element the most of atomic weight to the least of specific heat; but that with this difference: the conditions under which elemental matters are now formed about the center of the earth are the same as those under which were formed the earlier and denser matters nearer its center. That these systemic forces of the earth are realities, and as such are the essential beings of which are the matters of the earth, and which formed and placed these matters about the earth. And that thus, in fact as in theory, the earth is a reality. And that as a reality, therefore, there is the earth.

CHAPTER XVIII.

THERE IS A SPACE CENTER TO THE EARTH.

The earth, as to its exterior, is an oblate spheroid of solid matter, except to the extent to which it is covered by waters, and the impression is general, perhaps, that the solid matter seen at its surface, and known to be under waters, extends to its center. But there are reasons for believing that it does not. And that to the distance of three thousand miles, or more, from the axis of the earth, there is a region of non-matter to be termed space, or force, as we regard it, an existence merely, or a being in force, to sustain the solid earth in a hollow sphere about it. And the reasons for believing that there is this space or force are, that without this the earth were heavier than it is found to be. And that there is a weight upon the center of the earth which would sublime it to dynamic force if it were originally matter. And that there is no conceivable source of matter at the earth's center. And that there is the want of that space in force to sustain the matter of the earth about it, and to propel that matter into the earth's atmosphere, and through that into organic matters, and through those into plant, animal and man. And that there is such space within the sun.

And that without this the weight of the earth were greater than it is. Weight is the tendency of one of the systemic beings of the universe to the center of the universe. There are two beings of the universe to be termed systemic, from the fact that of their opposition to each other there is the system of the universe. Of these the one is dynamic and the other static; and the one eccentric and the other concentric; and the one from and the other

11

to the center of the universe; and the one the axle and the other the disk of every spheroid physiological. And the one is the space center and the other the matter crust of every planet, sun or star. And the one the specific heat and the other the atomic weight of the every molecule of matter in the crust of every planet, sun or star. And such and so related these systemic beings of the universe, the static being from its place in every such wheel physiological is in constant tendency to its center, and through its center and intermediate centers to the center of the universe, and is weight, therefore, to the other as the power which keeps it from its center on through intermediate centers, from the center of the universe.

And such the weight of a molecule of matter in the earth in its tendency to the center of the earth, such is the weight of the earth in its tendency to the center of the solar system; and such the weight of that system in its tendency, mediately or immediately, to the center of the universe. And such the weight of the earth, it is greater than it would be without a center of non-matter or space, and not so great as it would be with a center of matter.

Without such center the matter seen at the surface of the earth would extend to its very center, and the earth would then weigh as much as does the whole of its matter, and that but two and one-half times as much as would an equal volume of water, since the matter of the earth, as far as we can see it, is in an archaen rock of mica, quartz and felspar, or in the transformation of that rock from secondary forces on it, or in the detrita of that rock as they have been eroded, transported and deposited by water in geological formations, the average weight of which is but two and one-half times that of water. But the weight of the earth has been found to be five and one-half times the weight of water. And below that rock, therefore, must be a matter heavier than the rock. And for reasons given later, that matter must be metallic; and that the densest and most resistive known. That is, a metal in a group, of which platinum is the most conspicuous, and is twenty-one times the weight of water. And that, extending to the very center of the earth, would give it near twenty-one times the weight of water. And that greater than it would be with a center of space and not so great as it would be without. And to the extent that our estimates of the weights of the earth and matters are correct, there is a space center to the earth.

There is a space center to it also for the reason that there is a force upon its center which would sublime it to force if it were matter, and that matter platinum. Under force sufficient, any matter, even platinum, is raised to space in heat and light or lowered to space in cold and dark. And upon the center of the earth there is such sufficient force. There is upon it the weight of its crust of metallic and metallic oxide matters, more, perhaps, than one thousand miles in depth, the weight of any column of which would raise or reduce to space its own base. But, beside this, there is its atmosphere, the weight of which is fifteen pounds to the inch. And, beside this, the static being of the earth's system between its atmosphere and the orbit of its moon, the weight of which has not been estimated, and the moon itself, and meteorites possibly about the moon. And in the weights of these, all tending to the center of the earth, there were a static being in force sufficient to call into existence a dynamic force in space responsive from that center to counteract and sustain these beings at their places in relation to it.

And there is such center also for the reason that if not there is matter at the very center of the earth, and there is no conceivable way by which it could get there. If matter be the accident of consequence from no discoverable cause, or the miracle of purpose, executed without means, it might be at the center of the earth as it might be anywhere. But if it be not such accident or miracle, and is, therefore, the consequence of a discoverable cause and the purpose executed through means, those are the means through which the matter comes to exist as matter, and of these means the matters of the earth could not come to exist as such at the center of the earth but only in a crust about such center from the reactions of the earth's systemic forces, eccentric and concentric, into them. Which, therefore, were in a hollow crust of matter about a spherical center of space included.

And there is such space also for the reason that it is indicated in the movements of the magnet. This tends not around the earth as though it were a solid orb of matter, but through it, as if it were a belt of matter about its axis of space.

And for the reason also that such space is wanted to sustain and propel the matters of the earth. Whether true or not that force is of space, and matter of force, as this theory assumes, it is at least probable that there is a crust of matter static about the earth's center of space dynamic. And that in this position it is in relation to space as the boiler is to the steam which, through the boiler, runs the factory. And that this matter in successive strata of the earth's solid crust, and the waters of the earth, and its atmosphere of gaseous matters, and the compounds of these and the plants and animals of these, are the subjects into which that matter is forced by its included space, as the boiler, piston, wheels, spindles, spools and looms of the factory are the subjects into which the static being of the factory is forced by the dynamic being in its steam. And that as there were not these subjects of the factory, in their respective operations, without its steam in its boiler, there were not these static matters of the earth in their respective operations without its center of dynamic space.

And there is such space for the further reason that there is such space within the sun. It is as certain as any fact of science can be that the atmosphere of the sun, to the distance of many thousands of miles from its surface, is of the vapors of metals and metallic oxides. And nearly as certain that the crust of the sun itself is of the densest and heaviest metallic matter, which must extend to the very center of the sun, or stop short of it and about a center of space. Extending to the very center the sun would weigh twenty-one times as much as would an equal volume of water, while it is found to weigh but little more than would an equal volume of water. And without it, therefore, there must be space, if that were not apparent also in its necessity to the existence and operations of the solar system, as it is to the existence and operation of the earth's system.

And there is such space also for the further reason that it would exhibit heat in radiations from the earth's center through its crust, which we find, and which can come from no other conceivable source. There is heat in radiations from the earth's surface of 60° F., which increases towards the center of the earth and decreases from its surface. This is met at its surface by a cold in a pressure of fifteen pounds to the inch, which decreases towards the center of the earth and increases from its surface by a law the opposite of that in heat; and while we might conceive that the cold could fall from a source without the earth, as do matters, we can not conceive that heat can come from within the earth, but from a source at its center, or that this can be other than a center of explosive space. And as a fact, therefore, whatever its significance, we must rationally accept that there is a space center to the earth.

CHAPTER XIX.

THERE IS ALSO A METALLIC STRATUM TO THE EARTH'S CRUST.

Accepting that to the earth there is its center of space within its crust of matter, we must for the same reasons accept that its crust is in strata of matters unequally dense and obstinate. And that the first and nearest to the earth's center is metallic, and the next of metallic oxides in rocks, and the next of hydrogens oxide in water and the evolutions of water, and the next of an atmosphere of non-metallic matters gaseous.

And there is to the crust of the earth its stratum of metallic matter, and this the first to form about its center. The only conceivable reason for the earth's crust of matters about its center of space is in the intussusceptive reactions of its systemic beings different, the ones from within and the others from without the spheroid physiological of its original beings different reacting on its axis.

Of the original beings different, of whose reactions there were the moments of that medium of space in which the earth has formed, there will have been their segregations into systems of forces such as are the .minus and plus of electricity. These will have reacted on the axis of their neutral being intermediate, and in production of a spheroid of the one static about the other dynamic, as from the meeting of electricities on such axis, there is the thermophotal or electro-magnetic spheroid. But, from the axis of that spheroid forming, there will have been eccentric radiations of its dynamic being to disrupt and expel the static being forming on it. And from without that static being there will have been concentric radiations of static being to sustain that in place about the dynamic. These radiations eccentric and concentric, so meeting in that permeable septum of static being about the dynamic, will have reacted into attenuated physiologies of beings static about beings dynamic, in each of which the beings static will seize upon just so much of the beings dynamic as under the conditions they may be able to hold. And in each of these attenuated physiologies the beings dynamic and static will have been inversely to each other. And the being dynamic will have been as specific heat, to the being static atomic weight. And in the progress of the earth each such attenuated being will have become a molecule of matter, and these together will have formed into a hollow sphere of matter about a solid sphere of the earth's included space. And there were thus the reason for the earth's crust of matter about its center of space in the intussusceptive reactions of its systemic beings. And without this there were no conceivable reason for such matter.

And accepting this theory we must accept that of these molecular matters, the first to form about the space center of the earth, were of the most of gravitation to the least of levitation, and of the most of atomic weight to the least of specific heat. That these were metallic, and that of these molecular matters first forming about the space center of the earth there was a cordon of the densest and most obstinate metallic matter known or possible at this earth. And that of this there was the first stratum of the earth's crust. Such are the metals of the platanic group. And that of platinum or platanic metals, therefore, there was the first stratum of the earth's crust.

And to this truth of theory are the facts. In such stratum of the most atomic weight to the least specific heat there were the conditions of cohesion and density in such metallic matter necessary to its office of constricting its included force. And there is such stratum of metallic matter first about the force center of the earth for the reason that without it the earth were too light. The archaen rock and the detrita of that rock, of which are the earth's geological formations, are but the weight of that remaining; and this is of but two and one-half times that of water; and if this rock extended to the very center of the earth the weight of the earth were but two and one-half times that of an equal volume of water, while it has been found to be five and one-half times that weight. There is, therefore, a denser matter below the rock. This must be metal, and metal dense and obstinate to heat enough be be liquid, while other metals and metallic oxides of the superincumbent rock were in vapor. This metal can have been none other than that platinum or of the platanic group. And we must accept, therefore, that there is this metal below the archaen rock, that this does not extend to the very center of the earth. And that there is, therefore, a stratum of this densest metallic matter first about the earth's center of dynamic force.

And there is this for the further reason that there is this about the force center of the sun — analogously such being in such process as is the earth. And that this were necessary as is the boiler to the steam of the engine, that it be graduated to the work it is intended to perform. The earth was committed probably to the production of its moons as the sun is to the production of its planets, and is certainly committed to the production of its organic matters, and through these of its plants, and through these of its animals, and through these of its men. To this it will have been endowed with motive force which will have been at and from its center, but which can have operated thence, through such modulations only as it could take from such constrictive stratum of matter about it; as the steam, however explosive, can perform its work but through modulations of the boiler, engine and machinery about it.

There is this platanic stratum also in that there is platanic matter at the earth and below the archaen rocks. There is a group of metals, the typical of which is platinum, the atomic density of which in terms of hydrogen has been found to be one hundred and ninety-seven and one-half, and which from the peculiar relation of its specific weight to its specific heat will have been liquid or solid when all lighter metals and metallic oxides were in states of vapor.

And of this there is a stratum below the archaen rock, first for the reason that it is found only at fissures in that rock; and there but as it can have subsided from a state of vapor to which it will have been raised by the heat upon it at its place towards the earth's center.

And next for the reason that by no rational possibility can the matters of the rocks and waters have been formed before this platanic matter, or such platanic matter have been formed about the earth after the formation of its rocks and waters.

And there is this stratum also by reason of the analogy of the earth to the cell and membrane of organic beings, plant and animal, at the earth's surface. It is to be supposed that the earth is the cause of its organic beings, and that the means and methods of the cause of the earth are the same as those of its organic beings consequent. And that there is analogy of the every organic being at the earth's surface to the parent earth. And as to every organic being, plant or animal, there is its specific cell, and to every cell its nucleus, and about this its limiting membrane, to the exterior of which there is the further being possible of the parent cell; so to the earth, as a cell, there is its nucleus in its center of force, and about this, as its limiting membrane, its metallic stratum, and to the exterior of this in rocks and waters, the other beings of which the parent earth is capable. And from these considerations it is to be accepted that to the earth there is spherical center of dynamic force, and that about this there is a hollow spherical stratum of the densest metallic matter.

And the fact of this stratum is more conclusively attested by the movements of the magnet. Such stratum were deepest in the plane of the earth's equator, and in effect, therefore, were a belt and ring of metallic matter about the axis of the earth; in which there were the electrical reactions to produce such magnetic ring. But in this magnetic ring as conductor there were electrical reactions, about which there were magnetic moments moving as the ring itself were moving around the axis of the earth. Of these magnetic movements there were those in the magnet at the earth's surface from which it dips; and dipping tends to continue, not around the earth, but through it longitudinally by its axis, and in continuation of its elliptical orbit—not around the earth as a whole, but around that part of the earth's crust immediately adjacent, as though it were a ring about which, of some cause in the ring, the magnet moves. And this were reasonable if there were in the ring the cause of the magnet; and this were reasonable if in that ring there be currents of electrical reactions such as there are in the adequate conductor between the poles of the battery, about which move the magnetic moments produced by the electrical reactions in the conductor; and for the reason that there are magnetic movements about the conductor there were such about the ring of the earth's equatorial belt, supposing it a conductor of electrical reactions. And it were such conductor, if at the earth's center there be electrical reactions and about this there be a belt of metallic matter. In this there were electrical reactions such as are in the conductor between the poles of the battery. And about this there were magnetic movements, such as there are about the conductor. And of these magnetic motives there were the movements of the magnet at the earth's exterior surface such as we perceive. And without this the magnet and its every movement were a miracle or accident. And as it is neither, there is such belt, and this of such first stratum of metallic and magnetic matter first about the earth's center of electric space. And as there is the magnet at the surface of the earth, and platano-metallic matter, not as are other metallic matters in masses subsiding from vapors upon the exterior surface of the archaen rock, but of vapors through fissures of that rock, as from a mass of that matter under and pre-existing that rock. And as there were the want of such a stratum to contain and graduate the earth's explosive force, and thus to force the growing earth into its beings organic and inorganic, and as there is this, or the analogue of this about the space center of the sun; and as without this the earth, of archaen rock matter seen only at the surface, were too light, and as the supposable conditions at the start of the earth crust of matter about its included space were consistent with the formation of such matter. And as it is not conceivable that there could have been any matter in the earth but as it shall have started to exist under these conditions, or that it could have started under these conditions but as metallic matter, and as the densest metallic matter, and this continuously about the earth's center of space, there is reason for believing that there is a first stratum of matter to the earth's crust, and that this stratum is metallic, and that metal platinum.

CHAPTER XX.

There is a rock of the oxides of the basic metals — potassium, sodium, magnesium, calcium, silicium, aluminum and iron, in compounds known as mica, felspar and quartz — apparent yet at the earth's surface in places. And in places at which it does not appear there are the detrita of this rock in geological formations. of which is that larger portion of the earth's surface, not now occupied by the original rock. And it is proposed that this rock was once continuously about the earth; that it was, in fact, the surface of the earth next after that of the metallic stratum, and is thus a stratum of the earth; and that this is termed archaen from its being the first of rocks of whose detrita and transformations there are the earths and rocks seen at the surface of the earth. And that there is, or was, this stratum next after the metallic stratum, not only for the reason that there were then the conditions of such stratum, but for the reason that there is now that rock in places from which it has not been eroded, and that in places at which it does not appear there are detrita which can have come but from that rock disintegrated. And that these detrita in geological formations are consistent with the supposition that beneath them there is still the rock not entirely disintegrated, and still continuously about the metallic stratum of the earth's crust.

There were then the conditions of that stratum. Of the earth's essential beings physiological, eccentric and concentric, meeting and reacting about the earth's center of space into the molecules of that metallic stratum, there will have been eccentric radiations of dynamic being from its exterior surface meeting and reacting with concentric radiations of its static being still incident from without. And of these meetings and reactions in an atmosphere of these about the metallic stratum, there will have been molecules of matter about space, but different from those of the metallic stratum, not only in density but in diversity of densities, and in the proportions of their dynamic to their static beings. Some will have been of the most of dynamic to the least of static being possible, as is non-metallic oxygen; others of the most of static to the least of dynamic being possible, as is metallic potassium, while between these there will have been the relatively dynamic metals, silicium, aluminum and iron, and the relatively static metals, sodium, magnesium and calcium. Of these the ones were acids relatively to the others bases. And from their being so different their affinities for each other were so strong as' that even under the severities of the situation they could all unite with oxygen into metallic oxides relatively acid and base, which could also unite with each other into compounds able to unite with each other into rocks becoming liquid, while all other possible matters without the metallic stratum were in vapors. This rock matter becoming liquid will have subsided on the outer surface of the metallic stratum, and thus have become a second stratum of the earth's crust.

. And that there is such stratum is in the facts that there is a rock termed granite consisting of compounds termed mica, felspar and quartz. The mica consisting of the oxides of potassium, sodium or magnesium, silicium, aluminum, calcium and iron, the felspar of the oxides of potassium or sodium, silicium and aluminum. And the quartz of the doubled oxide of silicium merely. This rock appears at some places as gneiss, in which there are stratifications of its constituents subsiding without pressure, and at others as granite simply from which the gneiss subsiding on it has been eroded; while at other places it does not appear, but in its stead are its detrita as though it had been disintegrated and its detrita had been eroded, transported and deposited in geological formations by water.

In these formations there are beside the detrita of this rock the metals lead, tin, zinc, copper, silver, gold and others, which could not have formed with oxygen into insoluble compounds under the conditions of heat and pressure existing at the time the rock was forming. And which would seem, therefore, to have been there in states of vapor, and to have subsided there upon the outer surface of the rock when cool enough to admit them in a liquid state.

The facts suggest that at the time the metallic stratum began to form there were the intensest eccentric and concentric forces on and into them — the eccentric in a heat probably of 50,000° F. and the concentric in a pressure of 12,000 pounds to the inch. That the matter of the platanic molecule represents the pressure, and its included space the specific heat necessary to complement and neutralize each other into a consistent and indestructible molecule of both.

But they suggest also that of these forces much was absorbed by the metallic stratum. And that at the beginning of the archaen rock stratum the force of heat was not greater than 25,000° F. and the pressure not greater than 6,000 pounds to the inch. That for reason of these smaller forces there were not the formation of the densest metallic molecules simply, but the molecular matters possible of these forces from that of the most of specific heat to the least of atomic weight as oxygen, to that of the most of atomic weight to the least specific heat as potassium; that for reason that each of these was most in want of that the other had to offer there were their unions into an intermediate compound of both. And that potassiums oxides, therefore, were the first compound matters forming on the earth. And these liquid from an atmosphere of all other matters gaseous.

But that as the earth still cooled from such atmospheric absorption of its forces other metallic oxides, the most different from the potassiums oxides, formed with them into compounds more complex until upon the surface of the metallic stratum there was a stratum of liquid metallic oxides possible becoming solid in the fall of temperature from their own absorption of the earth's specific heat. And that of these liquid oxides becoming solid there was that granite and archaen rock which was then, as it is now, continuously about the earth, and which was then the second stratum of the earth's crust.

. They also suggest that at the time the rock began to form there was an atmosphere of metallic and metallic oxide vapors about the metallic stratum of the earth, as there is now such atmosphere about that stratum of the sun. And that it subsided from that atmosphere in opaque spots upon the incandescent surface of the earth as it does now upon the incandescent surface of the sun. And that the earth was then in the archaen stage of its being, as the sun is now. And that there is that stratum to the earth, as from the continued formation of archaen rock upon the sun there will be that stratum to the sun, however much, from the greater magnitude of the sun's system, it may be postponed.

And that at the completion of the earth's metallic stage there was the beginning of its archaen rock stage in an atmosphere of potassiums oxide, as at the close of its archaen stage there was the beginning of its organic stage in an atmosphere of hydrogens oxide. That there have been two stages of the growing earth, the one archaen and the other organic, and the one that in which were formed metallic oxides possible, and these into the compounds possible, and these into the rocks possible about the earth's metallic surface. And the other that in which are formed the hydrogens oxide possible, and these into the compounds possible, and these into the plants and animals possible, to be as analogously continuous about the archaen stage in use of the earth's energies transpiring that stage as were the rocks in use of its energies transpiring the metallic stage.

That oxygen, as heat or levitation, is common to both stages, archaen and organic, the potassiums, as cold or gravitation of the one, are analogous to the hydrogens of the other; and silicium of the one to carbon of the other; and aluminum of the one to nitrogen of the other; and calcium of the one to sulphur of the other; and iron of the one to phosphorus of the other; and potassiums oxide of the one to hydrogens oxide of the other; and silicium dioxide of the one to carbon dioxide of the other; and felspar and mica of the one in a matrix of quartz to the plant and animal of the other in a matrix of the provisions to subsist them.

That all matters are of the essential being physiological in teleologic evo-involution into the beings of them possible. And potassiums oxide of the one such, so is the hydrogens oxide of the other. And that felspar and mica in the one continuous rock about the earth are the results of the first form of archaen or metallic matter in such evo-involutions, and the plant and animal the results of the first form of organic or hydrogenic matter in such process; that these are the successive stages of the earth; also a being physiological, in teleologic evo-involution. And as there were not the archaen stage without the metallic stratum, so there were not the organic stage without the archaen rock stratum.

And that, as there was the archaen stage of the earth, there is the archaen stratum of its crust. And thus the existence of this stratum is established, not only by the predictions of theory, but by the inductions of phenomena.

CHAPTER XXI.

AND ABOUT THIS A STRATUM OF WATER.

Accepting that to the earth there was its archaen period, in which were formed its more obvious metals, and these into the archaen rock continuously about its metallic stratum, upon whose exterior surface subsided from states of vapor the less oxidable and more volatile metals seen, we must accept that after this there was upon it a stratum of water; and this of the same cause as that of which was the archaen rock; and that of which there is the earth itself, in teleologic evo-involution of its own essential being.

And this we must accept for the reason that the earth, through its archaen stratum, were capable of a water stratum, and that there is a water stratum possible of the earth.

The earth were so capable of such stratum. There was a time when the archaen rock ceased to form, and that was when, from their loss or absorption of heat, the metallic oxides previously in vapors became liquids, and before the inoxidable and volatile metals (also in vapors) had begun to subside upon them. The temperature of this period could not have been much less than 5,000° F., and the corresponding pressure less than one thousand pounds to the inch. This earth then, as to its exterior, was but a glowing globe of melted metal and metallic oxide matter, without one element of nonmetallic matter beside the oxygen of which were its metallic oxides. No one of the nonmetallic elements of matter—hydrogen, carbon, nitrogen, sulphur, phosphorus, the halogens, or others now found at the surface of the earth in waters,

12

rocks, plants and animals — were in that melted mass. No one of them is found in the archaen rock, as we now see it, and no one of them could have existed in it at the temperature indicated. No one of them can have been in an atmosphere about that earth, which can have consisted but of the heat in radiations from it. And if there shall have been, as there was, a subsequent envelope of water liquid about that rocky surface of the earth, it will have been an envelope of which the radiations of the archaen earth were capable; and this a stratum of the earth's crust in strict analogy to the strata antecedent of which it had been capable.

And of this the earth were capable, as is the cell of its limiting membrane, or the plant of its bark, or the animal of its skin. And this we must accept — possessed of the earth and its conditions — if we did not see it, or see that there was, or has been, the water stratum about it.

Into that region of what for want of a better name we term space, then insensible about the earth's archaen surface, there were radiations of the earth's being physiological in that mode of its beings which we term heat; and this the same but for the differences of conditions as was that in radiations from its metallic surface to the production of lighter metals, and these into metallic oxides. And of that heat physiological there were the beings dynamic and static, the ones in oxygens and the others in metals of which there were the metallic oxides of which there was the archaen stratum, so of this there were the beings dynamic and static, the ones in oxygens and the others in hydrogens, of which, under milder conditions, there was an atmosphere of water vapor becoming liquid from that static mode of the earth's physiological being termed cold, met with at a distance from the earth, and falling on it in the form of rain. This water vapor of oxygen acid and hydrogen base from the reactions of the earth's dynamic beings in radiations with its static beings in the air is in strict analogy to the metallic oxide vapors from the same cause. And with the difference only, the metallic oxide vapors were of the reactions possible under the conditions of the archaen time, and the hydrogens oxide were those possible under the conditions after the close of the archaen period. The oxygen of waters is the same as that of the metallic oxides. And hydrogen is static, as is metal, and is only not a metal for the reason that under the conditions of its original formation only two atoms of it were necessary to the one atom of oxygen, while under the conditions of the metallic time from the twenty-three equivalents of sodium to the two hundred and ten of lead were necessary to the wants of one atom of oxygen. But there is reason to believe that the physiological molecule of water is not only analogous to that of the metallic oxide, but is isologous and homologous with it. That there is no other reason than in the intensity of conditions why dynamic oxygen should hold more of static being at the rock than at the water time. And that the earth, able to form its rocks about it at the one time, was able to form its waters about it at the other.

This were true to us if the earth to us be the only dynamo-static being physiological in existence. Seeing it, of its own being, in production of itself to the one stage of its being possible, we would see it able to produce itself to the succeeding stages of its being possible.

But it is not only not the only such being in existence, but we see and have seen no being that is not such. There is no moment of thermal, photal, electric or magnetic force, or molecule or compound of matter, inorganic or organic, or plant, or animal, man or state of man on this earth, or on a planet, sun or star, that is not at its time and place of an universe of such being, and this the dynamo-static being physiological into the beings of it possible. And, however we incline to ignore the subject, yet gazing steadily we will see that the plant is not more able to form its wood about its axis and its bark about its wood, or the animal its flesh about its bones and its skin about its flesh, than is the earth to form its metallic stratum about its axis of force, or its rock about its metal, or its water about its rock. And this ability of the archaen earth to form its waters on its rocks we would see if we did not see the waters formed, or know that they ever did exist since seeing the earth capable of water without that water of which it were capable, were seeing the miracle of cause without consequence which we have not seen and of whose existence we cannot conceive. And from this necessity for this water stratum, we would see that there is or has been such stratum if we did not see it, or otherwise know that it ever had been. But there was and is yet in part a water stratum of this earth's matter crust.

At the close of the archaen period of the earth when its surface of metals and metallic oxides had radiated the heat of which they had been liquid, and when these had hardened into a solid crust about the orb, there was the fall of water upon that level crust to the depth of a mile or more. And this is established by the fact that the heat in radiation from that surface necessary to reduce it from a temperature of 5,000° F. to that of 212°, at which liquid water could rest upon it, will have produced such mass of water. And by the further fact that the disintegrations, erosions, and transportations of its matters necessary to the Silurian geological formation — the first and most extensive — implies the existence and operations of such masses of waters.

The radiations of heat from that incandescent surface were necessary. And it is equally necessary that this heat shall have been being physiological, and that being physiological which the earth's archaen stratum could express. The being physiological which the tree expresses in the production of its bark, or the animal in productions of its skin, is not that essential being simply of which the matters of the plant or animal consist, but is that being raised to the power of the plant or animal. And so that being physiological in heat, then radiating from the earth, was not simply that essential being of which the center of the earth consists and of which are its matters, but was that being raised to the power of the earth in its metallic and archaen strata. And this being in that field exterior to the archaen earth was capable of water and of the mass of waters necessary to so envelop the archaen earth.

It was capable of water. Water, whether gaseous, liquid or solid, is of the nonmetallic matter elements hydrogens and oxygens in the proportions of two hydrogens and one oxygen in molecules united at lower temperatures into bodies solid or liquid, but becoming vaporous, gaseous, and ultimately forces, simply dynamic and static, the one heat and the other light, and the one in representation of oxygen and the other of hydrogens, from successive increments of heat, or other dynamic force sufficient. And of this water the radiations from the earth's archaen surface were capable. And the archaen earth capable of these radiations were capable of water and of the waters of the Silurian seas. It was capable of water for the reason that through its radiations it was capable of hydrogens and oxygen in such relations to each other. And it was capable of these in such relation, for the reason that in its every radiation there were its beings dynamic and static, the one under the conditions to appear as central oxygen, and the other as peripherential hydrogens about it.

It were also capable of this water of hydrogens oxide, at that period, for the reason that at its metallic period it was capable of metals oxide.

And it were capable through its heat radiations of water for the reason that of the heat radiations of the earth there is now water.

It was capable of hydrogens and oxygen in relation for the reason that the earth's essential being is physiological, and of dynamic and static beings in reaction; that of this [advanced to its archaen state were its post-archean radiations; that these were to express in its further state its further purposes; that this expression were possible only in terms of its beings dynamic and static and in these but as the one be dynamic as is oxygen, and the other static as is hydrogen, in reciprocal limitations of each other. And that these were the terms in which the further purpose of the earth was expressed is in the fact that of this purpose were the waters of those seas which consisted but of these terms in reciprocal limitations of each other.

The earth were also capable of its Silurian waters through these terms, in that the hydrogens oxide, of which were these waters, is essentially the same as the metallic oxides, of which there were the archaen rocks.

Of heat, or other dynamic force enough, as I have said, on solid water it becomes liquid. And of further heat, or other such force enough, it becomes vaporous. And of further heat, or other such force enough, it becomes gaseous in the separation of its hydrogen and oxygen atoms. And if there be further heat, or other such force enough on such gaseous elements, they become forces in sparks of heat and light, in which those of oxygen are of the most of heat to the least of light, and those of hydrogen are of the most of light to the least of heat possible.

And so also of heat or other dynamic force enough on a solid metallic oxide—that of potassium, for instance—it becomes liquid.

And of such further force enough it becomes vaporous. And of such further force enough, gaseous, in the separation of its potassium and oxygen atoms. And if there be further such force enough on these they become forces in sparks of heat and light in which those of oxygen are of the most of heat to the least of light, and those of potassium of the most of light to the least of heat, so that between the oxides of hydrogens and potassium there are the differences only of the conditions of force terrestrial under which they came to exist, respectively. The oxygen the same in both. And the potassium of the one coming to exist in the post-metallic atmosphere of probably 20,000° F. in heat and of 4,000 pounds pressure to the inch, and the hydrogen of the other coming to exist in the post-archaen atmosphere of 5,000° F. in heat and 1,000 pounds in pressure. And the potassium atom consisting of thirty-nine units of static being to one of dynamic being in its oxygen and the hydrogen atoms, but of one unit of static being to the one of dynamic being in its oxygen, while the units of potassium and hydrogen are essentially the same, it is plain that these potassiums and hydrogens are but expressions of the force conditions of their respective atmospheres. And that there are more units of static being on the dynamic oxygen of potassiums oxide, and less on that of the hydrogens oxide for the reason that the conditions of the atmosphere in which the one was formed were more intense than were those under which was formed the other.

I instance for comparative analysis the oxides of hydrogen and potassium for the reason that they are in analogous positions with respect to the archaen and organic processes respectively of the earth. There was the archaen process in which were formed in a matrix of quartz the rocky matters felspar and mica into the rock, not accepted as organic. There was also afterwards the process in which were formed in a matrix of carbonic oxide the beings plant and animal, which are termed organic to distinguish them from the rocks termed inorganic. But, that of the rocks termed also archaen, this of plants and animals may be termed organic. And we may assume, therefore, that of the earth as we now see it, there have been two periods, the one archaen and the other organic. And that potassium oxide is to the archaen earth as is hydrogen oxide to the organic, in that, as there is reason that what we term the organic process of the earth began in hydrogens oxide, there is reason that the archaen began in potassiums oxide.

There can be no question as to that water of hydrogens oxide was the first matter to appear about the archaen rock stratum, and that these nonmetallic elements of matter were the first to exist, and that for a time they were the only nonmetallic elements that did exist beyond that stratum. Oxygen had existed as the acid element with the many metallic bases, but that oxygen which united with hydrogen in the waters of the silurian was not the oxygen previously existing in the rocks, but was formed, as was hydrogen, and with hydrogen, from the exterior radiations of the archaen earth. And though after there were these elements in water there were other oxygens with other basic nonmetallic elements into what are termed organic matters, plant and animal. There is reason that these did not come into existence of other than the physiological radiations of the archaen earth, or of these but through teleologic evo-involutions of hydrogens oxide.

There is neither time nor occasion for the argument necessary to establish the truth of this suggestion, but it is plausible that water be capable of such evo-involution, and that of this there shall have been the other non-metallic matters seen, for whose existence there is no other source conceivable.

And so plausible as it is that the organic earth began in hydrogens oxide, so plausible is it that the archaen began in potassiums oxide. The oxygen of both is the same, and the metal potassium is an univalent basic radical of which two atoms are necessary to one of oxygen, as is hydrogen, between which there is the difference only that while in the hydrogen alone there is but the one unit of static force, in the potassium alone there are thirty-nine such units; and, as potassium is the most basic and static matter known, and oxygen the most acid and dynamic, it is possible that, under the intensities of

the earth's post-metallic atmosphere, such potassium was
the first able to articulate, seize and hold the acid, oxygen,
and that there were then scales of potassium oxide in the
teleologic evo-involutions, of which there were the other
metals into their oxides, and combinations possible in
production of the archaen rocks, as under the milder conditions of the post-archaen, such hydrogens were the bases,
sufficient to articulate, seize and hold the acid oxygen in
seas, but of the teleologic evo-involutions, of which there
have been the other nonmetallic matters into their oxides
and compounds possible in production of the plants and
animals now seen at the earth's surface.

These oxides, therefore, were in analogous positions
with respect to the earth's archaen and organic periods
respectively. And for that reason, I have instanced these
matters for comparative analysis, to show that, in result
of dynamic force enough on the earth's nonmetallic matter, there is force the same as that in radiation from the
archaen earth, of which is water; and that the earth, therefore, through such its radiations, was capable of its silurian
waters, as of such radiations it had been capable of its
archaen rocks.

The earth was also capable, through its heat radiations, of its waters, for the reason that through such
radiations it is now in production of water in the earth, of
which are artesian wells, and in the atmosphere, of which
are rains and snows.

It is not realized, generally at least, that in the beings
of this earth themselves there are the causes of these
beings, and of these into these beings possible, and hence
there is science of phenomena but not of noumena, and of
consequences but not of causes. And hence, of the artesian waters in the earth, we assume the cause *ab extra* of
their being there, and find this in underground channels
from their fall on higher lands. And of waters falling in
rains and snows we find the cause of their being in the
atmosphere in their rising from evaporation of waters

previously upon the earth.   As though existing of a cause
quite undiscoverable, we are content to account for them
at these places through the heats and gravitations which
we find to have been upon them.

But it is to be doubted that there is artesian water
from the earth, or rain or snow from clouds, or other
than the causes of their existences, or that they rise from
the one or fall from the others, but of the causes of their
existences continued in them.

It is seen that of the earth's archaen heat radiations,
there were waters in that there was not water at first
about that earth, and that later it came to be about that
earth with nothing but such radiations to produce it, and
that they can produce water, therefore.   If they can, under
the static resistance of an exterior atmosphere, they can,
under the more static resistences of the matter crust of
the earth itself, such heat radiations, in passing from the
earth's center to its surface, will be obstructed by its
matter crust; in this they will find vacua, in which their
element may react, as they do in that vacuum beyond the
surface.   Reacting in these as in the earth's atmosphere,
the results were water; this would expand from the producing heat radiations continued, and tend to project itself
through any opening made for it.   And thus there were
the artesian wells of waters from its place, the existence
and operations of which were more consistent with its
being from the heat radiations of the earth than with its
being there through its gravitation merely, from its existence at the earth's surface of an undiscoverable cause or
course.

And seeing these reasons that the artesian waters are
of the heat radiations of the earth, there is stronger reason
that so, also, are those in rains and snows.   Without this
these waters must have existed at the earth's surface of
some undiscoverable cause.   Of this they must have risen
to the clouds, and of this have fallen again upon the earth.
There is no reason for the existence of water at the sur-

face of the earth, or elsewhere, or for its evaporation, or its rise evaporated, or its condensation again to a liquid, or its fall in rain or snow, but in that in it there is the start and course of its capacity to accept of the conditions to the continuation of its existence. Such cause of such capacity it can have but as it be in part of that cause of which there is the earth. The bark of the plant, or the skin of the animal, is in the position to accept of the conditions necessary to the continuation of its existence as such bark or skin but as it be in part of that cause of which there is the plant or animal.

And such the relation of its waters to the earth. Of these, whether within or without the earth, the earth is capable. And capable of these, the archaen earth was capable of its water stratum seen in its Silurian seas. And capable of this, it were cause of this, or it were the miracle of cause without consequence. And this were the miracle of consequence without cause, the neither of which miracles exists. And the earth was cause of its water stratum, and there was, and is yet in part, a water stratum of the earth.

And of these were its geological formations. There have been what are termed formations of matters at the earth's surface. These would seem to have been of the archaen rock continuously to considerable depth about the earth included by it, and this capped by the simple metals, subsiding on it from states of vapor. This would seem also to have been in longitudinal ridges highest at the earth's equator. The equatorial diameter of the earth was probably greater than it is now, its surface was probably of metals and metallic oxides melted. It was probably then in revolution on its axis, with an equatorial velocity greater than it has now, which is approximately one thousand miles an hour; to this the static matter liquid at the earth's surface will have been resistive. And it is possible that this passive resistance to the velocity of its surface revolution will have produced such longitudinal ridges, highest at the equator and lowest at the poles.

It is probable, also, that into water went the heat of its archaen surface from 5,000° F., at which metallic oxides ceased to form, to the 212°, at which water liquid could form and fall upon it; that in so forming and falling on it the surface was hardened to a crust about its interior, still liquid; that this interior cooled and, cooling, shrunk from the crust about it; that in keeping the touch of its interior this crust wrinkled and, wrinkling, was crushed into fragments no longer horizontal, but at angles to each other and the horizon of the earth; that these fragments yet heated, under the fall of an ocean of water possibly in blocks of ice when it began to fall, were disintegrated and eroded into pebbles, sands, clays, and soluble and indissoluble metallic oxides; that this eroded detrita was drained from the elevations and transported and deposited in horizontal strata by the water; that in such strata, of the pebbles first falling, there were conglomerate rocks; and of the sands falling next, sandstones, and of the clays, floating to greater distances, shales and slates. And that, of the soluble metallic oxides in contact with carbonic oxides, a product of the earth's organic period, soon to be noticed, there were the limes, chalks, marbles, dolomitis, and the silicates of these and others. Every such deposit were a geological formation, but there have been these at every point of the earth's surface, continually, from the first fall of water on it. This process of formation has been punctuated by the beings of the organic earth's coming to existence in it. These have been plants, from the alga to the oak, and from the seaweed's first existence in waters to the first trees on land; and animals, from the amorboid radiates, first existing in waters, to the two-footed and two-handed vertebrates on land. These have come to exist at different periods in the course of this modification of the earth's surface lands by water. These periods are distinguished by the plants and animals that have come successively to existence in them. And thus there are what have been termed geological formations from the primordium to the post-pliocene, inclusive. And to these there was not only an original stratum of water from its atmosphere on the archaen earth, but in part there is this stratum in seas and oceans now upon the earth.

It is not supposable that the waters now upon the earth are of that original fall. Of that much will have gone into the earths and rocks of which, to the depth of miles, are its geological formations. And much into the plants and animals, which for ages have come to live and die upon them.

It will be tolerably clear, from what has been said, that water is but force physiological of the earth, which, expended in such strata of its matter crust and in its rocks, plants and animals, will have ceased to exist as water. That in this way the original volume of waters have been many times expended, and that the waters now seen are of current radiations of the earth's physiological force, but it will be not the less clear that to the start of this majestic course of formations, with the lives and natures of plants and animals in them, there was the post-archaen stratum of water to the earth's crust.

CHAPTER XXII.

AND ABOUT THIS A GASEOUS ATMOSPHERE, AND BEYOND THIS THE MOON.

There is no question as to the existence of a gaseous atmosphere of the earth. And none as to the existence of the moon. But it may be questioned that the atmosphere is a stratum of the earth's crust of matter. And that the moon, while obviously not a stratum of that crust, is even of that process of being physiological through which there is the earth.

But the atmosphere of the earth is of matter, though it be gaseous, and if that shall have come to existence by that process of the earth's being physiological, through which have come the antecedent strata of its crust, or if it be about the earth in present relation to such strata, it is a stratum of that crust as truly as is any antecedent stratum.

And so the moon, though it be not a stratum or the part of any such actual stratum, yet if it shall have come to exist from the axis of the earth's system physiological, and by the same process of the earth's being such as have the antecedent strata of its crust, it is as entitled to consideration in determining the status of the earth in relation to the universe as is any one such stratum.

And the atmosphere is not only about the earth in actual relation to the antecedent strata of its crust, but is from the axis of the earth's system of being physiological, and has come to existence at its place about the earth as have come the antecedent strata.

It is of matters nitrogens and oxygens in the proportions of four to one at any distance from the earth's surface yet explored, while at or near the earth's surface there are percentages of gaseous waters, ammonias and carbonic oxides. And while it is clear that the waters, ammonias and carbonic oxides are of the essential substances of oxygen and nitrogen in that they react with those elements, there is ground for the belief that they have resulted from the reactions of those elements.

And thus it is clear that all of the gaseous matters of the earth's atmosphere are of the same essential substance, and probable, and demonstrable perhaps, that the compounds mentioned in the products of the elements, nitrogens and oxygens in reactions on the axes of their neutral beings intermediate, it is also clear, and for the same reason of their reactions, that these atmospheric matters are all of the same essential substance as are all the matters of all the antecedent strata. And that, being of the same essential substance, they are from the same source as are such antecedent matters. And that, as of the earth's dynamic and static beings in reaction on its physiological axis, there was the metallic stratum of its crust, and of their reactions on this there was the archaen rock stratum, and of their reactions on this the water stratum, and of their reaction on the water stratum the atmosphere; it is clear that this atmosphere of matter, gaseous and invisible as it may be, is a part of the earth's matter crust about its center of space included as is any antecedent stratum of that crust.

And that it is so physiological from being in continuation of the earth's being physiological is further apparent in the fact that it is itself physiological.

Its elements, oxygen and nitrogen, are so from their being of forces dynamic and static in reaction on their axes. And from their being forces respectively the oxygens dynamic and the nitrogens static relatively, and from their being in systems of one oxygen to four nitrogens.

It were not possible that there can have been one oxygen to four nitrogens at every point of the earth's atmosphere hundreds of miles in depth but as they be in systems of these elements, and but as these elements be of the same essential being; and but as they be respective parts of that being, and — that the word of God in space — but as they be materializations respectively of that space of dynamic and static beings there is about the surface of the earth.   And, as such, but as they be in reactions into spheroids and wheels of oxygen as axle and nitrogen as disk.   And — as that specific space can have originated but of the earth's eccentric and concentric energies meeting and reacting in it — but as these elements be materializations merely of the earth's forces physiological reacting at that surface.

And, physiological of these forces physiological, these elements are further so from their reacting into systems, such, of one oxygen as axle to four nitrogens as quadrants of the disk about it.   And from their reaction as axle and disk of such speroids physiological into the compounds waters, ammonias and carbonic oxides each, such being physiological of static being as disk about its axle of being dynamic.

And the atmosphere, as a whole, is physiological from its consistence of beings so delicately related as that a breath at one point is felt at every other, and the whisper at one point is heard at every other, if only there be instruments or organs fine enough to take them.

And that this is so is apparent in the telegraph and the telephone, and in sights and sounds of objects at a distance; and in the reactions of objects at a distance; and in the attractions, repulsions, inductions, limitations and gravitations of matters at or near the earth's surface.

There were not the electric telegraph but as the impressions made upon a continuous medium of being physiological at one end of a conducting wire are reported at the other.   Nor were there the telephone but as these impressions made in sounds at one end of such conductor be repeated at the other.   Nor were there sight of a distant object but of the impressions it makes upon a continuous being physiological intermediate that object and the eye piercing it; and this of the same essential being as the object and the eyes. Nor were there the sound of a distant object but of the activities of such object in disturbance of such being intermediate of the same essential being as the object and the ear. Nor were there the attractions of matters at a distance but as though reciprocally in want of the beings different in such being intermediate. Nor were there the repulsions of such matters but as they be not in want of such beings intermediate. Nor were there the inductions of matters but as they be of the same essential beings as the matters, and each, through such being intermediate, be able to force the other into a state of such being the opposite of its own. Nor were there levitation in any matter but as at the surface of a spheroid physiological it be in more of heat from within it than of cold from without. Nor were there gravitation in any matter but as at the surface of such spheroid, it be under more of cold from without than of heat from within. Such were oxygen as specific heat and hydrogen as specific cold at this earth's surface, and such were electricity as heat and magnetism as cold at such surface. And such levitation were the minus of electricity and such gravitation the plus; and such gravitation were the force of plus electricity left upon the trolley wire from which the levitating and supporting minus has been withdrawn.

Such are the matters and forces of the earth's atmosphere. And that is physiological from being of the earth such being and of forces such, and matters such, and from its exhibition of phenomena possible of such being, and of nothing else. The elemental matters—oxygen, nitrogen, hydrogen and carbon—are materializations of a physiological space about the earth which exists, therefore, as an elastic being physiological intensely sensible of impressions, or they are accident or miracles; and not either, they are beings physiological. And so is the

13

atmosphere. And so physiological the earth's atmosphere, it is of the earth's systemic factors, as is the earth. And a stratum of its crust. And to the earth, therefore, there is the center of space, and about this its crust of matters in strata, the first metallic, and the next archaen rock, and the next water, and the next a gaseous atmosphere, no one of which can have come to exist as it does but of the earth as a reality of the finite word of God in space.

Nor can there have been the moon but of the earth such reality. Though not a stratum of the earth's crust, it is, at its place and operation, in representation of such stratum. As of eccentric and concentric radiations of the earth's dynamic and static beings at the external surface of any one of the strata of the earth's crust, there is the stratum next in order, so of such radiations from the external surface of the earth's atmospheric stratum, there was that medium of being physiological in a belt about the earth, from which there is the moon, with the earth in its orbit about the sun. As of radiations of beings in forces dynamic and static, from the exterior of every antecedent stratum, there were the gaseous matters in an atmospheric medium from which there was the next succeeding stratum, and as of such radiations from the water stratum, there were the gaseous matters of the earth's present atmosphere, reacting through waters, ammonias and carbonic oxides into plants, reacting into animals, of which there is a dermal envelope of organic matters, plant and animal, as continuously about the earth's surface as is possible, and in the activities, possible to such continuation. So, of radiations from the earth at the archaen period of its process, there were the gaseous matters of a belt of such matters about the earth, at a distance from it and in the plane of its equator. And, as the matters of the earth's present atmosphere have resolved, and are resolving, into such envelope of plant and animal beings possible in their forms and activities possible to the continuation of their existences in relation to the earth, so have the matters of that belt resolved into the moon, and are resolving into the activities of the moon in continuation of the moon in relation to the earth.

It is probable that the radiations of which there was this belt were from the earth at the archaen period of its process. It is probable that there was an archaen period of the earth as there is now of the sun, and as there is, perhaps, of every planetary, solar or stellar being, at the time when, of radiations from its metallic stratum, it is in formation of its archaen rock stratum; that then the reactions of the earth's dynamic and static beings were the most intense; and that while those the nearest to earth reacted immediately into matters oxygenic and metallic, reacting into rocks, those at greater distance from each other, in emerging, did not so react immediately, but were radiated off to a distance from the earth, and in the plane of the earth's equator.

It is morally certain that these radiations, eccentric and concentric, are reciprocally refractive of each other. That while reciprocally attractive and repulsive of each other, their attractions are the stronger, and that while of such superior attractions the concentric radiations of every such physiological system are focused by the eccentric at the center of the spheroid forming, the eccentric radiations are focused by the concentric at the points possible in a belt of such foci about the earth, and this at a distance from the earth and in or near the plane of its equator. And that these foci of their superior attractions are drawn to four points equidistant from each other in that belt; and, each a quadrant of that belt and at a quadrant's distance from each other, that at and from the center of each such quadrant there are eccentric radiations of dynamic being as there are at and from the center of the earth, that these are eccentric from within and concentric from without. And that of these, the one as levitation and the other as gravitation, there is a spheroid of matter about its center of space. And that this is the moon.

This theory requires that there shall have been four moons about the earth. And, it is probable that there were. The moon is in relation to the earth as the earth to the sun. And it will have been as capable of a plurality of moons as is the sun of a plurality of planets. And, as the sun at its archaen stage has a plurality of planets, it is probable that so had the earth. And this the moon, since there is such plurality about outer planets at their archaen periods.

It is probable, as I have said, that the outer planets, Jupiter, Saturn, Uranus and Neptune, are at or are approaching their archaen periods, and that the inner planets, Mercury, Venus, Earth and Mars, are in or about their organic periods. And as Jupiter, which would seem to be at the close of its archaen period, is seen to be surrounded by eight moons in their orbits, there is ground for the suggestion that this earth was surrounded by four moons, and that these are the products of its archaen radiations, as the eight inner and outer planets of the sun are the products of its archaen radiations. And as moons would seem to be in relation to the planets as the planets themselves are to the sun, and as all planets would seem to have had, or be about to have, their archaen periods, it is probable that all planets have had, or are about to have, their one group of four moons, or groups of fours. It is probable that as about the planet, at its archaen period, there is the one belt of radiations focused in the plane of its equator, at a distance from the planet it may have others at successive distances, its archaen radiations being sufficient. And that these belts may each have broken into quadrants and that each quadrant may have formed into a moon to take its elliptical orbit about the planet as does that about the sun; and that in doing so, the first of such nebulous media to form into a moon may have taken its orbit nearest to the planet, and the others their orbits at quadratic distances to the exterior from their reciprocal repulsions.

But if this be not so, and that nebulous belt of focused radiations be the only one that formed about the earth, and this did not break into quadrants forming into moons to take their respective orbits about the earth, but only experienced a breach of continuity as such belt, the foremost parts will have been retarded by the attractions of the parts behind them, and the hinder parts will have been accelerated in their orbits by the attractions of the parts before them, in results of which these parts may have come together in one nebulous medium to form of the reactions of its dynamic and static beings eccentric and concentric on and from its center, into the one moon about the earth as the earth itself, may have formed of one nebulous belt about the sun.

But, however this may have been, enough remains to show that the moon is of the earth. There is this in the fact that the moon is of matters, and that these are the same essentially, as are those of the earth. It is reasonably certain that the moon, as to its surface, is of ice. And that this is of its atmosphere reduced to water, and that frozen. It presents the appearance of such frozen water: Its atmosphere, if it had one, will have been reduced to water by the cold there must be at the moon without an inherent source of heat; and although we must suppose that there was an archaen period of the moon at which, from its center, there were the radiations of the dynamic being in heat, of which were formed its crust of metals, rocks, waters and a gaseous atmosphere, we may suppose that it has passed that period, as Mercury and Venus at the earth have passed it with the loss, not only of their atmospheres of gaseous matters, but their moons. That the heat, therefore, of which every planetary body of the solar system consists, is not from the direct radiations of the sun upon it, but is inherent, and from the reactions of its dynamic and static beings on its center. That the cold, increasing in a constant ratio of distances from the sun as it does from the earth, is intense enough to freeze to static force even the metals of the nearest planets to the sun, and that Mercury, Venus, Earth and Mars exist, but of their own inherent heat not yet expended. But that it is so far expended by the moon that its atmosphere has turned to ice. It is the common opinion that planets have their heat only from the sun, and that those the nearest are the hottest. But this is quite unreasonable. If the direct rays of the sun be the only source of heat to the earth, 90,000,000 miles away from it, the sun were too hot and the earth too cold for any conceivable form of matter, and there can be the sensible existence of either only upon the supposition of an internal source of heat in earth sufficient to sustain its matters as we see them.

And such the status of the moon we must suppose that to its exterior surface of ice there have been the antecedent strata of solid matters such as are in the earth. And that these are of the same forces as are those of the earth. And that these are of the same essential being finite of beings infinite as are those of the earth. And that, as these can have come to the moon of radiations from the earth, and of no things else, we must suppose that the moon is of the earth. And that it is of the earth from its being with the earth in its orbit about the earth, as the earth of the sun is in its orbit about the sun.

And such the atmosphere and moon of the earth, they are equally conclusive of the truth that the earth is a reality of the word of God in space. It is clear that there was a period of the earth when neither existed; it is clear that, before the archaen period of the earth, the moon did not exist, and as clear that, at its archaen period, its atmospheres of gaseous matters did not exist. Nor did there at that time exist an element or compound of that atmosphere, save oxygen, existing in it now.

At that time when, at a temperature of 20,000° F. and a pressure of 5,000 pounds to the inch, metallic oxides were forming into incandescent rocks, there was, of non-metallic elements now existing, oxygen alone. The gaseous elements — nitrogen, hydrogen and carbon, now with oxygen in formation of waters, ammonias and carbonic oxides, also gaseous — did not appear. Nor could the one of them have existed for an instant under such conditions of temperature and pressure, and that they now exist in such relation to the antecedent earth were proof conclusive that they exist of that earth, if it did not appear that they are of the same essential being as are the oxygen and metals of the antecedent earth; and that that earth was capable of the radiations, capable of these elements, capable of these compounds. But seeing this, and seeing also that there were no other conceivable means by which these elements can have come to exist in such atmosphere, or other means than of these elements reacting, by which the compounds can have come to exist in it, we must see that the atmosphere of the earth is of the earth, as is its moon; that these were neither without the earth, without an essential being of the universe. And, that reality, without reality. And that as a reality there is the earth.

CHAPTER XXIII.

AND AS A REALITY THERE IS THE PLANT.

The plant is the produce of the earth's systemic forces reacting at the surface of the earth, the one from within and the other from without, and the one levitation and the other gravitation, and the one systemic heat and the other systemic weight; and these realities, the plant of these is a reality.

It is argued with reason that about the earth's center, though at a distance from it, there is a cordon of matter molecules, the atoms of which, the ones in representation of the earth's heats and the others of its weights, are so exactly opposite that they are fixed in rotation to each other and form into a metal. But that, transpiring this cordon, the earth's eccentric radiations of heat are met by its concentric radiations of cold which do not so neutralize each other but which unite into a molecule of the two as atoms, each retaining its specific tendency — the one from, and the other to, the earth's center — with the difference only that in their new positions the one tends also from, and the other to, the center of the molecule they concur in forming; that of these the one is oxygen and the other potassium in formation of the first metallic oxide matter in the earth's crust; that they grow through successive cordons of metallic oxide matters, the metals becoming of continually more specific heat to less of atomic weight as the distance becomes greater from the center of formation, and that of these formations is the archaen rock.

But it is also argued with equal reason that when these systems of metallic oxide, from want of heat to sustain the metals in a fluid state, become solid and fixed in the archaen rock they concur in forming continuously about the metallic stratum of the earth's crust, there are still eccentric radiations of systemic heat from their exterior surface met by concentric radiations of systemic cold at a distance from it; that these become the one oxygen and the other hydrogen; that to neutralize each other and react upon the point of their neutral being intermediate and as atoms form into the first molecule of organic matters, one molecule of oxygen unites with two molecules of hydrogen; that this first molecule of organic matter is the molecule of water; that this of forces from within met by forces from without enlarges through nitrogens and carbons forming on it, into a system of ammonias compound, acid and base, and that of these reacting from the persistence of the earth's systemic forces into them there is at every available point of the earth's solid surface the plant, cryptogamic, phenerogamic, endogenous and exogenous, possible.

It is further argued that as of vapors from the earth's metallic stratum there were the metallic oxides of which is the archaen rock, so, of vapors from the archaen rock there were the hydrogens oxide of which are now the gaseous matters of the earth's atmosphere; that, as from potassiums oxide there were the systems of metallic oxides possible, so from hydrogens oxides there were the systems of hydrogens oxide possible. That as from the potassiums oxide there were systems of metallic oxides possible, each upon its special base, through less basic metals to silicium, so from hydrogens oxide there were systems of hydrogens oxide through less basic hydrogens to carbon; that as of the metallic systems there were silicates of aluminum and potassium, so of the hydrogen systems there are the carbonates of nitrogen and hydrogen; and as of the metallic systems there were the physiological rocks of the earth's archaen stratum, so of the hydrogen systems there are the physiological plants which spring from the earth's solid surface and take the earth's central force of levitation by their roots from the earth, and the earth's concentric force of gravitation by their foliage from the air. That the plants are thus intermediaries merely of the earth's archaen and organic periods. And that without other cause than the union of the earth's systemic forces represented by these periods respectively, and these forces realities, the plant so consisting of them simply is a reality. And, such the argument, it will be found that this is in fact true.

And as a reality, therefore, there is the plant.

There is a being of organic matter at this earth's surface termed the plant. And this is a reality if it be of the earth a reality, and that be of the sun a reality, and that be of a star a reality, and that be of the finite word of God in space — the universal and causal reality of which there are the consequential realities of the universe. And as we have seen the reasons for believing that there is that universal and causal reality, and that of this, mediately or immediately, there is the star, and of this the sun, and of this the earth, there will remain to the question of whether the plant be also a reality but the question whether this be of the earth. And it will be of the earth if of radiations of the earth's energies in inertia there be the gaseous matters of the earth's atmosphere, and the organic matters in the plant be of these; and the plant be but of these organic matters. And as we have seen that of the radiations of the earth's energies in inertia there are the matters of its atmosphere, there will remain to the question of whether the plant be a reality but the questions whether the organic matters in the plant be of the gaseous matters of the earth's atmosphere? And whether the plant be of these exclusively? And it will be found that the organic matters in the plant are of the gaseous matters in the earth's atmosphere. And that the plant is but of these.

The plant appears to us in very different aspects. We see it *first* as a microscopic cryptogam; and next as a visible phenerogam; and next as an endogenous palm; and next as an exogens oak; but, however varied its appearances, we find that in it, essentially, whether as the cryptogamic seaweed only in water, or the exogenous oak on land, there are but the four matter elements, oxygen, hydrogen, nitrogen and carbon; and these in waters, carbonic oxides and ammonias.

In some and in all plants, perhaps, there are other matter elements, and of these other matter compounds, but these are not essential to the plant as such, and only enable it of its essential elements to vary to the conditions of a continued existence.

And such the plant the first question is whether, of the matters of the earth's atmosphere, there can have been its waters, carbonic oxides and ammonias. And to this the further question, whether with oxygen and hydrogen — the one energy and the other its inertia — there can have been of the earth's radiations also nitrogen and carbon? We can see how of such radiations there can have been oxygen and hydrogen, the one of the most of energy to the least of inertia, and the other of the most of inertia to the least of energy, but we cannot see quite clearly how, of such radiations, there can have been nitrogen and carbon, or these in carbonic oxides and ammonias. And it is possible and probable, in fact, that nitrogen and carbon are not immediately of the earth's radiations as are oxygen and hydrogen, but that the water molecule of hydrogen and oxygen in reaction is a natural being physiological of these kindred beings different in reciprocal limitations of each other into the spheroid and wheel of both, as is the being finite of infinite beings different, or the moment of electric force of its minus and plus, or the matter molecule of its atoms negative and positive. And that this is in teleologic evo-involution into its progeny of other elements possible, the first of which are nitrogen and carbon, as is the parent sun into its progeny of planets. And that thus therefore, but indirectly and mediately merely, there are of the earth's radiations nitrogen and carbon in its atmosphere. But as a fact, however we be unable to conceive the way of it, there is nitrogen at least in the earth's gaseous atmosphere, since that atmosphere has been formed to consist in the main but of oxygen and nitrogen in the proportions of one to four. And that in that atmosphere there is also carbon, is in the fact that in it there is a percentage, small it is true, of carbonic oxide. And though to this it may be argued that it did not originate there, but rose from the earth, there is to that the question how did the carbon get into the earth? There is the possibility, at least, of its existence in the atmosphere from teleologic evo-involution of the water molecule, but there is no conceivable possibility of its coming first to existence in the solid earth. That primarily is of metallic oxides liberated by disintegration of the archaen rock in which there was no carbon or other nonmetallic element of matter save oxygen. And, existing, it must have come to exist in some process of the earth's insensible energies into sensible matters.

That must have been a process after the rock, of which water first to form and fall upon the rock was the start, and that and its results can have been only in the earth's atmosphere beyond the rocks. And in that is the only conceivable source of either nitrogen or carbon, neither of which is found in the rock, but both of which are found in the atmosphere. And neither of which could have existed in the rock or at the earth's surface under the temperature at which the rock ceased to form.

We must accept, therefore, that not only oxygen and hydrogen, but nitrogen and carbon, and all other nonmetallic elements of matter, were formed of water in the earth's atmosphere of gaseous matters, or of these matters compounded and falling on the earth's crust of solid matters. And that the plant from its seaweed to its oak, essentially but of the elements oxygen, hydrogen, nitrogen and carbon in waters, ammonias and carbonic oxides,

has come to existence of some process of being physiological from its axis in the water molecule.

In every plant from the seaweed to the oak there are
other elements of matter and other compounds of these
elements, but these are the accessories merely of which
oxygen, hydrogen, nitrogen and carbon in waters, ammonias and carbonic oxides are the principals. And which
enable their principals to perform their functions in build-
ing up the plant to the plant possible.

And accepting this, and that the plant is of oxygen,
hydrogen, nitrogen and carbon, in water, ammonia and
carbonic oxide, we must accept that these are of the earth's
radiant energies in resolution, and so are realities, as the
earth is a reality. And that the plant, therefore, from
start to finish, is a reality if we can find that of these
essential constituents alone the plant has advanced from
the unicellular alga to the forest oak.

And we can, and do, find this. We find that the essential elemental and compound matters of the unicellular cryptogam are the same as those of the multicellular phenerogam; that each plant is a being physiological of energy
and inertia, the one life and the other nature, and that the
elements and compounds of the lowest cryptogamic plant
are sufficient for the highest phenerogamic plant. They
are sufficient, also, for all the variations by which the lowest, in accepting the conditions to the continuation of its
existence, becomes the highest; that as there are no essential elements of matter added to the plant, so there are no
powers *ab extra* to form the essential elements into compounds, or to vary it to the conditions of its continued
existence. And that in the whole course of its existence
it is but the medium through which the energies, eccentric
and concentric, of the earth and air react. That the phenerogamic plants take energy through their roots from
the earth, and inertia through their foliaged branches from
the air. That in the earth there are metallic oxides in
which the greater energies of the archaen earth have been

stored, and in the air there are the hydrogens oxide and ammonias in which the inertias of that energy are now stored; and that the plant, with its roots in the soil and its branches in the air, is to these but opposite reservoirs of forces physiological as is the conductor between the reservoirs of forces physiological at the opposite poles of the battery, and that, as there is nothing but opposite electricities to produce the electro-magnetic spheroids about the continuous conductor, or the spark of heat and light between the adjacent ends of the conductor discontinuous, so there is nothing but opposite energies in the earth and air to produce the plant, which, therefore, can be but of the earth's eccentric and concentric energies originally stored in the earth, and the gaseous matters of the earth's atmosphere. And the earth reality, and this reality, the plant, but of this, is a reality.

And it is true that the plant is such reality if it be true that of the earth there have been its two periods, archaen and organic—the one that in which it formed its archaen rocks, and the other that in which it formed its organic matters, plant and animal. And as for the reasons given there was its archaen period, the only question is whether there has been, or is, its organic period. And whether there be this is dependent upon whether of its radiations from its rocks there were its waters, and from the evo-involutions of its waters there were its nonmetallic matters found in plants, and of the evo-involutions of these there were the matters found in animals. And as of its radiations from its rocks there were its waters, since there were nothing else of which they could have come—and as of its waters there were its other nonmetallic matters, since there were nothing else from which they could have come; and as of these there were its plants, since there were nothing else from which they could have come; and as of the plant matter there was its animal matter, since there was nothing else from which it could have come; and of its animal matter there were its animals, since there was nothing else from which they could have come — it is reasonably certain that of the earth's post-archaen radiations there were its waters, and of these its nonmetallic matters, and of these its plants, and of these its animals. That these nonmetallic matters are termed organic from a supposed difference between them and those in the archaen rocks, termed inorganic. And that of these into animals and plants there is a period of the earth to be termed organic, as of those into rocks there was a period termed inorganic, but termed also archaen from its being that in which the earth began to form, as it is supposed, the matters visible to us at its surface. That there is the organic period, therefore, and the plant of the earth in this period of the resolutions of its essential being is also in resolutions of that being. And the earth, for reason of the resolutions of its own essential being, a reality, the plant, in continuation of such resolutions, is a reality.

In theory of the earth a reality from its existence of the resolutions of its own essential beings, termed realities, the plant in its existence of the continuation of such resolutions were a reality; and the only question with us is whether, in consistence with phenomena observed, we can accept it as such.

We see it starting as a cryptogamic and unicellular alga from a protoplasm of water, ammonia and carbonic oxide in the waters probably of the Silurian seas, then continuously about the earth, and by favorable variations rising thence through multicellular algas, still in water, to fungi, lichens, moss, equisetae and ferns on lands beginning to appear above the waters. And thence by favorable variations through endogenous phenerogamic plants to the exogenous phenerogamic trees of the forest. And seeing this we may doubt that it is of the same cause as the soil from which it grows; or that this soil is, in part, of an archaen rock disintegrated, or that there is a rock about the earth in the same relation to the earth as is the plant. To be this its matter must have started in a metallic oxide analogous to the hydrogens oxide in water. And of this in teleologic evo-involutions there must have been other metallic oxides; and of these in combination there must have been a first process analogous to that of the plant, which must have been felspar, the first constituent of the archaen rock; and a secondary process of which there must have been mica — the other constituent of that rock, of felspar and mica combined by quartz — analogous to the animal. And these, felspar and mica, in composition of the rock, the inorganic being possible, must have exhibited reciprocal activities analogously the same as these of the plant and animal in production of organic being possible. And it is safe to say that such analogies do not generally appear, and that not many are aware that the rock is of felspar and mica in a matrix of quartz, or that felspar is but of the oxides of potassium, silicium and aluminum, or their equivalents, while mica is of these and those of calcium and iron, or their equivalents in addition. Nor is it probable that any one has realized the separate existences and activities of these rock matters in preservations of their existences, analogously, as have the plant and animal.

But in that we do not see these analogies, there is no reason that they do not exist. We are in the one period, but not in the other; and we see the beings of the one period and not of the other. And while being ourselves of the organic period, and acting with its beings in preservation of their existences in preservation of our own existences, we see but the remains of archaen beings, and these in the rocks where they exhibit not more of those beings in life than do the remains of animals and plants in our geological formations.

These, to us, even of this period, would give but a faint idea of the plants and animals in life if we did not see them in life. And the remains of plants, animals and man will not give to the beings of another stage of the earth a clearer conception of the beings of this period than we have through their remains of beings of the archaen period. And while it is not probable that those of the archaen period whose remains are in felspar and mica were ever as discretely active as are plants and animals in the entire course of their coexistences, it is quite probable that they were analogously so active as are plant and animal and as are the successive orders of coral polyps, whose remains have given existence to the coral rock. And that in the nature of each felspar and mica there was a vital principle as efficient to the end of its being the matter possible, as is the coral polyp to its shell possible, or the plant or animal to its bark or hide possible.

But not seeing these analogies we do not accept the fact of their existence, or that there is an organic period of the same earth in teleologic evo-involution simply of its own essential being simply, as there was its archaen period, or that the plant of the one period is the analogue of the felspar of the other, or that the animal is the analogue of mica. And if there were nothing more to be considered than the appearances of these beings, respectively, it is to be doubted that anyone would accept them as such analogues, or for this or any other reason would accept the plant as a reality, still it is important that the analogy shall be realized, as in this way only can it be seen that the plant is in such process of the earth's essential being; and as such offspring of the earth a reality, is, itself, a reality. And it is important that we shall realize it as a reality, as without this we can have no science of it, and but empirical conceptions with respect to it. But if we see it of the essential being of the earth in teleologic evo-involution, under existing conditions, into the beings of it possible, we have the data from the deductions and inductions of which we can find what there is to be known about it—whatever that may be worth to us, and it is apt to be worth much. And there are facts through analyses of which the identity of the plant and

14

felspar as analogous constituents of the earth's organic and archaen processes respectively may be established.

Both are of matter in ultimate analysis of which there are the same physical forces. The matters of both are oxides, those of felspar metallic, and those of the plant nonmetallic or hydrogenic. Of those of the plant the first was that of hydrogen, in two of hydrogen to one of oxygen. And it is probable that the first of felspar was that of potassium, in two of potassium to one of oxygen, the atomic weight of hydrogen being one to that of potassium thirty-nine. In the plant there is the oxide of carbon, and in felspar that of silicium, and in the plant there is the oxide of nitrogen, and in felspar that of aluminum. In both, these oxides are sometimes substituted by their equivalents, and carbonic for silicic oxide and silicic for carbonic oxide. In both, the bases under condition unite with each other to become more specifically basic, while their oxygens are taken by other bases to become more specifically acid, as in the plant its hydrogens and nitrogens unite in ammonia, while their rejected oxygens are taken by carbon to become carbonic exides; and as in felspar it is probable; as do aluminum and potassium to become a more potent base while their rejected oxygens are taken by silicium to become silicic oxide. And it is probable that both plant and felspar take up — to their occasions for them — other oxides. But it is reasonably certain that the essential constituents of the plant and felspar are the oxides mentioned.

Of these the elements are the same, or analogous. Oxygen is the same in all, and hydrogen is analogous to potassium. It is an univalent basic radical as is potassium, from which it differs only in its atomic density, for which the differences of conditions under which they come respectively to exist sufficiently account. The heat at the archaen time when potassium formed was probably 20,000° F., and the atmospheric pressure 5,000 pounds to the inch, and under such conditions it is to be presumed that thirty-nine degrees of atomic density in each of two potassium atoms were necessary to contain the one of specific heat in oxygen. While the heat at the time and place at which hydrogen was formed was less ·than 60° F., and the atmospheric pressure less than fifteen pounds to the inch; when two hydrogens of but two degrees of atomic density was enough for· one of oxygen. It is reasonably certain that the waters of the Silurian seas were not formed at the glowing surface of the archaen rocks, but at a distance above them where the cold was as great as at a shorter distance it is now, and where the atmospheric pressure was less than at the surface of the earth it is now. And under these conditions it is probable that the two hydrogens were as capable of the one oxygen, as at the earlier period were the two potassiums.

So analogous, also, are carbon and silicium. Both are deatomic and multivalent basic radicals, of the atomic weights of twelve and twenty-eight, respectively, while of both the specific heats are not, as in all other elements of matter, inversely to their densities, but in proportions greater. Both are capable of two oxygens to one of either. And both as acids are able to unite with hydrogens as bases, though it is not seen that of hydro-silicates there is the abundance that there is of hydro-carbons. Nor is it seen that there are crystals of silicium as there are of carbons in the diamond. But that there are not the many hydro-silicates, or the crystals of silicium, is ·attributable, perhaps, to the conditions under which silicium came to exist.

At the archaen time, when in the process of potassium oxide into the oxides of the rocks, of which probably that of silicium was one, there were no basic hydrogens with which it could have formed, and if then, as an acid, it could have formed with a base, it must have found that base in some units of potassium as carbon finds its bases in units of hydrogen.

And so also while at that time there were probably liquid silicic oxides in solution, as at the water time there were carbonic oxides in solution, it is not probable that there were in any of its experiences the greater heat to discharge it of its solvents, and hold it discharged until, in the subsidence of the heat, it could harden into crystals.

At the close of the archaen time it is probable that there was about the still liquid rock an atmosphere of water vapor, charged with carbonic oxides; that this water fell in resistless torrents, and possibly in blocks of ice containing the oxides; that these penetrated the rocks, still liquid, and were held by them until, discharged of their oxygens, they hardened with the rocks into crystals of carbon. But to such experiences the silicic oxides could not have been subject, or if subject to them there was nothing conceivable to hold such crystals in their hardened state. There is thus the reason that, while the siliciums of the archaen times were the exact analogies of carbons in the organic, there were not the conditions under which these siliciums, existing in crystals, can have been exhibited to us.

And that there are not only analogies, but an essential identity in the beings of carbon and silicium, is in the fact that in organic and inorganic compounds they substitute each other. And if it be not seen that carbonic oxides take the places of silicic oxides, it is seen that in plant and rock matters the silicic oxides take the places of carbonic oxides, and that so woods are petrified and limestones become flints.

And so analogous also are aluminum of the archaen period to nitrogen of the organic. Both are multivalent acid radicals, as is oxygen. And both are basic to oxygen acid, while both are acids to all other elements of either period. And in this they are to each other as were two oxides, the one potassium and the other hydrogen, developed. Each of these were a wheel, of which the oxygens were axles and the potassiums and hydrogens were disks, respectively. But each disk were in quadrants, virtually, each a wheel of basic disk about its acid axle. And each in revolution on its acid axle, as the four were in revolution on the common axle, oxygen. And such the ideals of potassiums and hydrogens oxides respectively the element aluminum were in representation of the one quadrant of the potassiums oxide, and the element nitrogen were in representation of a quadrant of the hydrogens oxide. And regarding these oxides as representative of the beings archaen and organic respectively, we may regard aluminum and nitrogen as representative also, and performing analogous functions in the archaen and organic processes of the earth, and that they are essentially the same, and differ but as the conditions differ under which they will have acted.

The atomic density of nitrogen is fourteen in terms of hydrogen, while that of aluminum is twenty-seven and one-half. And these, therefore, are very nearly in relation to each other, as are carbon and silicium. And aluminum in archaen matters is in the same relation to silicium as is nitrogen to carbon in organic matters. And while it may not be seen that one aluminum unites with three other more basic elements to form an intensely basic compound, as does nitrogen with three hydrogens to form ammonia, it is seen that in all rocky compounds in which there is aluminum, that element is in such relation to others with it as it would be if introduced to them by such basic elements, and is to them as is nitrogen to others in all vital organic compounds.

Of all organic compounds nitrogen is the vital element. There are starch, sugar, lignin, and the like, without nitrogen and without life, but in all in which there is nitrogen there is, or has been, life, and in all in which there is, or has been life there is, or has been, nitrogen. It would seem to be to the life of the organic being physiological as oxygen is to its existence. And such would seem to be the function of aluminum in the inorganic compounds. If into that the aluminum can have come without its base, the compound could not exist without aluminum or the aluminum without its function. In the exercise of this it is to the existence of the inorganic compound, as nitrogen is to the life of the organic.

And as both are of matter, and that of force, and that of the radiations of the earth at its archaen and organic periods respectively; and as of nitrogen there was no other source than that of carbon through the resolutions of hydrogens oxide, it is probable there was aluminum from the source of silicium in the resolutions of the analogous potassiums oxide.

And as we must suppose, therefore, that the carbon and nitrogen of the plant and the silicium and aluminum of the felspar were of the evo-involutions of hydrogens and potassiums oxides respectively, and that of these oxides the one was the first materialization of the earth's post-archaen radiations, and the other of its post-metallic radiations, we must accept that the plant, of its hydrogens carbon and nitrogen oxides, is in continuations of the post-archaen earth. And that the rock, of its potassiums silicium and aluminum oxides, is in continuation of the post-metallic earth. And that as the earth, whether post-archaen or post-metallic, is a reality, the rock is a reality, and the plant a reality as is the rock.

This were the conclusion if we saw only the plant of the organic period and the felspar of the archaen. There were not these elements from the same source, at different periods, and so analogous, but as they be the successive outputs of the earth at the successive stages of its evo-involution. But this conclusion is the more resistless when we see the earth's organic period not only its plant but its animal, and of its archaen period not only the felspar but its mica. And that the animal and mica are as necessarily from the same source, and as analogous, as are the plant and felspar.

There were not the animal without the plant, and without the elements of the plant to which it has in addition only the elements sulphur and phosphorus, both basic as to oxygen, but with respect to all other matters metallic or nonmetallic, the one is a multivalent artiad acid radical, as is oxygen, of which it is twice the atomic weight, and the other a multivalent parissad acid radical, as is nitrogen, of which it is nearly twice the atomic weight. And in this sulplur is to phosphorus as oxygen is to nitrogen. And as neither existed at the formation of water; and as neither appears but as a by-product of the plant; and as sulphur is diatomic and just twice the atomic weight of oxygen, and as phosphorus is tetratomic and near twice the weight of nitrogen; and as both are polymorphic — in exhibition at different temperatures of different characteristics, as though each were of two beings in one — there is ground to suppose that both were produced by the plant, and that the one is but doubled oxygen, and the other but quadrupled nitrogen.

While sulphur is diatomic as is oxygen, phosphorus is tetratomic, as though consisting of four nitrogens united, and exhibiting in the animal analogously the functions of nitrogen in the plant. And as in the plant wheel physiological the oxygen is axle and the nitrogens probably the axles of the quadrants of its disk, it is probable that sulphur is the axle of a disk of wheels of the quadrants of which the four atoms phosphorus are the axles. And that the wheel physiological of these in the animal is analogous to that oxygen and nitrogen in the atmosphere. And that the animal therefore is to the plant as the sun is to its planets. To the single planet there is its axle and its disk in quadrants, while to the solar system comprehending its planets there is its axis and its disk of quadrants. And it is possible that the animal is to the plant as is the solar system to the systems of its planets. And that the cardinal functionaries of the superior animal system are its sulphur and phosphorus, as to that of the plant are oxygen and nitrogen.

Such the possible and probable relation of the animal to the plant in organic nature, such is the probable relation of mica to felspar in the archaen rock. It is assumed that in this there are the oxides of calcium and iron not in felspar. And there is the suggestion that, not existing before felspar, or as constituents of felspar, they were the by-products of felspar, and these through unions of its elements oxygen and aluminum. Calcium is a diatomic multivalent artiad, and basic radical with respect to oxygen. And possibly with respect to other bases as is oxygen. Iron is a multivolent porissad, and basic radical, with respect to oxygen, and acid probably with respect to other bases, as is nitrogen. And it is possible therefore that these in mica are multiples, the one of principles analogous to oxygen, and the other of principles analogous to nitrogen or their equivalents, produced by felspar, as sulphur and phosphorus are produced by the plant.

There are facts in the relation of calcium to magnesium of which it is near twice the atomic weight and of iron to aluminum of which it is more nearly twice the atomic weight, to suggest that calcium is the multiple of magnesium and iron, the multiple of aluminum, but of the histologies and histories of these rocks we are not so possessed as to speak with even the confidence of our conceptions as to the ultimate elements of plants and animals. And as to the physiological identity of the periods organic and archaen, and of the plants and animals of the one and the felspars and micas of the other, in expression of the organic and archaen earth, respectively, the most and utmost we can confidently say is that both periods are of the same earth at successive stages of the evo-involution of its own essential being, and of nothing else. That of the one period at its surface the only products besides its unaltered metals were its rocks, and of the other its plants and animals; that as these products of the organic earth are in successive sections, the one the condition of the other, so was the archaen earth. And that as the plant is the first product of the organic earth, felspar, or something analogous as were felspar to the plant, was the first product of the archaen earth. That either, of the earth, is as real as the earth. And that the plant therefore is a reality if there were nothing more to show its exist-ence of that earth and its relation to it.

But there is more; first, in the fact that plant is a spherical being physiological of dynamic and static beings in reciprocal limitations of each other as is the earth. And, next, in that the plant is in execution of a necessary office in the organic earth.

The every plant cell or germ, and the every plant and the plant kingdom, is in theory and in fact, as far as its features can be seen, a spheroid of relatively static being about its spherical center of relatively dynamic being in eccentric radiations of dynamic being to distend the static in concentric radiations of its static being to constrict the dynamic. And from the axis of their reac-tions in every such spheroid, there are radiations of their dynamo-static beings transpiring the exterior static crust, and forming on it into spheroids in every way, but in size the same as the parent spheroid. Such, as far as we can see it, is the plant cell in its nucleolus dynamic to its nucleus static, and its nucleus dynamic to the matters within its limiting membrane, static. And such is the fertile germ of which the sperm is dynamic and the germ static. And analogously such is the individual plant cryp-togamic, or phenerogamic, of which the spore or seed is dynamic and the plant static. And analogously such is the plant as a whole of which the cryptogam is dynamic to the phenerogam static. And the endogens dynamic to the exogens static, relatively, however it be dynamic to its exterior possibilities. In each there is cause and con-sequence, and life and nature, and life dynamic, to nature static—the central dynamic cause and life, of which can

have come into it only from the earth—an antecedent
such spheroid of life and nature. Such correspondences
were possible but as the earth and its plants be in teleologic evo-involution of its own essential being.

There is also further evidence that the plant exists of
the being of the earth in the facts that it performs an
office in that being. There is dynamic being in the earth
and static being in its air. In the soils there are acid
matters metallic and nonmetallic, not neutralized by adjacent bases. In the atmosphere there are basic ammonias
not neutralized by adjacent acids; these acids and bases
react through the media possible; those possible are the
plants which, therefore, perform for the earth the office of
uniting its internal and external energies, which they could
not if not themselves such energies. Through their
roots they take acid energies from the earth, and through
their foliage basic energies from the air, and thus are the
media through which these energies are united to the further possibilities of the earth. These energies react more
conspicuously through the higher plants, which draw them
from larger areas of soil and air, and to such channels of
reaction form themselves and the elements and compounds
of which they exist in performance of their offices. Nor
is that office exclusively or to a greater extent in the
larger and more conspicuous plants. The very lowest
orders are such intermediaries of the earth's eccentric and
concentric forces, and in their multiplicity make up for
their want of size. Nor do the matters or the elements
of the matters of which they exist to the performance of
their office, pre-exist. No being inorganic or organic, or
plant, or animal, takes to its existence or its growth,
existing matter. One rock of its existing matter under
changed conditions becomes another. But the one rock
does not come to exist of pre-existing rocks. It can come
to exist and, existing, grow to the rock it is but of the
forces of which its matters are. And, however the forces
of its matters may have existed in matters, those matters

must have been reduced to forces before they can be taken by the matter coming to exist of them. Nor does the matter taken as food by the plant or animal enter as such into the plant or animal, but is reduced to forces and then accepted. Nor do the waters of artesian wells in the earth, or those of rains or snows in the atmosphere come to their places as waters, but only as the forces capable of water. And it is not to be supposed, therefore, that the plants forming of the earth's eccentric and concentric forces do so of matters otherwise existing, but of these forces themselves which under the conditions, form the matters of which they ultimately consist.

And so forming its elements of the earth's radiant forces and its matters of such elements, and itself of such matters, intermediating the earth's eccentric and concentric energies the one from the earth's surface and the other from its atmosphere; and so consisting of the same matters as the earth, and so analogous to the earth and so concurring with the animal in the dermal envelope of organic matters about the earth, as is the foliage of the plant or the skin of the animal, there is ground for the belief that the plant is to the earth as is its cambium layer between wood and bark to the exogenous plant, or the true skin to the vertebrate animal. That at such it is part of the earth, and itself a reality as is the earth.

CHAPTER XXIV.

AS A REALITY, ALSO, THERE IS THE ANIMAL.

This truth is established in the showing that as a reality there is the plant. As there is the plant only of the earth's systemic forces meeting and reacting on centers intermediate the earth's archaen and organic periods, there were not the animal but of these forces acting through the plant. They are but successive stages, therefore, of the earth's reality in advancing from the earth's solid surface to its possibilities beyond. And both of the earth's systemic forces they differ only as the plant be sessile and the animal locomotive.

The plant, from being the subject of reactions between eccentric and concentric forces, the ones from the earth and the others from the air, is sessile upon the point of contact at the earth's surface, and is able, of these forces simply, to grow and vary into the plant possible of the primary elements, oxygen, hydrogen, nitrogen and carbon. But in forming to the possible of these, it is able to produce two additional elements, sulphur and phosphorus, both representing the earth's eccentric force, and the one the equivalent of two oxygens and the other of four nitrogens, which, not receiving their supports directly from the earth and air, are able to start with the primary elements into new processes, by which they may take the forces wanted already stored in the plant. This is the animal, which is locomotive, therefore, while the plant is sessile. But in its locomotion it is not more independent of the earth's systemic forces than is the plant. And the plant a reality from its existence of these forces, so also is the animal.

There is the animal radiate, annulate, articulate and vertebrate, and the radiate in polyps.and star fishes. And the annulate in worms, and the articulate in bees and ants, and the vertebrate in fishes, reptiles, and four-footed and four-handed, and two-footed and two-handed animals. Of these the radiate would seem to have come first, the annulate next, the articulate next, and the vertebrate last. And this in orders, the last of which is the animal two-footed and two-handed.

It would seem also that the radiate — the first and simplest form of the animal — is the unit in fact of life in nature of the animal; that the annulate is of the continuous reproductions of this radiate unit in the direction of its food; that the articulate is the annulate in sections reciprocally supplementing each other to its subsistence; and that the vertebrate is in the union of two annulates by a cartilaginous or bony section expressive of their contributions to the common being of them both. And that the vertebrates differ only in the means through which under different,condition they are able to procure the means of continuing their existences. The fish has fins with which to reach its food in water. The reptile projections through which to reach its food in marshes. The digitigrade the feet through which to reach its food from above the surface of the land; the plantigrade the feet with claws, through which to pursue and capture food escaping; the quadrumana, the hands through which it may climb and take its food from trees, and the two-footed and two-handed animal — the two feet equivalent to the four of the four-footed animal, and the two hands equivalent to the four of the four-handed animal — through which, under an organ of intelligence to coordinate the activities of its feet and hands, it is able to obtain a food and safety far beyond the reach of the animal four-footed or four-handed.

It would seem, indeed, that at the start of animal life there were waters continuously and to considerable depths about the earth in which fishes only could exist; that later there were marshes in which there was food for the reptiles crawling to obtain it; that later there were plants with fronds to be obtained only by animals standing on their toes to reach them; that later there was food to be had only by pursuit and capture; that later there was food to be had but by climbing and capture, and that later there was yet a wealth of food to be had by cultivation, climbing and capture, which, conserved and stored, was sufficient to sustain a race of animals indefinitely more abundant than any possible of other means.

Such the probable differences of conditions at the earth's surface since the animal began to be, it would seem that the vertebrate animals, at least, have differed in the means through which they have been able to comply with these conditions. And this so with the vertebrate animal that it is so with the animal as a whole, and that the radiate became the annulate of radiates, and this the articulate of annulates, and this the vertebrate of articulates as the means simply of continuing its existence to its extent possible.

And that thus the animal starting with the fall of liquid water on the earth in an automatic and autonomic protoplasm of the elements oxygen, hydrogen, nitrogen, carbon, sulphur and phosphorus, it has advanced by variations favorable to its existence under conditions favorable from the amoeboid radiate to the two-footed and two-handed vertebrate, in stocks, tribes and states of the animal we term man.

And such the animal it is a reality in teleologic evo-involution of the earth's essential being if it be in continuation of such evo-involution in the plant. And it is in continuation of such evo-involution in the plant if it be dependent for its immediate existence on the plant. And it is so immediately dependent on the plant if from the plant are the matter elements of which it consists, or if of the plant there be the food upon which it subsists.

And from the plant there are the matter elements of which it consists. The elements of the plant are oxygen, hydrogen, nitrogen and carbon, in water, ammonia and carbonic oxide reacting into ammonias compound, acid and base, reacting into the automatic and autonomic protoplasm of which there is the spore of the cryptogamic plant.

Those of the animal are the same, with sulphur and phosphorus in addition, reacting, it is to be supposed, into sulphosphammonias compound, acid and base, reacting into the protoplasm of which there is the amoeboid radiate. And from the plant are the elements of oxygen, hydrogen, nitrogen and carbon in the animal, if the plant shall have come to exist before the animal, or if the animal cannot originate these elements.

And the plant did come before the animal. It is reasonably certain that before either plant or animal there were Silurian seas of hydrogens and oxygens simply, and these continuously about the earth in which no other matter elements can have formed. But that about this there was an atmosphere of water vapor analogously such as is now about the earth; that in this of the physiological reactions of hydrogens and oxygens there were nitrogens and carbons, and of the reactions of these, carbonic oxides and ammonias; and of the reactions of these ammonias compound, acid and base. And of these, reacting in, or subsiding on waters, there was the protoplasm of which there was the spore of the cryptogamic plant by physiological reactions into the higher orders of plants. And that into the earth's cryptogamic plants went first the entire products of its post-Silurian atmosphere.

But that these reacting into the cryptogamic plants possible produced the elements phosphorus and sulphur, which, reacting with the elements of the plant, sessile or local, produced the radiate animal, originally local but becoming locomotive, to its food in plants.

And so, certain that both are of the same being, it is the more certain from the fact that both are of the same matters in that their matters react, as they could not otherwise. And that they do not start as parallel and independent processes of the same essential being is in the fact that the animal cannot originate its elements, or accept them self-originated of an anterior force. The amoeba can not, but can accept them only, and from the plant, as the offspring cannot originate the elements of its being, but can accept them only from its parent. For the elements common to them both, therefore, the animal is indebted to the plant. And to the plant also it is indebted for its sulphur and phosphorus. Of these the animal is not more capable than of its elements taken from the plant. And although these are not of the essential elements of the plant, which can exist apparently as well without them, they yet do appear in plants, and as probable products of the plants, and possibly as the duplicates and quadruples of oxygen and nitrogen respectively.

It is probable, as I have said, that the elements of matter, seen as substantive and sensible beings, are, in fact, but the insensible functionaries of those essential and universal beings physiological in wheels of static beings in involutions on their axes of beings dynamic. That the elements of these are units as well of function as structure.

And that of these elements ultimately becoming sensible in plants, oxygen is the dynamic and hydrogen, nitrogen and carbon the static functionaries. And that of these in wheels the oxygen is the axial and hydrogen, nitrogen and carbon, in possible relations to each other, the diskal functionaries. That any two of these plant wheels physiological may react, and, reacting, unite in a wheel physiological of both, in the axle of which were the functions of two oxygens, and in the disk of which were the functions of four hydrogens, four nitrogens and four carbons, and in the atmosphere and organic nature there are some

things to suggest 'that such are the relations of these
elements.

In the atmosphere of this earth there are four nitrogens to one oxygen, with the probable potencies of the
hydrogens and carbons, necessary to such wheels physiological throughout the atmosphere. There might have
been three such duplicates of oxygen, and quadruples of
nitrogen in the course of the plant as is required by the
elements sulphur and phosphorus. It is possible, therefore, and possibly true, that the animal is indebted to the
plant, not only for its elements in common with the plant,
but for its phosphorus and sulphur in addition, and for
these not as elements of matter, merely, but as the functionaries through which the plant becomes the animal.
Thus, reasonably certain that the animal exists but of
elements taken from the plant, it is as certain that the
animal subsists but upon food prepared for it by the
plant. It is true some animals subsist upon others, and
those upon others, but at last there are animals which
must originate the matters upon which they subsist, or
must take them originated from the plant.

And, as they can not originate their matters they
must take them from the plant, and accordingly we do
see the whole animal kingdom in subsistence upon food
taken mediately, or immediately, from the plant. And
from these facts, considered, it is as certain that the
animal is posterior to the plant, and dependent on the
plant, and in continuation of that being in the plant to its
beings possible in the animal. And so, posterior to the
plant, and dependent on it for its elements and food, and
so, in continuation of the plant, it is reasonably certain
that the animal is of that being of which there is the
plant. And this, that essential being of which the earth
is in teleologic evo-involution; and of which the plant, as
an offspring of the earth, is in such invo-evolution of that
same essential being. And the earth, for this reason, and

15

the plant, for the same reason, a reality, so also is the animal.

In theory of the earth, such reality. The animal, in such relation to the plant, in such relation to the earth, is such reality, and it is in fact such reality, if it be actually with the plant in composition of a dermal appendage of organic matter to the earth. So the earth, then, will have been several appendages analogously such as were that of the plant and animal. There will have been that of the densest metallic matter as a limiting membrane to the earth's radiating center of original force physiological. And that of the rock as the limiting membrane to its metallic radiations. And, analogous to these, there were such membrane of organic matter in plants and animals. And if the animal, with the plant, be in actual composition of such membrane, it were a reality as the plant is a reality, or either antecedent membrane a reality, if it be not apparent that the animal is dependent upon the plant for its elements of matters, and the food in forces of which its elements of matter are sustained to their work.

And the animal is with the plant in actual composition of such membrane, if there be such membrane, and for this the plant alone be insufficient. And there is such membrane.

There are from the surface of the earth its radiations of force physiological in heat of 60° F. under a pressure of fifteen pounds to the inch, of which there are waters and the elements of nonmetallic matters, and these into compounds, and these into plants from the alga to the oak inclusive. And if these were able to accept and chamber all such radiations to their capacities the plant alone were the membrane required. But it is not alone so competent. Through the matters of the plant transpires the energies of which from the unicorpuscular radiate to the two-footed and two-handed vertebrate, there is the animal.

And the animal, therefore, were the membrane to the plant, as the plant is to water, if it were not that either is incomplete without the other, and that both, as atomic and complementary parts, must concur in the membrane that exists. But the plant is incomplete without the animal to accept and raise its energies to higher powers. The animal is incomplete from its inability to exist but of such issues from the plant. They are to each other, therefore, as are felspar and mica in the rock, or oxygen and hydrogen in water, or the stem and foliage of the individual plant, or the head and body of the animal. And both are in reciprocal limitations of each other into the tissues of one continuous membrane of organic matters about the earth. And there is such membrane. And this of both, as there were not the one without the other. And if, therefore, it be not clear that the animal is a reality from its existence of food and elements taken from the plant, a reality, it is clear that it is a reality from its concurrence with the plant in such dermal envelope of organic matters about the earth.

But if there were not even this, the animal were a reality from its analogy to antecedent realities. Accepting that the plant is analogous to the earth and the intermediate beings on the earth, and is itself a reality for reason of its analogy to these realities, we must accept that the animal is a reality from its analogy to the plant. It is analogous to the plant in that it is of the same elements as the plant, and these of the same forces as are those of the plant, and that they react as do those of the plant, and into nonmetallic matter compounds in wheels physiological of beings static on their axes of beings dynamic, each a plotoplasmic unit, in each of which there is a nucleus of force, with its nucleus of matters possible about it, but differing in the number of matter elements involved. And those of the fewer elements being the germs of plants, those of the more, therefore, are those of animals. So analogously the same the germs of plants and animals, so analogously the same, also, are the processes of these germs. Those of the plant are through stages termed cryptogamic, phanerogamic, endogenous and exogenous. Those of the animal are through stages termed radiate, annulate, articulate and vertebrate, of which the radiate of the animal is analogous to the cryptogamic of the plant, and the annulate of the animal to the endogenous of the plant, and the vertebrate of the animal to the exogenous of the plant. To the fissiparous or hermarphodite animal there are obvious analogies in the cryptogamic plants. And to the higher animals, inclusive of the annulates, articulates and vertebrates, there are as obvious analogies to the seed-bearing and phanerogamic plants. And in effect, therefore, there is such substantial analogy between the animal and the plant, the one of which is sessile at the earth's surface in production of matters upon which the other is able to subsist and move, while of both it is the condition that they advance to the beings of them possible, and by variations possible simply, to their existences under the conditions they experience.

It may be that the animal does not apply to itself the specific matters taken from the plant, and it is rather to be supposed that, from whatever they be taken, it reduces them to force before such application from which are the matters of which it ultimately consists. And that in this view of the subject the animal produces its matters as does the plant. But, however this may be, it is certain that the animal is in a different relation to its forces taken in matter from the plant than is the plant to those in radiations into it from the earth, and that, however the animal may form for itself the matters of which it is and moves, it can only form them of matters taken from the plant, as the bark must take its forces from the plant, and the skin from the animal, however they may be able to form matters of them for themselves.

Nor is it in breach of this analogy of the animal to the plant that the animal, at the start of organic nature, was the more conspicuous, and passed the sooner through its stages of evo-involution.

It would seem, as I have said, that both started in the Silurian seas continuously about the earth, and the one in alga, the first in order of cryptogamic plants, the first in order of the plant, and the other in amoeboid radiates, the first in order of animals. But that while the alga in waters so continuously about the earth could get no higher than the sea-weed, the animal was able to advance through the radiate, annulate and articulate into the vertebrate stage of its existence. And that thus, therefore, there was not only not coincidence in their stages of advancement, but no apparent analogy between them. But upon such plant matters in waters the humbler marine animals could subsist, and the higher upon these, and the higher upon these, until of a supply of sea-weed sufficient for the lower orders of animals, there might have been all the marine animals there were when lands appeared above the waters. And there is reason that the supply of sea-weed was sufficient. The waters of those seas were more prolific of plant matters, it is probable, than any waters on land now. And as the plants in waters now, as humble as those, are able to support their fishes, so it is probable they were then. It is quite apparent that upon land plants land animals, not preying on each other, subsist, and that they must precede the animal to give it such subsistence; that from their first appearance together upon land they have advanced, and *pari passu*, by favorable variations under conditions to their states possible. And that so analogous to the plant, and so concurring with the plant in production of a limiting membrane of organic being about the earth, the animal is a reality, as is the plant; and as is the earth, of which there is the plant; and as is the sun, of which there is the earth; and as is the star, of which there is the sun, and as is the universal word of God in space, of which there is the star.

CHAPTER XXV.

AS A REALITY, ALSO, THERE IS MAN.

Accepting that as a reality there is the animal, we must accept, also, that as a reality there is man. Between the man and the animal there is but the single difference that in the one there is the family and in the other not. Both are of individuals in sexes proportioned to the largest offspring possible without the power in the individuals of either sex alone to continue the existence of the animal or man. Of both the individuals are of the same elements — material, moral, physical, chemical and physiological; both are charged with the preservation of their individual existences and the production of the offspring possible; and the animal and man are identical, therefore, to the point at which it is to be determined whether this being shall continue to be the animal merely as solitary individuals, dependent for subsistence upon the chance products of the earth, or shall become man in the collection and preservation of these products to the larger number of individuals they would support. Such conservation of products were possible only of groups of individuals in natural relations to each other in such conservations. Such groups could only be in families of offspring under the patriarchal power of human parents. And in such family is the only difference between the animal and man.

There is the suggestion and incipience in fact of such family in vertebrate mothers, which protect and find food for their offspring during the period of helpless infancy, and in this exert a kind of patriarchal power; but this ceases when the offspring is able to shift for itself, and there is only the family of offspring for life under the patriarchal power of parents in the human family.

And such the only difference between the animal and man, the man is a reality, as is the animal, unless it be that he achieves his family of some endowment not vested in the animal. And he takes no such supplementary endowment.

Such endowment were a miracle, and in this universe there is no miracle. The beings infinite, capable of an exclusive universe of being finite, were capable of man in families of parents and offspring united to the safety and subsistence of themselves individually and to the continuation of their race; and an endowment in addition, not of such infinites, enabling them to unite, were a miracle of consequence without cause, and as there is not such miracle there is not such endowment.

And there is not for the further reason that it were gratuitous. The individuals in use of the means to the preservation of their individual existences, could form into families agamic, polygamic or monogamic, as each became available, without the promptings of such supplementary endowment.

But beside this, the family of the lowest man in the union of parents and their offspring after the maturity of offspring is not essentially different from the flock or herd of bird or brute.

Each of these is of juniors under the authority of seniors to the safety and subsistence of the whole. And man in stocks, tribes and states of families not essentially different from these is a reality if he be of that being of which there is the animal, and be simply in enlargement of that animal.

And he is a reality if he be more than a conventionality. And if that more than a conventionality be but in enlargement of the animal, and he is more than a conventionality. There is a being we term man whose existence is independent of our recognition of it. And that being is but an enlargement of the animal. There is the animal of life in nature by variation from the radiate animal through the annulate and articulate to the vertebrate, and through the vertebrate fish, reptile, quadruped and four-handed, to the two-footed and two-handed animal, with an organ of intelligence to coordinate the activities of its feet and hands in the means to its safety and subsistence. Under the promptings of this organ it enlarges itself in becoming more and better that it may be more than it was as such two-footed and two-handed animal simply. In this it but continues that animal to the animal possible, and so but enlarges the animal nature of which it is in the lead. This animal, so enlarging itself, and the animal nature of which it is in lead is man, who is a reality, therefore, as is the animal.

There was the animal two-footed and two-handed before there was man. And there is now that animal in man a variation simply of the two-footed and two-handed animal, to the conditions of continuing its existence to the limits possible—those conditions consisting in the man to a larger safety and subsistence than had the animal antecedent.

And before there was man there was such animal. Not to go further back than to the start of the vertebrate animal. There were the first of these as fishes in the Silurian seas, which varied to their conditions of food and safety possible. And there were the next of these as reptiles in marshes beginning to appear, which varied also to such conditions. And the next of these were on lands as quadrupeds, varying also to such conditions. And the next were four-handed animals to the safety and subsistence to be had by climbing. And the next were animals two-footed and two-handed to the safety and subsistence to be had by climbing trees for fruits, or walking, or tilling fields for forage. And there was such animal, for a brief period at least, before there was man as certainly as that there is such animal in man; or that the four-handed animal could vary into an animal two-footed and two-handed.

There is such animal two-footed and two-handed in man. It may be argued plausibly that man is merely the animal two-footed and two-handed, complying with the conditions of a larger and better existence than had the animal four-handed. That as the arboreal ape was possessed of the food and safety there was to be had from trees, and as the anthropoid ape was possessed of the food and safety to be had by a four-handed animal from trees and fields, yet neither was possessed of that to be had by the animal that could not only climb and walk, but plan to its procurement. And this could the animal two-footed and two-handed. There were not such animal but as there be in it an organ of intelligence to coordinate the activities of its feet and hands in attainment of its objects, which implies the ability to plan its means to ends. Of such plans and activities there were food and safety much beyond that within reach of the ape, whether arboreal or anthropoid. And this without variation in structure of such animal. To become two-footed and two-handed from the four-handed animal it was necessary that there be structural variations. The two hinder hands of the one must have become the two feet of the other, which from them must have taken on that erect posture, and which from its larger brain necessary to its office must have had a larger facial angle, and so have been as different from even the anthropoid ape in Africa as is the bushmen; and so different and without further structural variations that animal was able to comply with the conditions of becoming more and better than the two-handed animal then upon the earth. And without contending now that it did comply with such conditions and so become the man that is, it is contended that in the man that now is there is such animal.

He may be more than was the animal two-footed and two-handed, and be more than of its life in nature simply that animal could be; yet, in that man, whatever his present grandeur compared with the animal two-footed and two-

handed, there is a two-footed and two-handed animal. In
ultimate analysis of man, monogamic, polygamic or
agamic there is such animal, and if man be more than
could be such animal in natural variations to the conditions of its subsistence that man were the consequence
without the cause in nature, and were the miracle therefore. And there is not such miracle. There is not such
miracle from the universe to man. And there is not such
miracle in man. That would imply that man is not of
that will of God in finite being from the universe, but is
of a special and supplementary endowment. It would
imply that the universal will of God through life in nature
of the earth, plant and animal to the animal two-footed
and two-handed, was not sufficient for such animal or for
the variatians of that into man. But that to man a further
will was necessary. That to the jurisdiction of man over
beings with him, a new order of beings had to be established, and that this is in his human races agamic, polygamic and monogamic existing now, or such other races
or divisions of these races as may possibly participate in
such jurisdiction. This were the special creation of man
and there is no such creation.

The will of God through life in nature sufficient for
the fish, reptile, four-footed and four-handed animals was
sufficient for the animals two-footed and two-handed.
And sufficient also for the possible variations of such
animal. And sufficient, therefore, for the unions of these
animals for their lives—these being tributary to their
enlarged existences—and for such unions of unmarried
mothers and their children, and for such unions of male
and female parents and their children whether polygamic
or monogamic.

From the unions for life of unmarried mothers and
their children in measures to the preservations of their
existences in common, there were continually more such
mothers and their children. This, therefore, were but a
variation of the two-footed and two-handed animal, sup-

posing its existence to its continuation and enlargement. Such also only were the unions by marriages of male and female parents, whether these be polygamic or monogamic. There were more individuals of the unions of unmarried mothers and their children than of the animal two-footed and two-handed, and more of the polygamic than of the agamic, and more of the monogamic than of the polygamic.

These orders of man, therefore, were but variations to the enlargement of the animal two-footed and two-handed, and were less in want of the miracle than were any one of the variations by which the lower animal advanced to such higher animal. In every antecedent advancement there were changes in structure, and the two-footed and two-handed animal could come from the animal four-handed only by changing its hinder hands into feet. But to the man, whether agamic, polygamic or monogamic, no such change was necessary. The agamic man is a savage, and the monogamic a civilian, and there are differences of appearance and capacity between them. But there are no differences of structure apparent between the savage and civilian. And such is the identity in structure and functions of the agamic savage, and the monogamic civilian that many sensible people assume that they are the same, essentially, being reciprocally convertible, and differ but in education, and that intentionally given by them to themselves.

And such the identity of the human race consisting but of the animal two-footed and two-handed, there was less of variation in man from such animal than in such animal from the animal four-handed. And as we may not rationally suppose a special creation of the animal, two-footed and two-handed, assuming its existence, the less may we suppose a special creation of man from that animal, or without that animal, consisting as he does but in unions of such animals. And while it may yet be doubted that man is of the animal, or but of the animal two-footed and two-handed, it can not be doubted that in man there is the animal two-footed and two-handed.

Life in nature of the animal four-handed were capable of the animal two-footed and two-handed, and the animal two-footed and two-handed were possible of the animal four-handed. And capability, cause and possibility consequence, the animal four-handed were cause of the animal two-footed and two-handed, and the animal two-footed and two-handed were consequence of the animal four-handed. And if the one capable do not actually cause the other possible it is the miracle of cause without consequence. And if the other do not actually consequence the one it is the miracle of consequence without cause. And as there are not these miracles there is, or was before it became man, the animal two-footed and two-handed, or there were the two miracles, neither of which is elsewhere seen in nature, or conceivable.

And so, also, if man be not of an animal, two-footed and two-handed, there were two other miracles. The two-footed and two-handed animal there is in man were capable of man, and, if not the cause of man, it were the miracle of cause without consequence. And man were possible of that animal, and, if not consequence of that animal, he were the miracle of consequence without cause. And thus, therefore, there were the animal two-footed and two-handed, or thus were four miracles, no one of which is elsewhere known.

Nor were the fact of its existence contradicted by the want of its geological record, if there were such want. In geological formations of the earth's surface detrita the remains of animals have been included. And if in these there were not the remains of the two-footed and two-handed animal that were not conclusive that such animal did not exist. It might have come later than other animals and after there were formations to take up its remains. And if there were the remains of this animal recorded, but not the record of its successive changes from the animal four-handed, that were not conclusive that such changes did not occur. Occurring they will have occurred at various places. The changes will have been minute and gradual, and there may have been at no one of these places a geological formation to contain a continuous record of them. Or if there were such formation the remains to a certain extent will have been taken for those of the anthropoid ape. And after that for those of the man. And if, therefore, there were not the record of the animal two-footed and two-handed, or of its changes from the animal four-handed, that fact were not conclusive that there was not, and before there was man, such animal. And the less were it conclusive that it was not by variation from the animal four-handed.

But there is such record at least of the existence of the two-footed and two-handed animal. We find the remains of such animal with those of animals now extinct, and we term them the remains of a prehistoric man. And they are such if they be the remains of an animal, the individuals of which were united for life in families agamic, polygamic or monogamic, but not without. The animal two-footed and two-handed were but an animal, without such unions as are the animals four-footed and four-handed. Though there be unions of animal mothers and their offspring during the infancy of the offspring, these are but animals, and so only were animals two-footed and two-handed until the unions of parents and their infant offspring were continued after such offspring had become adult. Then such animals first became agamic man, and then polygamic and then monogamic. And whether the remains of a being two-footed and two-handed be those of an animal or man will depend upon whether the individuals of such beings were or were not in unions for life. And to this question the record could make no answer. And we are forced to infer that whether they be the remains of man or not they are at least the remains of an animal two-footed and two-handed.

And of such animal there is man in that such animal were capable of man, and such man were possible of such animal. And if such animal capable of such man be not the cause of man there were the miracle of cause without consequence. And if man possible of such animal be not consequence of such animal he were the miracle of consequence without cause.

And such the reason for believing that before man there was the animal two-footed and two-handed, and that of such animal there is man, there is the further reason for this in that man is analogous to the animal as he were not if he be not of life in nature of the animal. And the yet further reason that through the antecedent animal only could the cause of being in this universe have produced man at the time and place of his appearance.

And such the reasons that before there was man there was the animal two-footed and two-handed, and that of this there is man, there is more conclusive reason in that it were capable of man. It were in individuals, male and female, capable, through coitions when adult, of offsprings male and female, and these were capable of unions for life — the adults male and female of those — termed marriage, and parents and offspring of others equally enduring. And of such unions agamic, polygamic and monogamic, there were the animal agamic, polygamic and monogamic, now existing with the possibility of an animal yet better and more abundant, from unions of any two of these races, than could exist in any single race.

And of such unions for life the animal two-footed and two-handed was capable. Consisting of individuals male and female capable, when adult, of coitions, and offsprings male and female capable of unions for life, termed marriage, of which there were offsprings, male and female, also capable of marriage and offsprings; of such unions agamic, polygamic and monogamic, there were man agamic, polygamic and monogamic, who now exist with the possibility of a man yet better and more abundant from the unions of these races than any now existing in any single race. And of these unions for life, whether with marriage or without, the animal two-footed and two-handed were capable. And so capable it were charged with the continuation of its existence through these ways becoming possible.

Of these unions the first possible was that of unmarried mothers and their offspring in provisions for their common safety and subsistence. The next were those of marriage between adults, male and females, in which there were several females to a single male. And the next were those of marriage in which there was one male to but one female, the offsprings of such marriages remaining for life under the orders of their parents, as did the offspring of the unmarried female parent. And such the unions possible, of these the animal two-footed and two-handed was capable. The individuals, without intellectual directions and under the proclivities of individual interests merely, were forced into them, and being in them they did that simply which was necessary to the continuations of their individual existences in consistence with the continuation of their race. That only does man. He may mistify himself with theology and metaphysics into the illusion that he does more. But in ultimate analysis of man through all the periods and vicissitudes of his existence it will be found that the individuals have but continned their existences through the unions possible to the continuation of the human race; that they have done this, not of their intelligences, but of their intuitions; that their unions and activities, therefore, and their families, stocks, tribes, castes and states have been not of the intellects of the man, but of the instincts of the animal, and that man has not, of any metaphysical endowment, caused the animal parts of himself in families, stocks, tribes and states. But the animal parts of him have made the man of him there is in such unions. And that the animal so making man was capable of the man it makes; and that the man so made was possible of the animal that makes him. And that thus of the animal, two-footed and two-handed, there was and is man.

And of such animal there is man for reason of his analogy to the animal. He is of a causal being termed life within a consequential being termed nature, as is the animal. And from his rudimentary stage to the man possible he is by stages analogous to those by which there is the animal from its rudimentary stage to the animal possible. The stages of the animal are the radiate, annulate, articulate and vertebrate, and those of man are the agamic, polygamic and monogamic, with a possibility and promise of a further stage from the unions of these races. And the agamic man is analogous to the radiate animal in that each is without the appearance of the male factor of its normal being. And polygamic man is analogous to the annulate animal in that each is in strings of its normal beings — the polygamic man in tribes, each a string of polygamic families, and the annulate animals the strings of radiate animals, each analogous to the polygamic family. And the monogamic man is analogous to the articulate animal in that each is in functional sections to its normal state — the monogamic man in sections executive, legislative and judicial, and the articulate animal in analogous sections cephalic, thoracic and abdominal. And the possible and promised stage of two races united is, or will be, analogous to the vertebrate animal of two articulate animals united, so that while each continues to exist it continues to exist in relation to the other in production of one animal of both. And such the analogy of man to the animal, this were possible but as he be of the life in nature, of which there is the animal.

And there is the yet further reason that man is of the animal two-footed and two-handed in that through that animal only could there be man. Accepting that there is an universe, and this of means and not of miracles, we must accept that of means there is the earth, and by means

of the earth the plant, and by means of the plant the animal, and by means of the animal four-footed the animal
four-handed, and by means of the animal four-handed the
animal two-footed and two-handed.   And, accepting this,
we must accept that by means of that animal only could
the universe of means have made the man.

Of an universe of miracles there might have been man
a miracle with no relation to circumstantial miracles. But
of an universe of means there is no other way by which
that universe could reach such man than that through
the animal two-footed and two-handed.   And that it did
so reach the man is in the fact that man, from his first to
his last, is but a variation of such animal.

And that he is of that animal is in the fact that he is
to the man possible.   Every antecedent being from the
axis of the universe is to its being possible, and this to
its most and to its best that it may be its most under the
conditions existing at its time and place.   And so is man
to the man possible, and to the most man possible, and to
the best man possible that he may be his most.   He is
under sexual feelings and maternal instincts, which force
him to the offspring possible in continuation of his race,
the every individual of whom is to his best and most in a
family to its best and most, in a stock, tribe or state to its
best and most. And of these conditions there is man to
the man possible, as of the same essential means there is
the animal to the animal possible, and the plant to the
plant possible.

And of that animal there is man for the further reason
that he is but to the man possible on earth.   If man were in
a natural life on earth to a spiritual life on some other
sphere that spirit were a miracle.   And that might have
caused man to be what he is, and other than he would
have been in life in nature merely.   And it is not now
contended that there is not in man such spirit, and that
this is not destined to an existence on some other sphere,

16

and apart from natural man on earth.   But it is contended
that in natural man there is a moral being, however we
may term it, as natural as is his being physical.   And that
this remains with physical man on earth so long as he,
through generations, shall continue physically on it.   And
in a moral being as real and organic as is his being physical in stocks, tribes and states; that of this is his law and
the government of his states and the civilizations of his
ages; that it is a moral being of the moral beings of all
the men who have lived to the betterment of present man;
that it is as tutelary and imperious over man, as a whole,
as is the mind of the individual man over the individual
man; and that as such it is a necessary part of man on
earth, and remains to brood and hover man on earth
so long as the race of man shall continue on the earth,
who will be, therefore, but to the race of man on earth,
however the spirits of that race, discharged of office here,
may leave to colonize some other sphere.

   And such the animal, of which is man, that is a reality.
And man is a reality as is that animal.

CHAPTER XXVI.

AND AS A REALITY, ALSO, THERE IS MIND IN MAN.

There is in every individual being, human or other, a sensitive being perceptive and reflective of the conditions incident to the continuations of its existence. And this not physical but moral. And not in its structure but in the functions of its structures. And not material as are the nerves, blood, flesh and bones of the animal, but in the consensus of these in concurrence to the animal under the conditions possible. This in the individual man we term mind, and in the race of man, civilization. And this in man, however we may term it, is a reality if it be of man. It is of man if it be of that life in nature of which is man. And it is of man if it be the means by which the individual or race of man is moved and directed to its being possible, and by which it accepts and reflects the conditions incident to its being possible. And to the continuation, under the conditions, of its existence to such being. And if it be as is the flower to the plant, which at the head of the plant continues its existence on to successive stages of its life, and as is the eye to the animal by which it sees its way to other steps of its progress. And as is the objectglass to the telescope of life in nature bringing to consideration objects otherwise insensible.

And it is of man, if it be of that being simply from the axis of the universe, and of which at this earth is man, and not of being from some other source. And if it be, therefore, of that original endowment of life in nature of which are all the beings of the universe, and not of a supplementary endowment to man alone of all the beings of the universe. And, finally, it is of man if it be of means and not of miracles; and if it be to man as man is to the animal, and the animal to the plant, and the plant to the earth, and the earth mediately or immediately to the universe — a stage in consequence simply of that precedent cause — and if man, therefore, were not naturally possible without this, or this so possible without man.

So of man, it were a reality as is man. And it is so of man. It is of that life in nature of which is man, as the functions of an organ are of the cause, in consequence of which there is the organ. And it is the means by which the individual man, or state, or race of man, is guided to the individual, state or race possible. And by which he accepts the conditions incident to the continuation of his existence possible.

And functionally to man it is as the flower to the plant projecting its further existence; and as is the eye to the animal, which, seeing objects, can not see itself; and as is the objectglass of the telescope, which focuses objects incident for observation on the eyeglass without the sense of its mediating office.

And it is of that being simply from the axis of the universe, of which are the beings of the universe, and of which at this earth is man. And it is not of being from any other source as a supplementary endowment. And it is thus of means and not of miracles. And is functionally to man as man is to the animal, and the animal to the plant, and the plant to the earth, and the earth to the sun, and the sun to the universe, in functional administrations through teleologic evo-involutions of an essential being of the universe. And man not possible without this, this were not possible without man. And as man is a realty, and as this were not possible without man, there is this mind as a reality, as is man.

It is not intended that man originates his mind intentionally, more than that of intention he originates himself, or than that his mind of its intentions originates him; but only that in every being finite of beings infinite reacting from the universe to man and mind of man inclusive, there is a finite product possible of such infinite factors. And this is a moral being potentially demanding of its factors the physical activities necessary to its physical existence; and that man and his mind, therefore, both of the same essential being of the universe, are both at their times and places in resolutions of that being into its beings possible, and in this reciprocate, and in such reciprocation reciprocally accept their existences in relation. And that the mind is as real as the man; and as real as is the sensitive substance on the photographic plate; and as real as is the seed of the plant or the ovum of the animal.

In the every plant there is its seed — a sensitive being susceptive of impressions from conditions incident in consistence with which, and of which, there is its development and evolution into the plant possible. And in every animal there is its ovum — a sensitive being susceptive of conditions incident in consistence with which, and of which there are its development and evolution into the animal possible. This in either is an organic matter analogous to that medullary matter in man susceptive of conditions incident, in consistence with which there are the development and evolution of man into the man possible. In the brain of man there is the germ of man, as in the seed or ovum there is the germ of the plant or animal. These are not strictly analogous. Of its germ there is actually the individual plant or animal, and of this germ of man there is not actually the individual man. But of this germ of man there are the beings and activities of man in becoming the man possible, as of its germ there are the beings and activities of the plant or animal in becoming the plant or animal possible. And terming by metonymy of cause for effect the brain of man the mind of man, we may, with the same propriety, term the germ of the plant or animal the mind of the plant or animal. And there is mind in man, therefore, as real as that sensitive being on the photographic plate which takes the picture of the landscape, and as is the germ of the plant or animal. It is not intended that the brain of man is the mind of man, as it is not intended that the germ of the plant or animal is the mind of the plant or animal, but only that their operations are so analogous as that terming those of the one mind, so also may we term the others. Nor is it intended that in any sense the mind of man is the brain of man, but only that the brain of man is capable of those operations in acceptance of the conditions of man's existence, which we term his mind.

And such the mind of man, there is such mind as there is man himself, in families, stocks, tribes and states of man, no one of whom could have so existed without mind, more than could the plant or animal without its germ.

And that mind is a reality, in that it is the natural mode of the reality. The every reality, as we have seen, is a being physiological of beings different in reciprocal limitations of each other, of which the one is energy and the other its inertia, and the one force and the other matter, and the one life and the other nature. And such the reality of which is mind — the correlative of conscience — these are to each other as are life and nature. And conscience life, the mind of man is the nature of that life. And as nature is a reality from being of the reality in life, so is mind reality from being of the reality in conscience.

And the mind of man a reality from its being the natural mode of human life a reality, it is also a reality from its being the initial mode of energy; and the matter mode of force; and the moral mode of physical man. Each of these beings, energy, force, life and man, is a being physical, of which there is its mode of being into the beings of it possible, to be termed moral. And such energy the moral mode of that which in physics we term inertia; and of force to be termed matter; and of life to be termed nature; analogously, such is the mind of man, the moral mode of his physical being into the individual, family, stock, tribe, state and race of his being possible. And the moral modes of energy, force and life realities, so also is mind the moral mode of man.

We do not see it to be such, or that as a real being there is mind. We see in the activities of individual men to the preservation of their individual existences, and in their entrances into families, and in the entrances of families into stocks, tribes and states, that which implies the existence of a moral being such as were mind in the disposition of man to his best and most, but we do not see the thing itself. And this, I suggest, for the reason that the thing itself is that instrument through which we see the ministrations of this moral being, and therefore, seeing such ministrations of itself, can not see itself in such administrations as the eye, the instrument through which we see objective beings, can not see itself. Nor can it realize that the insensible being through which it becomes sensible of such objective being is the same as that of which these beings consist and react with each other. Itself a reality, it can not realize that other beings so different from itself in their appearances are but modes of that reality of which it is itself. Or that it is sensible of them only through its reactions with them, as the eye is sensible of objective beings only through the reactions of an insensible being in itself with an essential being equally insensible in them; or that it itself is a being of energy and inertia, and force and matter, and life and nature, as are all objective beings; or that its impressions of objective beings are but the limitations of its own indefinite being, as are those of inertia upon energy, or matter upon force, or nature upon life; or that in such limitations they are in moral administrations of their physical beings respectively, as is mind in administration of its physical man. But if there be mind in man, such is its office. And there is mind in man as the condition of his existence at any stage above the animal, as there is inertia to energy, and matter to force, and life to nature; and the seed to the plant and the ovum to the animal; and as there is consequence to cause in every being physiological of this physiological universe, and as such the moral mode of physical man a . reality, the mind of man is a reality. And as a reality, therefore, there is the mind of man.

CHAPTER XXVII.

AND AS A REALITY, ALSO, THERE IS LAW.

If, as I have assumed, law be a rule of being, and of the activities of beings in relation to each other and the universe of being of which they are in part, and if being be finite of infinites in limitations of each other, and this be the word expressive of the will of God in the beings of it possible, and this be reality, there is law as a reality, if there be beings in such activities. And there is being in such activities.

There are stars about the axis of the universe, and suns about stars, and planets about suns. And at the surface of this earth, a planet, there are forces, and of these matters, and of these plants, and of these animals, and of these man, and in man mind. And in each of these there is the rule of its being as it is, and the rule of its beings in relation to the beings with it.

There is the star but as it be a being, and under a rule that it be as it is; and also under the rule that of its activities in being it be as it is in relation to the axis of the universe. And so is it with the sun in relation to its star, and the planet in relation to the sun, and the force at this earth's surface in relation to the earth, and the matter in relation to its force, and the plant in relation to its matter, and the matter in relation to the plant, and the man in relation to the animal, and mind of man in relation to the man.

No one of these is original or self-existent at its time and place, but is of an antecedent being in which there is the rule that at its every time and place about the center of its being it be its possible. This being under such rule of its being were the law of such beings. And there is. such law.

There were this by hypothesis in the being finite of beings infinite. And this in the word expressive of the will of God in such beings of it possible.

And there is this in phenomena of these beings in their reciprocal activities. There is no planet but as it be under the rule that it be an orb of matter in its elliptical. orbit about its sun from whose periods it can not, of itself, depart for a single instant. Nor at this earth's surface is. there a force but as it be in appointed activities with. respect to other forces and matters adjacent. Nor is there an atom of matter, but as it be in appointed activities with other atoms in the matter molecule. Or the molecule of matter but as it be in appointed activities. with other molecules in the matter compound; or a compound of matter but as it be in appointed activities with. other compounds.

There are not hydrogen and oxygen but as in definite proportions they form water, or chlorine and sodium but as in definite proportions they form salt. Or water ammonia and carbonic oxide but as in definite proportions. they form ammonias compound, acid and base; or these but as reacting they form plant matters; or these but as. reacting they form plants; or these but as reacting they form into the plants possible. Nor is there animal matter but as of this there be the animal and of this the animal possible. Nor is there man but as there be of him the man possible; or mind in man but as of this there be the man possible. And this under the rule of an essential and universal being, that at its time and place it be the being possible. This being under rule were law. And. there is law therefore as well by inductions of the phenomena as by deductions from the hypothesis of an essential being in the finite word of God. And as the finite word of God is the reality there is law as a reality..

And it is contended that as. there were not being finite of the word of God, or space, or force, or matter, or life, or nature, or the universe, star, sun, earth, plant, animal, man, or mind, or mind in man, or law, without such essential being of the universe; and as there is not only the one but the every one of these there is that being. And that the truth, therefore, of the first of the two propositions of this work is thus established—"that there is an essential being of the universe"—and in that there is established, also, the three following propositions: "That in this essential being there is life, and of that nature;" and "that of nature there is man;" with but the one remaining—"that man of nature is to the man possible," and not to the individuals of any dominant human race who of their own means and in their own ways may be pleased to continue their existences. And in that there will have been established, also, the truth intended in the first part of this work that the beings of this universe are of the resolutions of that essential being, simply, and not of the manipulations of an exterior and personal cause upon it. In that exclusive universe of infinite being finite there will have been, necessarily, all the power, and all the purpose, and all the force, and all the matter, and all the life and all the nature, appearing or possible in that universe, or in any being of that universe. And these from motives of infinite beings becoming finite in their reaction on the axes of that universe, and without the possibility of other agency to the power and purpose of that word and will of God. And that man at this earth, therefore, is not more under a tutelary genius in administration to him of special providences than is the animal or plant. And in this conclusion ends the first part of this work.

PART SECOND.

CHAPTER XXVIII.

MAN AT THIS EARTH TO THE MAN POSSIBLE.

It must be admitted, however, that the truth of the conclusion in the first part of this work is not accepted generally. And in fact that a very large proportion of the people of states the most advanced assert, in practice if not in terms, that not only is there to them a tutelary genius apart from the resolutions of infinite being finite, but that this accords to them that they be not what they must from the resolutions of such universe, but individually what they would like to be. And not, therefore, the man possible, but a man supplemented by his individual intelligence to what he should be. And that they may continue or discontinue the existence of the race of man on earth as it may please them without awaiting the final resolutions of the universe. And that making states, not of nature but of their own invention, so long as that may be agreeable, they may take their departures to eternal existences in some other sphere. But this assumption is controverted in this second part of the work, in which there will be proofs to show that man on earth is there to the man possible and but to the man possible.

The truth of which proposition is affirmatively established in the establishment of the proposition that man is of nature.

He is of nature only as he be of the will of God. He is of the will of God only as he be the finite product of infinite factors. And of this will of God he were to the man possible. God were the cause of being from the universe of infinite beings finite to man, in finite being at this earth. And there is every reason why every being from that universe to man should be its possible, with no single reason why it should not.

And every reason, therefore, why man should be his possible, with no reason why he should not. There is also every reason for believing that every being from the universe to man is its possible under the conditions at its time and place. There is every reason that the earth is the earth possible; and the plant the plant possible; and the animal the animal possible. And there is every reason, therefore, why man, if of the same will of God in nature, should also be the man possible.

But this is more clearly so if man be of a nature not only of the will of God but of infinite beings finite. Each being were then the finite product of infinite factors which at the time and place of man could produce nothing else but man and him the man possible.

But besides this if man be to other than the man possible it must be through agency other than the will of God in nature. There must be an anthropomorphic Theos attendant on the nature of the will of God in process from the axis of the universe with power to modify that process. And as a tutelary genius to take charge of it in man and make man not simply his possible in nature, but a something he would rather be. This something were a mass of absolutely equal individuals in no natural relation to each other, and under no law but that they see proper to impose and that by force of majorities over minorities of adult males. This is the state to which the man of the earth now aspires. And if man is not to be the possible of God in infinite beings finite, he must have or find such tutelary Theos. And he can not either find or have it. It must exist in and of the will of God and to execute that will and this in modifying it to the extent expressed. And there is no such Theos unless it be that in the will of man himself. And in the will of man there is not such Theos.

In the will of man himself there is an agency of the will of God in nature to the man possible. Any agency of the will of God is a Theos and in the will of man there is such Theos. But that a Theos to the man possible is not a Theos to the man not possible. Beside this in man himself there is no other Theos apparent or conceivable to execute the will of God in man. And this sufficient for the man possible is not sufficient for the man not possible. But while sufficient for the man possible and not sufficient for the man not possible of the will of God in infinite being finite, man himself assumes that it is not sufficient for the man possible, but is sufficient for the man not possible of such being. And hence it is that, while man at no time or place strives as a whole to be his most possible and his best possible that he may be his most, at every time and place of his existence he asserts his individual being against those of other individuals and his stock, tribe or state against other stocks, tribes and states; in the hope, it would seem, that he may come to a state of moral being not derived from the nature of the universe, but original in him and fitting him for a nature of his own — from which illusion there are absurdities innumerable and these the most conspicuous in the most conspicuous man.

That Theos of God in man is sufficient for the man possible. There are conclusive reasons for believing that the original of man was the animal two-footed and two-handed, with its organ of intelligence to coordinate the activities of its feet and hands in provisions for its safety and subsistence. There are reasons equally conclusive that this animal was, by variation to its means of subsistence, of the antecedent animal four-handed. And reasons as conclusive that this animal two-footed and two-handed took its entire being physical and moral through antecedent beings in radiation of nature from the axis of the universe.   And reasons as conclusive that in this its being it took in power and purpose of that will of God all the being necessary to its becoming what else or more under subsequent conditions might be possible.

And to its becoming agamic man in stocks of the unfathered children of unmarried mothers; and polygamic man in tribes of the families of several wives under the patriarchal power of single husbands; and monogamic man in states of the families of single wives under the power of single husbands, and compound man in states of monogamic families in unions with the families of lower races in which the monogamic families were in exercise of the patriarchal power over those of lower races as their proletariates; and in this the being to become the man possible who can be no other than the most man possible of these races united.   Such being in radiation of the will of God in nature from the universe were in itself the Theos of which is man.   And of this there were the man possible, and of this there were not the man not possible.

But the men themselves, conscious that to them individually has been committed the preservation of their individual existences, are not conscious of any obligation beyond.   Or that to them there is any thing more than their individual existences which they may use here on earth for a time and then take with them to another sphere.   Or that while here they are to provide for those coming after them.   Or that there shall be others coming after them.   They seem to regard those at any time existing as the only ones to be considered, and that these may start or stop as they please.   And that these be under the patriarchal power of majorities of adult males, who may form them into states to be and act in independence of the laws of nature.   But so far these conceptions have been illusive.   No real state has yet been formed by any compact of its adult males.   And no artificial state has been other than it would have been of its nature under the conditions. And thus it is that while man assumes autonomy he does not possess it, and while able to provide the means to the preservation of his individual existence he has individually no more effect upon the course of man in nature than have individual plants upon the course of the plant, or individual animals upon the course of the animal. Such man as man individually conceives of and proposes is not the man possible. But there is to be such man possible of nature as surely as man himself is of nature and not of the anthropomorphic Theos of his own invention. And while we may doubt as to the magnitude of this man or the date of his occurrence or duration, we can not reasonably doubt that at some time, however distant and for a period however short, there will be the man possible upon this earth. There will be upon every spot of the earth's habitable surface the utmost man it will support, and him of all the races in the relations of their fitnesses for the works of a common safety and subsistence. And to this, the end of man on earth, there will be the man possible.

And he is to the man possible in that he is of being which in every instance of its existence is to its being possible.

There is an universe of being, whether that be being finite simply or the word of God, or being merely without the being finite or the word of God. And of this there is an universe; and at every time and place within that universe the being possible. Without this there were not the universe. There were not the whole of beings but as there be the beings possible to comprise that whole. And man, a being of that universe, were, or were to be, the man possible, if it were not as being simply he were, at his every time and place, the being possible. But if he be being in that simply he is at his every time and place the being possible under the conditions then and there existing, and to become the further being possible under

17

these conditions changing. And if man be not to the man possible, he is not of the being of this universe, and as he is of the being of this universe, he is to the man possible.

And if he be not to the man possible through unions of unequal races, rising from the plane of individual men into organized bodies of men reciprocally supporting each other in cultivating the earth to its capacity of provisions, and in conserving these provisions to the population it is possibly able to support, he is here on the earth to himself, and each individual man or woman is the end of that providence producing him or her. Neither were under obligation to continue the race, or continue in it, or do other than that to please himself or herself. They were the flowers of the human plant, without cross-fertilization of each other to the seed of man; and to lives of indolence and self-indulgence, not only while here on earth, but in an after life of dissipation elsewhere.

But he is not so to his individual self on earth, but at the every instant of his existence on earth is tasked to the exertions necessary to the preservation and transmission of that existence, and for any neglect of that task is punished to the extent of his dereliction.

Nor is it apparent what use the cause of man could have for him as such unconditioned individual. It might be suggested that one use were in his self-regulations to the execution of the intentions of his cause. But in that state there could be no further intentions of his cause with respect to him. Nor would such individuals execute the intentions of their cause, however clearly these might be expressed. But as such unconditioned individuals, some would war upon others for power over them, and would recognize their cause but as an anthropomorphic Theos to authorize their doing what of their selfish instincts they had resolved on. Such anthropomorph to prompt man to indulge his inclinations on others were not the cause of man. Nor could the cause of man have use for him in execution of the orders of his imaginary anthropomorph.

And for these reasons, with nothing to the contrary, man on earth is to the man possible on earth, and but to the man possible on earth. It may be assumed, as I have said, that while the plant and animal at this earth are to the plant and animal possible, man is not simply to the man possible, but is also to the production in him of moral beings for another sphere of existence elsewhere, and apart from man on earth.

But this assumption is unwarranted, These moral beings were the souls of men who will have helped the man on earth to be the man possible. And they may unite upon the deaths of the men so helping into a moral being attendant on living men to brood and hover them on the way to the man possible intended. And they have united in such moral being. There is over the families, states, races, and the race of man, a civilization, and this a real moral being, as potent in ordering these families, states and races of men as is the government of any existing state in ordering its constituents. And it is not to be supposed that these moral beings so attendant yet on man can have gone, or been intended to go, to other spheres. Nor can it be supposed that men have other souls, or, if so, that these are cultured in the living man. They were those that prompt stocks, tribes and states to war upon each other. And they were most and best in monogamic states, more advanced than polygamic and agamic states. And in these they were most and best at the periods when the commons become possessed of the patriarchal power, and when the one victorious party begins, through an imperator, to subjugate another. And they were most and best at Rome, when, as a republic, she trampled upon prostrate provinces, and when social conservatism became relaxed, and marriage was abated and children went to waste, and when men in the habilaments of women, and women in the habilaments of men, drunk at noonday, reeled about the market-places.

And they were most and best in this Republic, the grandest since that of Rome, now, when it takes foreign provinces, and marriages become belittled, and children are remitted to the state to be educated, and men take the employments of women, and women those of men, and aspire to vote and take political and professional offices and when wives aspire to contract even with their husbands. And when the government is in the hands of the victorious party, who think nothing wrong that keeps the other under, while the other thinks nothing wrong that can bring the victor down. And if living men, therefore, be but culture tubes for human souls to form into a moral being on some other sphere, the conditions were singularly unfavorable for the productions of such souls as were fit for a moral being elsewhere. The souls of men now struggling for political supremacy in this Republic were the best perhaps the human world has known. And a moral being of such souls were not useful or attractive. And it is not to be supposed that man is here but to such impotent conclusion, while for every conceivable reason it is to be supposed that he is here to the man possible who were not possible of such moral beings. Nor if man merely had been the object of man would there have been more than the first agamic man. In him there would have been man as truly as in the polygamic or monogamic races. And if men as butterflies and not as bees shall have been intended there were no reason for a higher than the agamic race who could as well have so gone to waste.

Nor are men individually the ends of man on earth as they were if only to the pleasurable enjoyment of their individual lives. Since in fact at no period of their existences on earth have men stopped in their course of being what they could be to such enjoyment. Of the sexual feelings and maternal instincts of men and women, as I have said, there have been coitions, and offspring, nurtured and educated, to survive them; and who, surviving their parents, have been as much the ends and objects of the cause of man as were their parents, and as forced to continue the race as were their parents. And in consistence with these facts it can not be assumed that the individuals so succeeded were the ends of the man continued thus to other ends in his further being.

Nor can there be an end of man on earth while yet of his industries the earth is able to yield provisions for his subsistence in his abundance possible.

Nor while on earth are the men but the culture tubes of human souls for existences in other spheres. There is in every man a moral being to be termed his soul, which, intuitively sensible of what the cause of man intended him to be, is instantly prompting him to what he should be; and to the opportunities of his becoming what he should be; and which continually puts before him the pictured plan of what he should be that he may work up to it; and which acts in this as a tutelary moral genius in the man. But analogously such moral being is also in the plant and animal. In every plant or animal there is a moral being conceptive of his conditions and wants and prompting instantly to the variations proper to its becoming the specific plant, or animal intended; as does that moral being we term a soul in man. And this soul in man is — not more than that in the animal or plant — of other than that endowment of finite being originally in the man, animal or plant. But is a moral being finite inseparable from that physical being finite whatever it be, to instruct it what to be and do. And not in addition to that physical being finite of which is man it can not make man to other than the man possible, more than can that in the animal or plant make the animal or plant to other than the animal or plant which, under the conditions possible, it can be.

There is in every man, therefore, a moral being to be termed a soul. And one end of man may be said to be the production of such moral beings, but that can not be said to be the end of man on earth. Such man goes on from generation to generation in such production, while yet, himself, advancing immeasurably from the animal from which he started.

Nor can it be said that these souls are for another and distinct state of existence. It is not seen what state of existence there is beyond that of the finite of infinites in which, at this earth, man now is. Nor is it seen that there is such state; or that there can be such state of that finite being, simply, there is in man; or that there can be a state of man beyond his present finite state, without other endowment, or other being than that now in man. And there is ground to doubt, therefore, that there is a state of man in another sphere than that on which as a finite being he now is, to which, leaving this, he goes.

And the more may we doubt this, when we see that about physical man at this earth there is a state of moral being exactly such as there would be if about him there were the moral beings of all the men through all the ages working to compose it. This we see in what is termed the civilization of every human state.

The state may have its civil government of the moral beings of its present people; but every such government is under the orders of a higher power consisting in what is termed its civilization, which is, itself, a state of moral being more imperious than the civil state which must submissively accept its orders. This were such as were the moral being of all the moral beings of all the individuals of the race, who have lived up to it, and into it; and who, living to the advancement of ·man, will have· so lived. And as there is such state of moral being now about man, which can be but of the moral beings of man, who have lived and died to its production, it is not to be supposed that these beings have been, or are to be, exiled to another state of existence elsewhere, but are to continue here in tutelage of man. This moral man is to physical man as nature is to life, and the cause of man will not have separated moral from physical man more than it will have separated nature from the life of other beings.

And there is reason, therefore, that, whatever be man's conceptions as to the end of his being on earth, he is to the man possible, and but to the man on earth possible, and to such end he will attain. The individuals of a family, or the families of a state, or the states of a race, or races, even, may neglect or misuse these opportunities, and so drop out of the march of man into an oblivion of nonexistence, always yawning. But the march of those not so failing will continue to the most man possible, and the best man possible that he may be his most upon this earth.

And if in the preceding chapters, affirming the first proposition of this theory, it shall have appeared that there is in space of the finite word of God an essential being of the universe, it will appear in this, affirming the second proposition, that man at this earth of the life in nature of that being is at his time and place to the man possible, and but to the man possible; as are all ante-cedent beings to their beings possible of such infinite being finite, from the axis of that universe in space.

And to the theory of man at this earth in continua-tion of his life in nature to the man possible, there will remain in question but the fourth proposition — that he can do so, not through any single human race existing now, but only through unions of the individuals of these races in relations of inequality.

CHAPTER XXIX.

BUT NOT OF ANY SINGLE HUMAN RACE.

The races I have said are, first, the agamic in stocks of the unfathered children of unmarried mothers; and, next, the polygamic in tribes of the families of several mothers under the patriarchal power of their single male parents; and the next the monogamic in states of the families of single mothers under the patriarchal powers of their single male parents. And though of these the agamic race be capable of the agamic man possible and the polygamic race of the polygamic man possible; and the monogamic race of the monogamic man possible neither one is capable of the man possible of all in complementary relations to each other. Each exists and runs as it can upon its own peculiar mode; and the agamic upon that of the orders of unmarried mothers; and the polygamic upon that of the orders of polygamic male parents; and the monogamic upon that of the orders of a government by appointment of proprietory male parents. Each running upon its peculiar mode is to be termed a race. And as neither can take the mode of another each must run in exclusion of the others to the continuation of its own individual existence. And in thus antagonizing each other neither can be what it would be without those races impeding it. And the less can it be what it would be if with its own it could adapt to occasions for them the modes of others. For this reason there can not be the man possible of any single race.

And there can not be this also for the further reason that the races are unequally able to sustain themselves in the race to the man possible. The ability of races is in the human lives they can produce and mature to their respective continuation in the race of man. And the agamic is less able than the polygamic and the polygamic than the monogamic. For this reason the polygamic supersedes the agamic whenever they come in contact, and so also does the monogamic the polygamic, which therefore were destined to supersede both lower races, and to occupy the earth exclusively and give to it the man possible of that single race if it were not that the monogamic race at the period of its maturity is upon the verge of its dissolution.

This race of the states of monogamic families under orders of male parents has, as has every natural being, its periods of infancy, adolescence, maturity and dissolution. And so also has the every one of its several states, each of which becomes mature when the class of its people termed commons become possessed of the patriarchal power originally in a superior class termed lords.

The patriarchal power is that of human parents over their offspring, and that is the condition of the human family, and that is the condition of the human state, and that is the condition of the human race. And the reason for it is that man, at the every stage of his progress, shall have the discipline and direction possible. But this power of natural parents, sufficient for the family, is not sufficient for the state of families — naturally equal — who were without that regulative power if it were not that in the experiences of these some have the ability to procure and conserve the provisions for the support of themselves and others and some have not. Of these the capables assume that power over the incapables, and thus there is that power not only in families but in states. Without this the individual, whether male or female, or parent, or offspring is but an animal two-footed and two-handed, with an organ of intelligence to coordinate the activities of its feet and hands in preservation of its individual existence. And it only becomes man when forced into the family by the patriarchal power of the parent. Nor even then is

the individual a normal man. He can not originate himself, or, as man or woman, alone, can not give existence
to offspring. And the unit of man, therefore, is the
family, no one of which could exist without the patriarchal
power. Nor could a state of such families. exist without
that power, which may be said therefore to be the condition not only of the state of man but of man himself.

These classes of lords and commons form in every
nascent monogamic state. In every such state, at its
earlier periods, there are these human units unequally
capable of the provisions necessary to their safety and subsistence. These are made and held as property by the capable families, who allow the use of them to those incapable
only upon the terms of their submission to order in such
use. In such order, then, were the patriarchal power.
And this in the class of lords were originally absolute.
But in time the commons of the same race as their lords
contest with them the patriarchal power, and, being the
more numerous, by proscriptions force the lords to the
modus vivendi of a common law. To this the commons
have forced the lords of England. But, not content with
this, the colonists of this Republic, by revolution, have
abolished lords and taken to themselves the patriarchal
power. In this it has attained to its adult stage as a monogamic state and, as the animal, plant, or other adult
being in nature, has but to await the period of its dissolution, with such provisions as it can make to protract that
period. These it has made in vesting that power in its
adult males. These, achieving the revolution, were possessed of that power taken from the lords, and can exercise
it only through parties of such males, the major of which,
for the time of its majority, shall have the patriarchal power
of government, while the minor shall have for its time the
proletariate powers of offspring, subject to its parents.
And in this there is a dissolution of the monogamic state.
Of these parties the one will represent the state and the
other the people, and the one property and the other labor,

and the one despotism and the other anarchy, and in this contest one or the other must succeed, when there will be the end of the state in despotism or anarchy, or its extinguishment in the extinguishment of both parties.

Between these parties of adult males there can be no compromise : *First*, for the reason that they are not of lives in nature, and can not, therefore, reciprocally support each other to a higher human nature as lives in nature do. And, next, for the further reason that they are parties in contest for the funds of the state, each claiming jurisdiction of the whole, and neither able to renounce or abate its claim.

. Of lives in eccentric radiations from the axis of the universe into the concentric natures receiving them, there are their resolutions into such natures such as that of the two lives, there is a nature of both; but this capable of differentiation into two other lives capable of such resolution into a further nature, and so on to the ultimate nature possible. It is so that of atomic individuals as lives there is the human nature intermediate. And of this, differentiated into parents and offspring as lives, there is the family nature intermediate. And of this differentiated into monogamic families, capable and incapable, then is the monogamic state of such families. And of this, as one life united with a lower race as another human life, there is, or may be, the compound state of such unequal races united, in all of which natures the lives of the same cause and to the same end of the nature possible reciprocally reinforce and sustain each other.

But they do so only as they be of that infinite being finite in the resolutions of which is that will of God from the axis of his universe which we term nature, and without which no one of them could have a sensible existence. Without this there were nothing but the will of the individual men themselves to take the monogamic state of commons possessed of the patriarchal power into a state of adult males. And that volition could not so continue a natural monogamic state more than it could start it. And in theory, therefore, of nature from the resolutions of an essential being of the universe, the simple mono- gamic state when its commons become possessed of the patriarchal power is at the end of its natural existence. It could then continue its human life in human nature by uniting on lines of inequality with a lower race over which it could exercise the patriarchal power. But without this it can not make normal human lives of parties of its adult males. Nor of such lives can it make the nature of a normal human state. Nor can such factitious state con- tinue its existence longer than the contest of parties for the patriarchal power. The one party must claim that power is the condition to the organized existence of the state, the other party must claim it as the volition of the people of the state, the one therefore, must affirm power and the other liberty, and the one the power of the state to rule its people and the other the right of the people to rule the state. And without natural relations each is absolute and exclusive of the other. There were not only no disposition to compromise but no ground for com- promise. Each must extinguish the other; the state can not survive the extinction of its factors. And the state, therefore, however abundant of blessings and prodigal of promise is as destined to fall between despotism and anarchy as is the individual man at maturity between the principles of progress and decay in him as in every natural being.

And this the precept of theory, is also the induction of phenomena. When the colonists as commons by their revolution from their English lords became possessed of the patriarchal power there was here an immense subject for its exercise. There were varied and fertile lands from the Atlantic to the Pacific and the Gulf to the Lakes, every habitable acre of which when properly cultivated could yield subsistence to an average family. There were man in every monogamic state of Europe, and in stocks and tribes of agamic and polygamic people ready to come or to be brought, the every one of whom on coming was worth $500 in value to the state. Upon this fund for human life, the largest ever known on the earth before, the adult male then existing or coming to exist were let in. Of this they took possession in parties, each taking what it could get and claiming its right to the whole, but to be taken by the major parties through the government and by the minor through the people. This claim neither can abate, nor would either abate it if it could, but both are linked into an inexorable contest for existence, with the perfect certainty that neither can survive it; with the certainty, also, that with the extinction of these parties there must be the extinction of the state.

I am quite aware that this truth is not accepted generally. And that our most able men in pulpit, press and parliament are persistive in the assertion of this republic as the human state the more replete with prosperity and promise than any other that has yet existed. But whether it be this or not will depend upon the question whether individual men of their volitions can give existence to a natural state of man. And whether, therefore, this is a natural state of man. And it must be admitted by all reasoning people that it is not. It exists of no natural factors. The parties major and minor of its adult males are not such factors. They are in fact the agencies to its dissolution — each claiming the whole to the exclusion of the other. Nor has it exhibited a function of a natural state. It has not given existence to a human being or to a family or to a state of families; nor has it caused any one of the changes through which the major of these parties has become supreme over the other. It did not arrest the foreign slave trade, nor did it cause immigrants to come in the place of slaves. Nor did it cause the secession of the South and the invasion of the South by the North, and the subjugation of the Southern States and the liberation of their slaves. Of all these acts the republic was quite innocent, and each has occurred from the efforts of the major party of adult males to support itself in possession of the patriarchal power against the minor seeking to regain it.

Nor has the constitutional compact under which it has assumed to become a normal human state made it such. That was an unilateral instrument and was not binding longer than the party making it was willing to be bound. And it means but that, the power to interpret it, would have it mean. And instead of being a natural ordinance in preservation to its ends of a natural human state it has been a blind or fig leaf merely to the perversities of either party in its attempts to take from the other the patriarchal power.

Nor have the constitutions assumed by the several states been more real or effective. The majority of votes secures that power to the party obtaining it. To that power every thing is right which tends to sustain it and every thing wrong that tends to defeat it. And while, therefore, we rejoice in our possession of the finest human state that ever was, it is rationally demonstrable that we have no natural state at all, but only an imaginary state of adult males in parties struggling for the government; and, certain that the state can not survive its parties, it is certain that neither party can survive the other. And that there is the end of the state in the extinction of these parties.

The monogamic race is to be that of which there is to be the man possible if of any single human race there is to be such man. In no state of that race can there be the man possible while in it there is the contest of lords and commons for the patriarchal power. Nor in any such state can there be its existence to the man possible of the parties of adult males. And of this state, therefore, alone there can not be the man possible.

Nor can there be of any human state or race existing now.

The races now existing, as I have said, are the agamic; polygamic and monogamic. And the agamic in stocks of unmarried mothers and their unfathered offspring. And the polygamic in tribes and castes of polygamic male parents and their wives and families. And the monogamic in states of monogamic families under governments, at first by appointment of proprietary male parents, and at last not by appointment of proprietary male parents, but of adult males. And though there is to be the man possible, there is not to be such man of either race alone. And not of the agamic race, for the reason that that is without the male element of manhood. And not of the polygamic race, for that that is without initiation or autonomy. And not in the monogamic race for that in that there is an excess of the initiation and autonomy, of which the polygamic is in want.

The agamic man — the man without marriage — is without the male element of manhood, in that to the offspring of such man the male parent is officially unknown.

And the polygamic man is without initiation and autonomy, in that the course of his existence in tribes and castes is inexorably prescribed by the conditions under which it starts.

And the monogamic man is under an excess of initiation and autonomy, in that the course of his existence in states is determined by the volitions of its individuals in assertion of their individual interests in preservation of their existences.

In the stocks of agamic peoples, without males in office to supplement unmarried mothers in support and regulation of offspring, there is, perhaps, the *agamic* man possible, but not the *man* possible. And that there is not is in the fact that, though these modes of man were the first to appear upon the earth, they not only did not give it at all times and places the population possible, but at no one time or place did they give it such population. And so certain that of these there is not to be the most man possible, it is equally apparent that of these there is not the best man possible that he be his most, since an abler than such agamic man is the polygamic or monogamic man, the either of whom subjugates or extinguishes the agamic whenever they come in contact.

And in the tribes and castes of polygamic peoples, without initiation or autonomy, there is perhaps the *polygamic* man possible, but not the *man* possible. The tribes are without initiation or autonomy, in that of the families of the polygamic male parent there is, of necessity, the tribe, without the power in such parent or family to make it otherwise.

And the castes of polygamic tribes are equally without initiation or autonomy, in that castes occur from the subjugation of tribes, becoming peaceful and productive, by hill tribes, still predatory, adjacent. These, becoming peaceful and productive, are in turn subjugated by other hill tribes, still predatory, until there comes to be a stack of tribes, priestly, militant, industrial and servile, without the ability in either to make it otherwise. The tribe, or caste of tribes, is as without initiation and autonomy, as is the plant in becoming the plant possible from its seed, or the animal in becoming the animal possible from its egg. And as from the seed of no one plant — endogenous or exogenous — can there be, without initiation and autonomy, the plant possible, or from the egg of any one animal the animal possible of the polygamic family — the unit and seed, or egg, of the polygamic man — can there be the *man* possible, but only the *polygamic* man, who is not such man.

And in states of monogamic man, in which there is initiation and autonomy from their courses and activities being determined by the proclivities of their individuals, there is perhaps the *monogamic* man possible, but not the *man* possible. And this for the reason that in such state there is an excess of that origination and autonomy of which the polygamic man is deficient. The polygamic man can not alter the course of his being by any self-originated activities. But so can the monogamic man. He is in states of families, of individuals related in the production of their families, in production of their states, in production of their race. And the individuals are in preservation of their individual existences in production of their families. And the families are in preservation of their existences in production of the state, and the states are in preservation of their existences in production of the race. And in these productions each is egoistic, and concurs in the necessary activities only as these may seem to be consistent with its individual interests in continuation of its individual existence.

The individual, however he may have come into the monogamic family, continues in it as he finds it, and of his own volition; and the family so continues, of its volition, in the state; and the state so continues, of its own volition, in the race of monogamic man. And the monogamic man, therefore, at the later stages of his existence — so in relations of his volition — is able to alter his relations, and so has an initiation and autonomy the polygamic man has not. But these functions of initiation and autonomy come to be, ultimately; not in the individuals, families or states, but in adult males, who become possessed of the supreme political power.

In every such state through its earlier periods, however they be named, there are lords and commons, the lords holding the lands, and the commons the use of them upon terms; and the lords holding the government and the commons the liberties the government may admit.

But in time, the commons prescribe the lords; and by prescription, or revolution, take the Government, and thus become themselves lords, as well as commons. And as these prescriptions, or revolutions, are by adult males, they retain to themselves the places and powers secured, and thus the state becomes the subject, not of monogamic families, but of adult males.

This state is termed a democracy. And thus, the monogamic man, originally in a state of lords and commons under a king, or other hereditary chief-magistrate, exhibits his initiation and autonomy, in establishing such state under government of adult males.

But these, as a body, can exercise their powers of self-government only through majorities, each, at its time, being a party in representation of a special policy, and each, for its time, therefore, being the artificial lord over the beaten party as its commons. And thus, of such initiation and autonomy, the natural state of monogamic man becomes artificial. And as such is not only not capable of the indefinite duration necessary to the man possible but is not capable, during the brief period of its artificial existence, of the most and best man there could be of his normal human nature.

The man of parties struggling for the government can not successfully struggle for the means of subsistence possible; or for the peace and order necessary to such means. Nor, while they may be the best men for their parties respectively, at war with each other, can they be the best men of a state not of parties warring with each other. But beside this, such war must ultimately end in the possession of the state by the one of these parties able to hold it from the other, which, able to hold it, will hold it from, and over, the other. And this under a leader who, whatever be his pretexts or protestations, will be practically absolute, and who will look, not to the enlargement of the population of the state, but to the stability of his power over that population he may safely let exist. And such the initiation and autonomy of the monogamic state, it is apt to be more inconsistent with the man possible than is the want of it in polygamic man, or the want of the male element in agamic man. And, inasmuch as monogamic man, even under such conditions, supersedes polygamic man, and polygamic man the agamic, while yet of him there may not be the man possible, it is reasonably certain that while there is to be the man possible, he is not to be of any single race of men existing now.

And for this the more conclusive reason is that the cause of man is not in the individuals of the state or race, but in the state or race of individuals. The individuals are simply charged with the preservations of their individual existences to whatever state or race that preservation may take them. But the state or race is charged with the regulation of individuals to the state or race possible. The individuals, therefore, are as is life to the nature of the state or race, and the state or race is as is nature to the life of its individuals. And as the life of no finite being can, of its own motion, elect its nature, so can not individuals elect their state or race. And while, therefore, of any state or race there may be the individuals possible, of the individuals of no one state or race can there be the man possible.

If of any existing race there is to be the man possible, that race is obviously the monogamic. That race is of the two unions of individuals for life, of which is man above the animal. And these of parents and offspring, and of male and female parents to the production of offspring. But of these unions of parents to the production of capable offspring, the much more efficient is that of a single husband to a single wife. From this, the monogamic union, there are more children possible of such marriages. And these, under the care and culture of both parents in correspondence to that end, are better fed, clothed and educated, to the end of being most and best, than are the children of agamic or polygamic parents. And of these conditions there is the possibility, at least, of a larger and better population at every portion of the earth's surface than is possible of either of the lower races.

And beside this the monogamic state. supersedes, in fact, the stocks and tribes of agamic and polygamic peoples whenever they come in contact. And as the monogamic race is capable of unlimited increase and expansion, it is reasonably certain that in time it will overspread the earth, to the exclusion of all other races, except to the extent that in such expansion it shall take them up and conserve them to the ends of man in the man possible. And it is reasonably certain, therefore, that if there is to be the man possible of any single human race, that man is to be of the monogamic race.

But that race, while able to dominate the earth, is not able to populate the earth to its capacity. It is not probable that its population at any place can become more dense than it is in monogamic states of Europe. Already those states are throwing off their too-abundant populations upon lands in occupation of lower races. In all these are contests of lords and commons. for their patriarchal powers, from which the commons are willing to recede in order that they may exercise that power over themselves and natives in other lands. But without this it is. reasonably certain that in every monogamic state of Teutonic Europe this contest will continue until the commons shall possess the supreme political power, as they virtually possess it in England, and as they actually do in this Republic; when they will not be further concerned as to an increase of population or as to the assertion of these rights in their states, but only in the exercise of their power imperially over other races and monogamic states. In this they will not advance the population of the earth, which it will be their effort to diminish or extinguish.

And if the monogamic race alone shall become the man possible, it must be through the enlargement of some one state of that race to supremacy over all other states and races. And in its production from within itself of the population possible.

And of this no single state is, or will be, capable. It must be a republic, in the possession of its patriarchal power by its commons, to be exercised by majorities of adult males. And such republic, if it could preserve its integrity, might dominate the world, as Rome very nearly did at one time, and as this Republic has hopes of doing now.

But no such republic, however powerful, will be able to preserve the conditions upon which will depend its power. These will consist in parties, in the one of which, at any time becoming stronger, there shall be the Government, to which the other, then the weaker, will be willing to submit in the hope of itself at another time becoming stronger, and so, in turn, the Government.

But such alternating equilibrium of parties in any republic cannot long continue. The party in power, to sustain itself, must reward its partisans. This for a time it may do at the expense of the weaker party; but in time it must conquer provinces. To do this it must have a standing army, of which there must be a commander, who, as the leader of the dominant party, will hold the Government, however elections be against them. Nor would the party in power allow him to renounce it. In such government there will be large emoluments, upon which its partisans will have come to live. Renouncing their power, there will be no such means for them in sight. And they will not allow their leader to renounce the powers upon which their means of living depend. Submitting, the leader becomes emperor, and the republic an empire, to exist so long only as it can sustain itself against armies from without and insurrections from within. The period of its existence, under such conditions, must be brief. It can not enlarge its own population, or the population of the outer world. And it is quite unreasonable that of one monogamic state becoming a republic, or a kingdom on its way to a republic, there can be on the lands it holds either the most man possible, or the best man possible that he be his most.　And it is even the less to be supposed that on the earth, beyond such state, at ceaseless wars in support of its supremacy, there can be the man that would be possible without such wars.　And in reason, therefore, there is not the man possible of the monogamic state.

If, of any such state, such man were possible, he were possible of this Republic, and of this he is not possible.

The conditions of this Republic are singularly favorable to its becoming what a monogamic state can be.　Its people are of the Teutonic stock, in which there is more of manhood than in any other; and they have been trained to self-government as no others have been; and they have a chart of self-government, deduced from the experiences of the race; and under them is a continent of most varied and fertile lands, their title to which is unquestioned — but by Indians, unable and unwilling to assert rights they have surrendered — while they enjoy the respect of all other peoples of the earth from deserving and being able to command it.　And it is hardly possible that any other monogamic state has ever been, or will ever be, in conditions so favorable to its people becoming the man possibly able to subsist upon the products of the lands they live on and transcend these lands to those in the hands of other people, and so become the man possible.

But it is as certain that of this state there is not to be such man.　And for this certainty the capital and conclusive reason is that its supreme political powers are not in proprietary male parents, but in adult males without the qualification of either parentage or property.

The normal monogamic state is of normal monogamic families, the properties and powers of which are in the male parents, actual or potential, of such families.　The actual male parents of such families are those males who have married and have children, and the potential male parents are such males as have married but have not children, or who have property and intend to marry and have children if it be possible.

Of these families, actual or potential, some, of their order, industries, economics and self-denial, have acquired provisions for the support of their families, and some have not. These provisions are properties, of which the medium of exchange is money, and the power of use and disposition of such properties is rightfully in such male parents. And as the state must use these properties to the continuation of its existence, the parties to direct and regulate that use should be the male parents of families owning such properties, who also should control the actions of such state to the affirmance and preservation of their monogamic mode of man.

And in this proprietary male parents only should participate. And it is not clear that a state of proprietary male parents could not exist perpetually, and to the density of monogamic population possible.

But the revolution of the colonies was achieved through its adult males, without the qualification of either parentage or property. And these, thus taking the patriarchal power from the lords of England, have kept it to themselves, and have continued to administer it through majorities of adult males. And of such administration there can not be the perpetual existence of the monogamic state. There can not be the perpetual existence of such state of adult males. To such administration there must be parties, the major of which for the time must hold the government, but subject to the minor becoming major to take it from them, who, in turn, will hold it subject to the same contingency, so that, for a time, the state will be the battle-ground of parties for the spoils of government, without consideration by either of the advancement of the state, but only of the issues upon which the one can turn, or keep the other down.

And such, in fact, has been the case. All men of ability and enterprise become politicians, with such following as, from promises of participation, they can get. All things profitable become proper, and in such scramble

for the government there is no consideration of the interests of the state, which can not advance, if it can last, under
such conditions.

But it can not last under such conditions.   The one
party or the other must take a hold upon the government
it will not yield, and which its partisans will not let it
yield, and which the other party can not make it yield.
The party holding the government is supreme over the
party not holding it, as was seen in the Civil War.   And
at some period not distant a party will hold the government who will use the powers of the government to sustain themselves in office, and against such party the efforts
of the outs, with no other cause than that of wanting to be
in, will be vainer than was that of the confederated states,
who had the moral right, at least, to the independence
demanded, and who acted under governments, which a
defeated political party will not have.

It is reasonably certain, therefore, that the republic
of adult males will not, as such, live long.   And even more
certain that it will not live long as a normal monogamic
state.

To the normal monogamic state it is necessary that
at the proper times there be the marriages of adults, male
and female; that these be unions for the life of such adults,
and dissoluble only for the adultery of either party; that
of these marriages there be the children possible; that to
this the husband and wife shall have respective offices in
the family— that of the husband being to shelter and support the wife in giving birth to offspring, and to support
and train such offspring to its fitness for duties in continuing the family, and that of the wife being to give birth
to offspring, and to nourish and raise it to the hands and
orders of the husband; that to this the man and woman
have respective spheres of activity, the one without and
the other within the family; that thus the children possible shall be subject to no other authority than that of these
parents, and be taught to be that only which their parents

would have them be, and to do that only which the parents would have them do, and which their parents may have for them to do, and that thus the family be an automatic and autonomic human unit physiological, of which units simply there is the state, without the power to make or alter them of its intelligence, more than the individual man of his intelligence can make or alter the physiological units of his own body. Such were the normal monogamic state existing and acting in consensus of such units, and not in consensus of any class of the individuals of its units whose every act were not in conservation but in destruction of such state. And though it be true that the state, in intervening its units, might make them better, and itself better than it would be, as the individual intervening his units might make them better, and himself better than he would be, it is quite certain that it would not make itself better as a monogamic state.

And such the normal monogamic state, it is clear that this Republic, not being such from its being and acting not of its proprietary male parents but of its adult males, is not such from its not requiring the marriages of adults, male and female, and that these be for life and indissoluble but for adultery; and that of these there be the children possible, and that these be nourished in infancy by the mother and trained later by the father to what he has for them to do. And that in this the husband and wife have respective spheres of activity. And that the husband shall shelter and support the wife to her maternal office in continuing her race. And that to this men and women generally shall have respective spheres of activity, and men the outdoor and women the indoor employments.

And that every capable woman shall be secure of a husband, able and ready to support her without her being required to contest employments with men that she may support herself. And these things this republic of adult males does not require.

Its sentiments in practice are that adult males and females shall not marry but as it may please them, and that marrying, they shall not have children but as it may please them; that their marriages shall be not for life, but shall be dissoluble for any cause that either party shall urge with sufficient force, and is not, therefore, a rite of man to the continuation of his race on earth, but only a contract, to be kept at the pleasure of parties, or to be broken under the penalties that either may be willing to incur. Nor is it required that wives and husbands have respective offices in the family, or that the children be educated by their parents to what they may have for them to do in support of the family, but are to be educated by the state to what it has not for them to do.

And in these ways the state exhibits the sense that the cause of man, in bringing him up to a republic, is done with him, and has turned him over, completed, to his own inventions; that the volitions of its majorities of adult males are sufficient to make him what he should become; and existing of this volition, and discharged of the orders of his cause in nature, he is loose on earth, as individuals, to no duties, and but to the enjoyments of his unconditioned situation. And, such the situation, this Republic is not only not to the man possible, but is not even to the monogamic man possible.

And that of neither the agamic, polygamic or monogamic race is there to be the man possible is in that either race is unilateral while the man possible is bilateral, and is as impossible of either race alone as is the man of man or woman alone. The man or woman alone is the bilateral product of his or her unilateral factors in the male and female principles of his or her parents. But so bilateral of his or her parental principles, each is unilateral with respect to the bilateral offspring intermediate of both united. And so bilateral are the races of their unilateral factors, parents and offspring, while each is unilateral with respect to the bilateral man possible of any two united, no one of which alone is more capable of man possible of both than is the man or woman alone of the offspring possible of both. Each race — agamic, polygamic and monogamic — may live to its opportunities of living, as may the man or woman, and may grow and mature itself and seed and then die without giving existence to another race.

And so the man or woman may live, grow, mature his or herself, and seed, and then die without giving existence to another man or woman. And in this, such man or woman, however either be bilateral of unilateral factors as well as such race, is incapable of the bilateral man or race possible without such union of unilateral factors to the man or race.

And in this the man possible, as the bilateral product of unilateral factors, is in strict analogy to every antecedent being of the universe. There is not the bilateral moment of electric force but of its unilateral factors, plus and minus, or the bilateral molecule of elemental matter without its unilateral factors, positive and negative, or the matter compound but of its factors, acid and base; or the plant but of its factors, stamen and pistil; or the animal but of its factors, male and female; or man but of his factors, parent and offspring; or the state of man but of its factors, dominant and servant. And so there were not the man possible but as the bilateral product of unilateral races united as its factors.

And accepting, as for reasons given we must, that man at this earth is to the man possible, we must accept that to such man possible there must be unions of unequal races, since of no single race can there be such man. And we must accept that of no single race can there be such man, for the reason that while of each race there can be that man of that race possible, of no single race can there be the man possible. And this for the reason that of no one unilateral factor can there be the bilateral product possible of both.

CHAPTER XXXI.

There may be unequal human races. These may unite, and of such unions there may be, if not the man ultimately possible, at least a more and better man towards the man possible than now exists in any single human race.

And if there be such unequal races, they can unite in a race of any two or more. And, as they can unite, they will unite, in such race of two or more. And, of that race continued, as it will be, there will be ultimately the man possible.

And they can unite. Each race will be the projection of a radiating human energy, from the axis of man, into the universe of human inertias, in its way. And, to the progress of this radiating energy towards its possible, there must be its reaction with the inertias obstructing and accepting it. In this reaction there is the union of these beings into the being of them both. Such radiation of human energy were the one race of man; such inertia were another race of man, with less of energy. Such were inertias agamic or polygamic, to monogamic man, and such energy, with either of these, the monogamic man may unite into a man of both, as may every radiating energy from the axis of the universe with its complementary inertia into the being possible of both, as does the minus with the plus of electricity, or the negative with the positive atom of the matter molecule, or the acid with the base of the matter compound, or the stamen with the pistil of the plant, or the male with the female of the animal.

And as these that can, must unite for reason of their reciprocal wants of each other, so, for the same reason, must these races unite.

But only in relations of inequality. These races, as I have said, are unequal in ability to become the man possible. They are unequal in ability to produce and mature offspring, and to provision and protect themselves and offspring. And so unequal, they can unite only in relations of inequality such as that, while to the monogamic race there shall be what may be termed the patriarchal powers, to the agamic or polygamic there shall be what may be termed the proletariate, or offspring powers. And to the ones, therefore, the functions of government, and to the others the rights, privileges, and immunities, consistent with such functions. Such were the relations of inequality intended, and there can be unions of such races only on such terms. If the conditions of inequality could be eliminated, and the agamic man could become polygamic, and the polygamic monogamic, as seems to be considered possible, the individuals of all these races, indistinguishable from each other, might be in the same states. And so the individuals of these races might be together, but in this there were not the unions of these races, and only the obliteration of distinctive differences. But to their union it were necessary that both should continue to exist in assertion of its original individuality, so far as they might consist with their existences in common. But so that neither can withdraw from such coexistence, or its consequences.

Such is the union of adults, male and female, in production of offspring. They may not regard it as an indissoluble union for their lives. But it is such. They may separate while alive, but they can not withdraw their separate contributions to their intermediate offspring. Those are irrevocably vested in the race of such offspring, not to be recalled, however the adults, male, and female, may assert that they are not acting in advancement of human life in human nature, but only in amusement of themselves.

And such were the unions of unequal human races. They were as unequal as are adults, male and female, to the production of the man possible. Their contributions to the intermediate race in families, dominant and servient, were as irrevocable as are those of adults, male and female, to their offspring, male and female.

These unions, therefore, were as indissoluble as are those of parents; and of parents and offspring in the monogamic family; and of lords and commons in the monogamic state.

And such, in fact, are the beings infinite in every being finite; and the stamen and pistil in the plant; and the male and female in the animal; and partners in the copartnership; and the corporators in the corporation; and metals in amalgamation. Each such life in nature must contribute individually to the life in nature intermediate of both, without the ability to withdraw from it to such individual existences as it had before; and without the ability to withdraw from it, that of itself, which it will have given to the being intermediate. Every such union is irrevocable, therefore, and domestic in its consistence of the unions of individuals to the beings intermediate of both. And such were that between adjacent human races. Individuals must unite in an individual race intermediate of both, as do husband and wife in production of the monogamic family of males and females, in representations of themselves respectively, And the unequal races will be represented in their respective families, dominant and servient, as are parents, male and female, in their children, male and female. And the families of such adjacent races will be in natural relations of reciprocal dependence, such as are those which give consistence and tendency to the

monogamic family of males and females in the monogamic
state.

And there can be such unions as surely as that the
monogamic race is stronger than the agamic or polygamic
race; and, as being so stronger, it will overspread the
lands occupied by those races; and as overspreading
these lands it must absorb or exterminate the natives.
And, not exterminating, it will absorb them.

Not absorbing, it must exterminate them. Absorption would consist in accepting the individuals of these
weaker races to offices they can fill in provisions to the
safety and subsistence of a state of both; extermination
would follow their expulsion from their lands without the
ability to find others, or others to be found. And such
expulsion will be necessary. The invading monogamic
race, if Teutonic, as it must be, will not miscegenate the
native races, nor can it remove them to other territory;
nor can it assimilate them, nor would it assimilate them if
it could, more than the husband would assimilate his wife.
Nor if it could and would assimilate them, would they be
assimilated, or be less offensive to it than were wives
assimilated by their husbands to an obliteration of their
sexual differences.

And lower races, educated up to be in every way the
equals of the higher, and to be indistinguishable from the
higher, but in their having distinct individual existences,
which they were ready to assert in opposition to those of
the higher race, were as repulsive to that higher race as
were women so educated up to men to the men with whom
they were so in competition. The only possible condition
of coexistence between such races were that of their having
relative positions and offices in domestic economies of
both, as have men and women in the monogamic family.
These they can have but as the ones, individually, be subject
to the orders of the others. Without this, the order of the
monogamic race to other races in its way were imperial.
It would allow them to exist so long only as they could

sustain themselves under its exactions. And under such conditions they could not long exist.

The encroachments by the monogamic race upon other races on the earth are imperial or patriarchal. By the imperial process, it enters upon states of lower races under order of its home government, to exercise discretionary jurisdiction over such subject people, without reference to their ability to sustain themselves under it, but only to the wants of the parent state. By the patriarchal process it enters through emigrants from the parent state under no other order than that they do the best they can for themselves, which will consist in their unions with natives into states of both.

Or if in the state invaded there be classes unequally able to preserve their individual existences the order of imperialism is that these be equally subject to the authority of the invader; while that of paternalism is that the superior class shall take domestic jurisdiction over the inferior while it, itself, shall exercise its authority under direction of the invading state. Of these processes the imperial is destructive and the patriarchal conservative of the invaded state. And by the imperial process, there is the order to exterminate the lower races, unable to sustain themselves without such unions. And by the colonial process, they will not always be extermination, but the natives will, under favorable conditions, be preserved. And, as in such preservations there will be the unions of the races concurring, there can be such unions.

There are these races agamic, polygamic, and monogamic now. They are unequal in their ability to produce the man possible. And the agamic, unequal to the polygamic, and the polygamic unequal to the monogamic. There is the monogamic in Europe and America, and the agamic in Africa and the Pacific Islands, and the polygamic in Asia. The monogamic states are now moving upon the peoples of Africa, Asia, and the Pacific Islands. There can be the subjugation of these lower races at these places by the monogamic race, and in this there can be the unions of these races in fact, as in theory there can be.

But it must be admitted that man is averse to any compromise of his egoistic individuality, whether agamic, polygamic, or monogamian, or Andoman, Bushman, Negro, Indian, Chinese, Egyptian, or Latin, or Teutonic, he would be what he is, and not more, or less. He is as averse to sharing his individuality with others as is the man or woman with each other. But he aspires to the creative office of making man what he would have him be, and to help God, and be the cause, rather than the consequence, of man in nature.

This appears in the efforts of religious sects, to make man, not what he can be, but what they would have him be. And of lords in monogamic states, to make the commons, not what they can be, but what they would have them be, in subjection to themselves. And the commons in monogamic states to make the lords what they would have them be, in subjection to themselves; and in the declaration, by the colonists, of their independence of Great Britain, in which they announced the absolute equality of human individuals, however they may differ, and the inalienable right to life, liberty, and the pursuit of happiness in every individual, at any time, place, or state in which he may find himself, however he be unable to exercise such right; and in the promulgations of constitutional compacts by which it is intended that succeeding generations shall be regulated; and in the edicts of majorities in democratic states, by which it is proposed that the states should run, not on natural laws, but upon bases furnished by the ingenuity of the men composing them.

But there is not natural vitality in any such artifice. And the states of man today are as simply natural, involuntary, and the results of human lives in relation, origi-

19

nally involved, as is the individual man or woman, of his or her parents, male and female.

And, as there can be union of unequal men and women in production of the man intermediate of both, there can be the unions of unequal races in production of a race intermediate of both.

CHAPTER XXXII.

AND, AS THERE CAN BE, THERE WILL BE SUCH UNIONS IN A RACE OF BOTH.

This follows from the truth announced that man is to the man possible but only through unions of unequal races, which, therefore, must occur to the production of such man. It also follows from the truth proclaimed throughout the universe that there is cause to consequence, and consequence to cause, and these so exactly adequate and equal as that what can be will be. And unions of unequal races will follow from the truths that the races will be the better of them; and so can not decline such unions when the opportunities occur. And, accepting such unions, they will not be able to depart from them.

And they will follow also from the fact that there are existing races—the agamic, polygamic and monogamic—and that these are unequal in their ability to produce the man possible. And that the monogamic—the superior—must transcend the others when they come in contact; that each is capable of indefinite expansion on its own plane; but that the monogamic—the superior—must extend its plane over those of the others; that in doing this it must absorb or exterminate the others. And that, as it will not exterminate, it must absorb them. And that in absorbing it must combine with them so that they will continue their existences in common. This will be possible but as the individuals of the higher race shall have domestic discipline over those of the lower.

This will be in the union of these races to the man possible of the races so uniting. And, as there can be such unions, there will be such unions. And as there can be such unions of the monogamic race now in Europe and

America with the agamic races in Africa and the Pacific islands, and with the polygamic races possibly in the tribes and castes of India and China, there will be such unions — certainly with the agamic states of Africa and the Pacific islands, and probably with the tribes and castes of India and China.

The certainty of such unions with the states of Africa and the Pacific islands is in that ultimately, if not in the near future, there will be emigrants from the monogamic states of Europe and America to them. Of every such emigration, continued, as it will be, to land held by agamic peoples, there will ultimately be a colony, and the colony amid such peoples will be inclusive or exclusive of them. It will accept natives to the offices they are fitted to hold in an economy of both, and will exclude them only as they be unable to hold such offices. And natives — savages as they may be — will be able to take and hold offices in subordination to the colony of monogamic immigrants. Each colonist can take a native and make him work and live as he had never lived before. And the immigrant will be better, and the native better, and the colony better than either could be without such taking. And as it is the interests of each to live to its possibilities of living, and as interest is the declivity of human action, there will be the acceptance by the immigrants of the native to the colony of both. And this for the further reason that the colonist must accept the native or exclude him. The Teutonic colonist at least will not miscegenate the native; nor can he assimilate the native, so eliminating the differences between them. Nor would he so assimilate the native if he could. Nor would the native be so assimilated so as to lose the sense of his separate existence. Nor were they so assimilated without the loss of reciprocal interests in each other, and without the repugnances there were between man and woman so assimilated, as they were without their sexual differentiations. And so unable to miscegenate or assimilate the natives, there were nothing left to the colonists expanding but to remove them. Their removal to other lands were onerous without any interest to compensate the labor. They will not be removed, therefore, but in their extermination. And this expensive, and their retention profitable, it is reasonably certain that, by every such colony of monogamic immigrants in territory occupied by agamic peoples, these will be retained, and there will be unions of immigrants and natives to its production. Profitable to the immigrant, it will be the condition of existence to the native. These unions will be domestic in their consistencies of individual colonists over individual natives, and predal in the forcible ownership by one individual of another. But predal and domestic, they will occur when crowded monogamic states shall send, as they will, their emigrants to lands sparsely in occupation of agamic races. This they may not do for some time yet. In no monogamic state is there yet the population possible. In all there are lords and commons in contest, the ones to hold and the others to take the patriarchal power. And on this they are so intent that there is not generally the dispositions in commons to seek relief through emigration.

But emigrants from European states have colonized this Western continent. And they are now colonizing Africa. And while it is not yet determined that these colonies shall accept to continued life and usefulness the natives of Africa, it is reasonably certain that they will ultimately do so.

There will be the colonists wanting the services of natives; there will be the natives able to subsist but in rendering such services. These can be rendered and accepted but upon the conditions that the natives be subject, individually, to the orders of the colonists, individually. The colonists as a body could not act upon the natives as a body without each be an organic state capable of an individual existence in relation to the other state; of immigrants and natives there can not be such states.

And the relations of coexistence in Africa, therefore, will not be those of states in relations of inequality but of individuals in such relations. Such were these unions, and the unions of individuals of different races into a race of both. This were domestic and patriarchal in the sense of a superior in power over the inferior as his offspring. And such unions there can and must be between agamic and monogamic races intersecting each other as they must.

It is not probable that these will so unite voluntarily. The immigrants as a body will not make such overture to the native. Nor will the natives make it to the immigrant. Nor, meeting, will the one propose or the other willingly accept such union. But upon the same land from which the one must remove the other, or absorb him, they will accept absorption. And that, the unions of these races, there will be the unions of agamic and monogamic races as certainly as that these unequal races now exist.

But it is not so certain that there will be unions of the monogamic and polygamic races in Asia. There is the disposition of the monogamic race to turn back upon the polygamic castes of Asia, as upon the agamic stocks of Africa. Monogamic states of Europe are acquiring jurisdiction over lands in Asia. And this republic is acquiring it over Pacific islands. But so far neither has started a colony of emigrants. And they at present are content to exercise their authority through force of military, or proconsular establishments; and not upon the individuals of those states but upon the states, as did Imperial Rome over her conquered provinces. These processes of the monogamic upon the polygamic race are not patriarchal, therefore, but imperial. And not of the individuals of the one race upon those of the other. And in this there were not their union in any proper sense, but only such as there are between polygamic castes.

It is probable that the polygamic caste has not originated at any place from the natural development of any

one polygamic tribe, but from the superposition of successive tribes. That originally the every tribe was predatory. But that some, on fertile plains and deltas, found
it easier and safer to make, than take, provisions for subsistence; and so became peaceful and productive. That
so they became subject to the incursions of hill tribes
adjacent — still predatory; that these become masters
of the peaceful tribes but, themselves becoming peaceful,
to be subjugated by other hill tribes still predatory, but to
become peaceful to be subjugated, and so on to a stack of
tribes related, such as is seen in the polygamic caste.
And it is probable that so as was the predatory to the
peaceful tribe, so will be the monogamic states of Europe
to the polygamic castes of Africa and Asia in states of
both in which there will not be the individuals of the races
in relation to each other, and these domestic, therefore,
but only the one race as a caste over the other as a subject caste; and with the one to inflict what the other may
not be able to endure. And with the certainty that such
imperfect union can exist so long only as both may be
able to continue their existences under such conditions.
And, as these were not the unions of these races in the
proper senses of that term, it is certain that of these
races, as such, there will not be their union until both be
wasted, as were Rome and her conquered provinces.

But it may be that of the survivors of these races
there may be such unions. Neither state of cast can exist
perpetually in such relation to the other. Polygamic
tribes may exist through extended periods in castes
priestly, militant, industrial, and servile. But so could
not the monogamic states and polygamic caste. The
state would exact what the caste could not perform. The
state will be to the caste, not as is the individual to the
property he owns, but as he is to the property he hires.
And he can not so conserve the property he hires of
another as he will the property he owns. Nor will the
caste as such subject be able to stand the treatment the

state can give it. Consisting of tribes in relations of reciprocal dependence on each other these relations will give way to such pressure from without. And the caste will become a mass of unrelated individuals, each pre-serving as he can his individual existence. And this, however considerately the state may press upon it. But the state can not press upon it considerately. The state, if owner of the caste, might act upon it so considerately as that its existence might be continued to a lengthy period, or without such ownership, if it were a natural individual, it could so act. But it were not so natural. The every monogamic state of Europe is in a contest of lords and commons for the patriarchal power. And in this republic there is the contest of parties for that power. And in every encroachment of the monogamic upon the polygamic race there will be such state of the one upon such caste of the other. And such monogamic state, whether it be as is England and the other states of Europe in which the contest of commons for that power in lords has not been decided, or as in this republic in which it has been ended in the commission of that power to majorities of adult males, the conduct of the state to the caste will depend, not upon what shall be to the well-being of either the state or caste, but what shall be to the well-being of that party which would control the state. And upon such contingency the caste will not long continue to exist, if the state, itself subject to such contest of parties, can long continue to exist.

But ceasing to exist, as have the states of monogamic Rome, with the subject tribes and castes of the outer world, an unarticulated mass of human beings must remain, each of whom will be charged to continue his existence as he can, the means to which will consist in such domestic relations of the races monogamic and polygamic as of their reciprocal wants of each other, and fitnesses for each other, may be possible. And thus, though it be impossible that there can be directly unions
f mono amic and l amic races there ma be unions

of the remnant of these races in states and castes disintegrated. And as there may be such unions there can be
such unions. And as there can be such unions for the
reasons stated there will be such unions—not only of
agamic and monogamic races, but of polygamic and
monogamic races. And this for the reason stated that
the cause of man on earth requires the man possible.
And as there can not be such man of any single race
existing now, there will be such of unions of these races
to the man possible of both.

There is the disposition of the people of every monogamic state approaching its maturity, in the possession by
its commons of the patriarchal power, to assume that they
can make their state what they please, and make agamic
Africans and polygamic Asiatics monogamic Europeans
by receiving them into their monogamic state and giving
them the rights of monogamic citizens. And if this
assumption be correct there will not then be unions of
unequal races to the man possible. For then there will
be no human races, and no man possible of those races
if there were. There is no race of man but as there is of
the animal or plant. And this the process of energy into
inertia, and life into nature. And there is the race of man
but as it be a process of human life into the human nature
of it, under the conditions possible. And of such self-
made man there were no such human race. Nor, if these
modes of man agamic, polygamic and monogamic be so
self-made and be termed races, were there of these the man
possible, or more, or other than each might see fit to
make of itself. Nor so the creature of its own volition
were it to the man possible. But so improbable that man
is so the creature of his own invention, and so probable
that he is of life in nature, as is the animal or plant, it is
reasonably certain that he is under a mistake in supposing
that he is not of human nature but of human art. And it
is so certain also, that he is to the man possible and that
he will become such man by unions of existing races no
one of which alone is com etent.

CHAPTER XXXIII.

AND CONSISTENT WITH THESE CONCLUSIONS ARE THE EXPERIENCES OF THIS REPUBLIC.

The position of this Republic is important. It is the first of monogamic states to attain to its maturity. In all such states there are classes, the ones as lords and the others as commons, in contest for the patriarchal power. That is the power of monogamic government, and in any state is the aggregate of powers in the male parents of the monogamic families composing the state. These parents, holding the properties and powers of the state, are natural lords of their offspring as commons, who, themselves, in the course of nature, must become possessed of the powers in their parents. But in no state, before this, had this power by nature come to the hands of its commons. In no other state before England had the lords and commons in parliament cyphered down their issues to the rule that the government of the state should be in the majority of the commons house, with a negative merely in the king and lords. And in no state before this Republic had there been the withdrawal of its commons from that negative in king and lords. It is the first instance on record, therefore, of the natural and orderly possession by the commons of a state of the supreme political powers of the state. And the first instance, therefore, of normal self-government in man.

And such the position of this Republic in the lead of the monogamic race, itself in the lead of all other human races; its experiences are important to the question, whether there be a race of man? — whether that advances to the man possible? and whether that advancement is, or shall be, through unions of unequal races?

There was originally in this Republic, as I have said, the institution of domestic slavery; and this an union of unequal races in relations of inequality. There were agamic negroes under monogamic whites. And in this there was the union of agamic and monogamic races. They were in respective families, white and black, but both under the authority of the male parent of the white family. And this for life; and so that to every member of the compound family there was assigned the duty it was best fitted to do in providing for the safety and subsistence of the whole. This were their union to the man possible of both. And to the possibility and propriety of such union the experiences of this Republic were not averse. They were not averse to its possibility, since in it, this union did in fact occur; and in its occurrence there is proof conclusive that it can occur under analogous conditions elsewhere.

Nor were they averse to the propriety of such unions to the ends of man on earth. For though, while originally existing in every state, these unions came to exist only in States at the South, and from these were ultimately abolished, there is much to show that they were not of disadvantage to the whole Republic originally, or to the States of the South later, or to the individuals of those States. And they were abolished, therefore, not from any evil in themselves, but only from the occurrence of political conditions not necessary to unions of unequal races elsewhere, and not likely to occur in human experience again.

Before the Revolution the regions of North America now within this Republic were populated by white immigrants from Europe and negro slaves from Africa; and, after that, immigration was promoted and the trade in slaves suppressed. The immigrants tended to the North and to the arts, the slaves to the South and to agriculture; the arts became established at the North and agriculture at the South, and these sections played into each others' hands, the South producing the raw material to be manufactured and commerced by the North. But, with the slave trade closed and immigration open, there came to be a larger population at the North.

After the Revolution, as I have said, the government of the Republic came to be in majorities of adult males. That majority was at the North, not only for the reason of its larger immigration, but for that the male slaves at the South were not fully represented. From the larger voting population, the North was, in effect, the Government. This fact is asserted in its taking the Presidency and the majority of Congress. In this it had to antagonize slavery; from this that institution fell, without a fact to suggest an evil in it. And without the probability that, reestablished elsewere, it will be so again suppressed. There was no natural reason for the suppression of the slave trade, or the encouragement of the white immigration exclusively, or the larger population at the North, or its repugnance to the slave. Without this it is not probable that such a state of things will again occur. And it is reasonably certain, from the experiences of this Republic properly considered, that not only will there be such unions of unequal races elsewhere, but that they will not be suppressed, and that of these there will be the states of the future world. There is ground, in fact, for the belief that not only the grandeur but the existence of this Republic is due to its union of unequal races. There is ground for the belief that if at the close of the Revolutionary War all the colonies had been without slaves they would not have united under a common government. That each colony becoming a state and capable, and in exercise of self-government, would not have delegated that government to a majority of individuals appointed by the several states. But each state conscious of self-government and of its ability to exercise it in its own individual interests, and each not assured that it would be exercised by such majority to its own individual interests, but apprehensive of its exercise in the interests of others at the expense of its own, would not have entered into an union of which this were possible. But as all the states held slaves, and as each such holding was a natural municipality of the individuals engaged in it, and as in each of these there was a natural self-government, and as the state was the consensus of such municipalities in which there was no disposition of the one to infringe the other, and as this also, therefore, was under such natural self-government, and as in this there was a natural bond of union from the representation of which in a common council there was nothing to be feared, they formed an union without misgivings, or with reluctance only on the part of the states holding the fewest slaves.

But to be doubted that there had been union and the one Republic without slaves, it is quite certain that there would not have been the union that there was without them. There would not have been the constitutional stipulation that the powers not delegated should remain in the states — or that the foreign slave trade should not be arrested before a period then distant. Or that the right to slaves in one state should be respected by citizens of every other. And, doubtful that there had been union and certain that there had not been such union as there was without slavery, it is the more certain that there would not have been the Republic that there is without it. There would not have been its present population of 80,000,000, extending from the Atlantic to the Pacific and from the Gulf to the Lakes. Nor of this would there have been 8,000,000 negroes. Nor would there have been sections North and South in one of which there was slavery and in the other not. And in the one of which there are now free negroes and in the other comparatively none. Nor had the immigration of whites from Europe been encouraged and the importation of negroes from Africa been prohibited. Nor had the South from having slaves been agricultural, and the North from having immigrants been mechanical and commercial. Nor had the

North from influx of immigrants become the more populous. Nor had the North from its larger population, merely, taken the government. Nor had there been the secession of the South and its subjugation by the North. Nor had there been a war of classes at the North, and a war of races at the South. Nor had there been an absolute government of the Republic, and this in the volition of a victorious party. Nor had this Republic, now the most powerful nation of the earth and possessed of foreign territories, been unable to give to the unequal races on them the necessary governments. There had not been such Republic as there is, and has been, without slavery. And to its slavery, therefore, must be attributed its grandeur if without it there had been its existence in the union of the states, is ground to question whether without it there had been the union of the states.

To such union of races, therefore, the experiences of this Republic are not averse, since from the dependent colony of a foreign state it had advanced, of this, in little more than one hundred years to be one of the strongest, if not the strongest, nation of the earth.

And not for these reasons averse to the existence of slavery established, the experiences of the Republic are not averse to its establishment, or to the continuation of its existence.

They show in fact that unequal races can unite, and when they can that they must unite; and that when united they will not be parted by any evil in the union, or separate from motives of their own.

They show also that the whites were better of such unions than they were without, and that the negroes were better of such unions than they were without, and that the states were better of such unions than they were without. And they forcibly suggest that of such union is to be the man possible. That other states must adopt such unions and not discard them. And that the state that first adopts and holds to such unions will become the leading nation of the earth. But that that will not be this Republic, which while based on such unions was easily in the lead of other states not so based. But which now discarding such base is not in the way of advancement from it, but is only in the administration to individual uses the funds of property and power accumulated by the Republic while it was upon that base. And that while, therefore, of its slavery it became the leading nation of the human world, from its abandonment of slavery it will not continue in such lead, if as a normal human state it will long continue to exist. It will exist as such state so long only as it shall exhibit the results of its individual human lives in common. And it will do this so long only as the party exercising the government shall be appointed by a popular vote. But, of parties alternately possessing the government by such vote, one must become able to hold it from the other, however that other may secure the larger vote. When able to do so it will do so. And the state then will not be in the volition of its individuals, but in the volitions of the leader of that party. As such, it will not be a normal human state. Nor, existing only in the volition of such irresponsible individual, can it long continue its abnormal existence. To these conclusions are the experiences of this Republic. They show that unequal races can unite in a human state of potency and promise, but also present grounds for apprehension that the state of neither race alone can long survive the dissolution of such union; that the whites can not long sustain a state under the orders of a victorious party appropriating the state to the uses of its individuals; and that the negroes can not form a state of themselves, and could not sustain it formed for them, and can not sustain themselves in the state of the whites, rejecting them; and that, however whites and negroes existing here may find the enjoyments they would individually have, they will not long find them in states of either to the man possible.

CHAPTER XXXIV.

THEY SHOW THAT UNEQUAL RACES CAN UNITE INDISSOLUBLY.

There was no reason for the unions of whites and negroes here that may not exist for their union or the unions of unequal races elsewhere. They were not in contact. Nor were the negroes in occupation of a territory wanted by the whites, who must absorb them or remove them. They were brought from distant lands and at much expense. While in the necessary expansion of monogamic whites over the portions of the earth's surface in occupation of agamic or polygamic peoples there will be contacts in which the incursives must absorb the natives, or remove them, or exterminate them. Their absorption will be possible only in the acceptance of them to subordinate positions in economies of both; and to such acceptance the inducements will be stronger and the opportunities of existence better than existed in the acceptance by the whites of the negroes here.

In every such an incursion there will be colonization, and in every such colonization there will be the want of labor by the colonists, which, as the conditions of their continued existence, the natives can supply. That will be the conditions of existence of the weaker race; and from the ones wanting labor and the others subsistence to be had only by supplying that want, there will be not only the stronger reason for their unions in relations of inequality than existed here, but the reasons conclusive that they will unite.

And the experiences of this Republic show also that when unequal races are so united in relations of inequality they will not be disunited from any evil in such union, or from any motives or activities of their own. There was no evil anywhere exhibited. Every such union was a natural municipality, of which the individuals, white and black, were members, each elected to his place by his fitness for its duties, and of which the male parent of the white family was chief magistrate, under whom there were the whites as peers and the blacks as commons. In this the whites and blacks were fitted for their offices — the whites were elevated, able and considerate; the negroes respectful, ordered and loyal. Neither wanted the place or office of the other, and both engaged in provisions for the safety and subsistence of both; each was in want of that the other had to offer, and neither was in want of that which the other had not to offer. And that there was no evil in the union, therefore, to part them.

And they show, also, that when united they are not parted by motives or activities of their own; that there was no repugnance of the whites to such union, as is seen in their efforts to preserve and defend it. Nor was there repugnance of the blacks. Whatever their individual feelings, their human nature was not averse to it, as is seen in the fact that of the 450,000 imported the descendants, within two hundred years, amounted to 8,000,000. Nor in feeling were they averse to it. It was the condition of their every well being. They were as proud of the master's standing, and interested in the advancement of his estate, as he was. They looked with contempt upon negroes without masters, and dreaded nothing so much as to be sold. Nor of any evil in the union, or of aversion to it by whites and negroes in it, was it dissolved.

Through the Revolution the colonists had become possessed of the patriarchal power, still exercised by the kings and lords over the commons in England. This, acquired by adult males in arms, was retained by them to be exercised only by majorities. From the exclusion of negro slaves from Africa, tending, for the reasons stated,

20

to the South, and the admission of white immigrants from
Europe, tending to the North, the Northern section had
come to have the larger population and the larger vote of
adult males; this they cast for the President and Congress-
men nominated by themselves, who, thus elected, took the
government, not only of the North, but of the South.
Nor did they do this from any repugnance to slavery at
the South, from the manufacture and commerce of whose
products they had so prospered, but simply to secure the
common government, from the use of which they hoped
for more emoluments. And possessed of the government,
the emoluments of which would have been greater of slavery at the South—if they could have done so, they would
not have allowed the subjugated South to liberate her
slaves, and so reduce the spoils of victory.

The slavery of the Republic was not abolished, therefore, of any evil in itself, or of repugnance of the parties
to it, or of the repugnance to it even of the men in that
section in which it did not exist, who, simulated repugnance merely that they might take the government.

Nor was it abolished from the repugnance to it of an
outer human world, since in such world there is no repugnance to it. There is none to it in the agamic and polygamic men of Africa and Asia, who, as far as they are able,
practice it. Nor is there repugnance to it in the monogamic men of Europe. In all such states there are contests
of lords and commons, as I have said, for the patriarchal
power. And in all the Teutonic states of Europe, at least,
the lords are losing ground and the commons gaining it.
The lords holding that power contend that all men are not
so naturally equal as that, in a state having institutions to
conserve to individuals the provisions they have made to
support themselves and families, those who have not contributed shall equally participate in the uses of those funds,
or in the governmental powers of distribution. But pressed
by the commons in assertion of a natural equality involving these conditions, they are induced to concede the

natural equality by way of compromise, while withholding
their assent to the proposition that in this equality there
is the immediate right of such participation in the provisions of the actually existing state. And while quite ready
to concur with the commons in assertion of the abstract
wrong in the holding by one man of another as his slave,
and passively to unite in measures to suppress the foreign
slave trade, there is ground for the belief that this seeming repugnance is provisional and passive; and that in
their acceptance of the discipline of offspring by parents
and of school children by teachers and of culprits by mag-
istrates, there is the recognition of the truth that all individuals, however naturally equal, are properly under the
restraints necessary to their usefulness in the state of
their actual existence. And that so simply are those of
a week race in a state of a stronger. Nor does it appear
that the commons are more earnest than the lords, or that
either, while willing to sacrifice the rights of others in
such philanthropy, is willing to compromise its own. Nor
in the Civil War, when the North and South were fighting,
the one as a free and the other as a slave state, was the
feeling of the European world against the South.

And as it does not appear that the South was at disadvantage from practicing slavery, or that there was any
impediment to the establishment of that union of unequal
races in the repugnances to it of the races themselves
involved, or that it was abolished from any evil in itself,
it must be admitted that unequal races can unite in such
relations of inequality, and that these unions will not be
dissolved but through intervention of a foreign force not
likely to occur again. And that of these unions there will
be the man possible, and not only the most man possible
and the best man possible that he be his most at the some
one point of the earth's surface at which that union may
occur, but at every point upon the surface of the habitable
earth — all of which is consistent with the experiences of
this Republic, which, considered properly, exhibit also

that what of good there has been in it has been due to its slaves, and what of evil to the want of them. The tone of the Republic, from its start, was singularly elevated and sustained, as it would not have been had it not have been of a master class.

There was a general tendency to agriculture — the nearest way to human well-being — which there would not have been if there had not been slaves, of whom that was the most profitable employment.

In consequence of this was the tendency of enterprises from the towns to the country. And in further consequence, there were abundant provisions for the support and comfort of the population possible.

And in further consequence there was a peace and order for near a hundred years that has not been known in any other human state. And all from the fact that at the start of the Republic there were slaves enough to support a class of masters able to direct the state to its proper ends.

But upon the suppression of the African slave trade, while European immigrants still came without the ability to procure the slaves of which they could be masters, the conditions became greatly altered. Without slaves they could not sustain the tone of a master class. Nor could they engage in agriculture, the arts being more immediately profitable ; nor could they tend from town to country, but only from the country to the town. Nor could they sustain the peace and order that had theretofore existed. They put themselves in opposition to the slaves and drove them to the South, where for a time they were willing they should stay in production of provisions for their use. But in time this was not enough. The government of the state was in a majority of adult males, they came to be that majority and for a time were content with burthens upon slave products to the benefit of themselves. But in time even this was not enough. Their population gave them the majority of adult males through which

they could take the Presidency and the majority of Congress, and they took them and with them the government
of the slave states as dependent provinces. And the
slave states not submitting to this they invaded and subjugated them, liberating their slaves. And in this there
have been evils. There was evil in the liberation of negro
slaves without other provision for them than that they
could extort from their former masters. There was evil
in depriving masters of their property without compensation. There was evil in such breach of the peace that
had been so perfect; and in the loss of lives in the war;
and in the reduction of the state from a self-governing
republic to a conquered province with no rights or liberties than those a popular majority may allow.

All these evils were due to a want of slaves. The
immigrants had taken slaves if they could have gotten
them; and with them they had been as peaceful, ordered,
rural and agricultural, and as ready to sustain the Republic
against such raid upon it, as were the masters of the
South.

And thus it is that what of good there was in this
Republic was due to its slaves and what of evil to the
want of them.

And that this is so will appear from a comparison
of this Republic when it held slaves with itself when it
ceased to hold them. But more clearly from a comparison of one of the states of the South while it held slaves
with itself when it ceased to hold them. Such typical
state is South Carolina. It was one of the first to take
slaves imported and it held them so that at the beginning
of the Civil War the slaves were in the proportion of
four to three of white, while in but one other Southern
state was their number greater than of whites.

And from a comparison of the Republic with itself,
and of South Carolina with herself at these different
periods it will appear that at the one period of both there
were not only the possibility and promise of the man pos-

sible but the facts of a better white man and a better negro and a better state of both than had been possible of a state of either race alone.

And as of the Republic before and after slavery enough has probably been said to show that the whites were better and the negroes better and the state better, then, when it had slaves, than either is now without them. I will now proceed to show that such were the facts of South Carolina.

CHAPTER XXXV.

THE WHITES OF THAT STATE WERE SO BETTER BEFORE EMANCIPATION THAN THEY ARE NOW.

They were then the masters of negro slaves employed in agriculture, and in monogamic families of whites and blacks reciprocally dependent, of which the blacks were in subordination to the whites. And these in natural municipalities, of which the actual or potential male parent of the white family was chief magistrate.

Now they are not the masters of slaves employed in agriculture, or in families reciprocally dependent and in natural municipalities, of which the white male parent is chief magistrate, but are in monogamic families of whites in no domestic relation to families of blacks. And these in artificial municipalities from which the black families are virtually excluded. Then the whites were in care and custody of the blacks, and were sharing with them — still agamic — their superior monogamic civilization, in consideration of the help the blacks could give them in provisions for the safety and subsistence of them both. And both, intuitively, if not intelligently, sensible of the situation, were instant to accept and make the most of it.

- And the masters were just, considerate and humane and the slaves docile, obedient and loyal, and there was a peace, order and propriety rarely seen in any state; and the state itself was the respected member of a confederacy of states admitted to be sovereign.

But now it is not the respected member of a confederacy of states admitted to be sovereign. The supreme political power of the Republic has been seized by the one party of its adult males to the subjugation of the other. And its government is as absolute in that party securing

a majority of such males as is that of any state in any
usurping monarch.   In such subjection the state is not
now sovereign.   Nor, in the contests of parties for the
majority to rule the state, is there the peace, order and
propriety there was.   Nor is there the consideration of
whites by blacks, or the loyalty of blacks to whites, there
was.   And however it may appear that the negroes are
better and the state better than they were, it will not
appear that the whites are better than they were.

They were then the members of a ruling race.   And
while it may be doubted that it be right that any one
human race shall rule another, it will not be doubted that
the white men of that race were the better of their superior position.   They were exempt from the servile offices
to which some had been subject in ministering to the
wants of others.   They were free from the frictions of
classes contesting for position and from strikes of labor
against capital and the combinations of capital against
labor; and from the strifes of parties to possess the
government; and from the bitternesses and demoraliza-
tions of such strifes.   And while it may be questioned
that races are unequal and that the individual of any one
race can rightfully take jurisdiction of the individuals of
any other, it will not be questioned that the individuals of
one race having actually acquired jurisdiction over another
accepting it and the better of it, are themselves the better
of their place and office.

They were also the better from being primarily
engaged in agriculture.   Agriculture is the business in
which slaves can be the most profitably employed.   It is
a business which will not admit of strikes, necessary if
labor be by contract, and a business in which all from
earliest infancy to extremest age can be usefully employed.
And a business which furnishes immediately abundant
provisions for the comfortable subsistence of those
engaged in it.   And a business necessary to the start of
every state, and without which no state can advance to

arts or commerce. And while, therefore, the men of that state were the better of their superior position they were the better, also, that this position was over a race engaged in agriculture. They were also the better that in their position they were sustained by natural relations, and not by contracts. They were naturally related to each other through their respective families and as naturally related to the blacks through the unions of families black and white. Among them there were duties, not obligations; and duties imposed by their relations to each other in the state and not obligations incurred only by contract. In the male parent or one in *loco parentis* of the white family there was the patriarchal power to which there was the obedience not only of the members of his white family but also of the black. He did not have to contract or pay for service to sustain the compound family to its best and most. And he had little use for money, therefore. And the proprietors of large estates were often and for long periods with as little money in his purses as in that state now has the clerk or journeyman mechanic. What was wanted by the individuals of the estate was made upon it by them or was taken by barter from estates adjacent, and thus there were from within themselves families to the families possible, in a state to the state possible, without. artificial contrivances or the exaction from the individuals more than that they accept the situation.

They were also the better that they were in tutelage of a lower race to share with them the advantages of their superior state. The negroes were better then in relation to the whites than they had been in Africa. And to that extent they shared with the whites their superior state. And of this tutelage the whites themselves were better. Superior position gives to man the superior powers required to its duties. He also loves that he has helped and is the better of his affections. And the whites of that state were instant and persistent in exhibiting

the character and conduct becoming a ruling race in production of the man possible.

There were the most and earliest marriages possible.
The every adult male was in want of a wife, not only to
the indulgence of his natural affections but to help and
supplement him in his office of caring for the slaves with
which he was, or expected to be charged. And these
increasing naturally both man and wife were in want of
offspring to supplement them who could do so best but
as they also married early. And from a sense of interest
as well as of the sexual feelings of individuals becoming
adults there were the marriages possible and at the earliest periods possible.

And of these there were the children possible. To
the male parent in charge of the municipality his children
were as importont as his slaves. And as in him and
wife there was the natural want of offspring, and as for
these there were offices, and as they were not incum-
brances, therefore, but helps to their parents, there were
few men and women who did not marry, and who, marrying, did not have the children possible.

And these were educated to the work there was for
them to do.

From its earliest intelligence there was something the
child could do to help its parents, or to fit it for the duties
of its maturer years, and to this its attention was addressed.
The male children were with their father in his outdoor
duties, so that when adults they were as possessed of them
as he was, and could relieve him when he was ready to be
relieved. The female children were with their mother in
her indoor duties, and when adults were as possessed of
them as she was, and could relieve her when ready to be
relieved, or could execute such duties in homes of their
own. And in such their respective positions and offices
the parents and their offspring exhibited characters and
conducts eminently proper for the coming man, and as
proper for the masters of a race of slaves.

In every such white family there was acceptance of relative positions, and decorum and order in such acceptance. There was no contest for position in that family, the order of that having been established by nature. Nor were there contests of families for position in the state; for there was virtually no artificial state, in fact, with respect to the vital center, of which the families were grouped, each of itself being a natural state upon a vital center of its own. And such the situation. All were elevated to dignity and composure by a sense of their superior position. And the individuals of families were respectful of themselves and of their families, and the families were respectful of themselves and of the state existing but of their voluntary concurrence in it. And the men were brave and honorable and the women virtuous and humane, and in both secure of their superior position in the compound family there was the magnanimity the consciousness of superior position inspires. Each was respectful of himself and others with him in his family, and of other such families, and of the state of such families. And so perfect in all was this sense of their relations to each other in the family and state of families, and so perfect their acceptance of its dictates, there was no need of other law. Nor in fact was there other law in that state than that of public sentiment. There were legislatures meeting annually, four weeks before Christmas, which enacted civic duties, some of which, affirmed by public sentiment, were retained upon the statute books, and others of which, not so affirmed, were repealed by succeeding legislatures. And they then went home to their Christmas dinners, while the state went on as it would have done without them.

But these formal legislatures were admirably ordered. The House of Lords in England is perhaps the most ordered legislative body known. The every member in it is there for life, by inheritance or by appointment for meritorious service to the state; and, each secure of his position and of the respect it gives him, is respectful of himself and of that body.   But the members of the House of Lords are not so respectful of themselves, and each other, and their house, as were the legislators of this state.   Of these each was a slave-owner and the representative of slave-owners; and each, therefore, was the natural chief magistrate and lord of a natural municipality of commons, acquired by his fitness for that office, and within which realm his authority was practically absolute — and more absolute, in fact, than is that of the sovereign of any monogamic state.   And of these, meeting in legislation, no one had the disposition to assert himself, or the occasion to assert himself over others.   And respectful of himself, he was respectful of others, as he required others to be respectful of him.   And he was respectful of the body that it be respectful of him.   And he was fitted to command respect from his having acquired his position, not by inheritance or appointment for service to the government — not always meritorious — as have some members of the House of Lords, but by his ability to build up and govern his natural municipality.   And a body so ordered and decorous has been seldom, if ever, seen as was the legislature of that state.   Its sentiment of what should be the rule of conduct was the rule.   There were no irregularity of deportment or personalities in debate permitted.   No one member was named by another, or by the presiding officer.   There was no electioneering for office.   Each had a more profitable office in his estate than the state could give him.   Nor was any one dismissed from office who, learning its duties, had filled it properly.   Nor if the office were elective, could the incumbent, learning and discharging its duties, be defeated.   Nor did candidates for Judge, or Governor, or other office filled by the legislature, venture to canvas for votes, or to appear, without business, at the session in which the election pended.

And such the deportment of these men in legislation, analogously such was their deportment in public and at home.

In public they were equally courteous and respectful of each other and themselves. There were no bickerings, trials, feuds, factions, or personal collisions, comparatively. The duel was admitted. And if, as rarely happened, there was an irreparable wrong to one, he had the right to call the perpetrator to that field of arbitrament without involving others.

But the duel itself was under law. The sentiment of the state admitting the duel required that there be no such arbitrament of a wrong which the perpetrator was willing to repair. And in every community there were men of standing to act as a board of honor to determine whether there was a wrong, and if so, what reparation were sufficient, and that the one make and the other accept it. And rarely did either disregard the determination of that board; and disregarding it, he was sent to coventry. So also was sent from social recognition the individual, however gifted, who violated willfully a principle of social morals. And while it was objected to this slave state by states without slaves that in it there was this code of honor in exclusion, or supplement even, of the legislative law, it is to be doubted that there was ever a state of equal population in which there was so little mortality from violences of individuals on each other.

The negroes were not involved in duels, or allowed to own or carry arms. The few whites themselves who carried them secretly were shunned. Their collisions, therefore, not requiring the duel, were with natural weapons, while the duel itself involved in its risks only the principals at issue. In other states, prohibiting the duel, there were constant collisions with artificial weapons, in which were involved not only the principals at issue, but the friends and followers of each, and often in these states have fallen in feuds within a single year more than fell on the field of honor in that state in the course of its existence before the war.

And, besides this, its public peace was singularly perfect and its social morals singularly pure. By peoples interested in repudiating slavery it is assumed that the state was a house for the debauchery by the males of one race upon the females of the other. And it must be confessed that there were illicit intercourses.

There are monogamic men whose sexual wants are not supplied by the indulgences a single wife can give them. There are also youths in every monogamic state who are under the impulse of sexual feeling before they are allowed to marry. These, in states without slaves, must indulge those feelings by seductions of females on the same plane with themselves or by self-abuse, and from this there is demoralization, damage, disorder, and the deterioration of the state.

But in the state of unequal races united there were not these. There were inferior females ready to respond to the wants of superior males. In this they were not injured. Their chances of mating with males of their own race were improved. The offspring of such intercourses were not at disadvantage. It was more competent to the task of subsistence and was more considered than was offspring of the same mother by a father of her own race. No wrong was done; and there was no sense of wrong. Wives and mothers were conveniently blind to such necessary transgressions of conventional morality. Transgressions were confined by the sentiments against them to the narrowest limits possible. And confined to these limits it was conservative of the peace and morality of the state. And it is to be doubted therefore that there was ever a state in which the order was so perfect or the morality so pure.

And such the conduct of these men to each other in public, analogously such was their conduct in their families at their homes.

Practically absolute in authority over the persons and properties of their individual municipalities the instances were phenomenally rare of their abuse of either. The parent's individual family was protected by his affection for it. And his slave family by his interest in it. Under bond, as I have said, to his every slave in the precise amount of his value that he should come to no harm from which the master could protect him, the master was considerate of that bond in his treatment of his slave. He was considerate of his slave, also, from that affection which the thing that we have helped and its helplessness inspires; and also from the loyalty of the slave, and from that honor which, not permitting him to wrong an equal, was absolute in its prohibition of wrong or injury to his slave so completely at his mercy.

And so, was it in fact. The master may not have given to the slave all the privileges he may have wanted, but, giving to him all he considered proper, he was respectful of these gifts. And the last of his acts had been the defrauding of his slave, or the withholding from him, but for cause, a right that had been conceded.

Not realizing their union with a lower race over whom they exercised the patriarchal power, and that they differed, therefore, from other whites not in such relation, and that in preservation of their individual existences they were not to strive for individual advancements with others in the state, and to share with them the property of the state, they were singularly inconsiderate of themselves and the state as a member of an artificial Republic. Nor did they exhibit eloquence or practice statesmanship, or do anything heroic or strive for individual advancement or form parties to take to its uses the property of the state, nor did they seem to realize that there was a property in the state which a dominant party possessed of the government could take. Nor did they simulate or pretend to anything for effect, or exhibit the impatient or mischievous activities of a people under no other rule of law than that of their individual volitions through majorities, but were content to be or seem in contrast to be the

practical and commonplace constituents of natural and
normal human states.

And this not from real inertia or inability to participate in the affairs of an outer human world, but from the
intentness of their attention to a world of their own. . The
white man who could possess a slave became a master and
thenceforth became charged with the family of the slave
as well as of his own. And as both enlarged naturally,
and the slave family the faster from its greater fertility
and the purchase of other slaves, there come to be of both
a natural municipality under offices appointed by the
master, the regulation and supervision of whom so tasked
him that he had not time or inclination to any other
subject.

And such, and so situated, the men of that state
were not considerate of themselves from having so much
else to consider, nor did they indulge in oratory from
there being no one to be moved by it.

There were men of that state in the councils of the
Republic who were known as orators, but in the men of the
state there was no oratory. Nor in their own affairs did they
exhibit or aspire to statesmanship from there being nothing
to be done to change for the better the state of such municipalities, or to change the relations of them to the state or
of the state to other states. There were men of that
state in the Congress or Cabinet of the Republic who did
as much, or more, perhaps, to shape its fortunes than did
an equal number from any other state, but they did nothing of statesmanship in the state itself, which drifted on
an even keel to ends of its own natural existence. Nor
were there parties in their common sense from there
being no fund of property and power in the state for
them to act on. The funds reserved by one generation
of monogamic families for the generations succeeding it
had been invested in the compound families themselves
existing and were not subject, therefore, to the volitions
of a victorious party. A victorious party, if there had

been such, had been as powerless to act upon the state as upon any one of its families. And as powerless to act upon that in alteration of any part of its state in relation to the whole as is the mind of individual man in alteration of an organ in relation to his body. There was nothing, therefore, to be done by parties. And from want of a subject of partition there were no real parties, such as are in democratic states, more than there is in any natural body.

And for this unusual elevation of character and conduct there was a reason not commonly considered in the fact that their current means acquired to the ends of human life were instantly invested in human life.

Individual men in monogamic states are considered and considerable in the proportions of their ability to make money and make investments of that money in properties to the support of human life. Some men can make money but can not make investments of it in such provisions from their dispositions to use it on themselves. And some, able to make investments of it, are not able to make investments of it in provisions for a larger human life. But to the whites of this state as a ruling race it was the peculiar fortune that while able to make money as few had done, and to invest it in provisions for a larger human life, they were able to invest it directly in human life, with every motive of individual interest to do so.

From the surplus products of every estate there were annually moneys for which there were no investments so ready and remunerative as slaves, and the lands for them to work in enlargement of their lives. In thus enlarging the lives of slaves there was proportionate enlargement of the lives of masters dependent on their slaves, as there is not now.

Now in men of that state there is a growing indisposition to investments in taxable property.

That subject to the uses of the party in government, if the state is liable to assessments, its owners are unwilling to incur. And that they may not, they shun the property, as they can in not becoming the owners of it. And thus it happens that real estate is avoided, and annuites, government bonds and life insurances are indulged in. Men of large incomes insure their lives with portions of them and live in splendor on the balance. And in this, and in various other ways, there is evinced the common disposition in the whites of that state to quit the harness for the car of human progress.

But such was not the disposition then. The owners of estates had no other use for money but to reinvest it in slaves. And related as masters to the operatives as slaves, able, under the directions of masters, to do all the works required by such estates, the whites were under no obligations to contract, and under no want of money, therefore. And thus it was that the owners of large estates in extensive operations were as without money in their purses, and for long periods, as in other states are clerks or journeymen mechanics. Nor were they perturbed by strikes or trusts. In every monogamic state becoming democratic in the possession by adult males of its patriarchal and proprietary powers, there are necessarily perturbances from the disposition of some unpropertied to share the properties which others have secured.

Of these males so possessed of the powers of the state, and so its rulers, therefore, some, of their industries and self-denials, have become possessed of properties which they would hold exclusively to the wants of themselves and families, except as they be necessary to the support of the state. Others, not practicing these virtues, are without such property, but, sharing the powers of the state, would share, through these, the properties of others; and not content to be laborers for hire, are instant that the government shall require of capital that it give them more pay for less work. And when the government is unable to give them all they would have of the capital employing them, they combine to strike against it, and so stop its operations until their exactions are complied with. And capitalists, to protect themselves, also combine, and in trusts, to the resistance of these demands; and while each is using its available means, the one to take and the other to hold the capital of the state, the state itself is much perturbed. Industries are interrupted; enterprises are not undertaken, or abandoned; capital seeks security at low interest in the bonds of the government, and operatives who would share the property existing, while having ample income, will not invest in it from their unwillingness to share by taxation in the expenses of the state, which they thus would put upon the property of others. Such disturbances there were in all the states not holding slaves, to a slight extent, before emancipation, and such are coming to an alarming extent in all the states of the Republic since.

But such there were not in any Southern state before emancipation. And especially were there none in South Carolina. There every white man could own a slave, or could hire a slave of his master to help in his work. So possessed of a slave; he was a capitalist or an employer. There were none, therefore, to strike against capital, and no capital in want of trusts to its protection against strikes. And no classes to antagonize each other, and no parties to contest for the property accumulated. There was not a class or party arrogating the right, in virtue of its numbers merely, to administer the state, and so execute on man the will of God in man. But all, with the faith of children, felt that in accepting themselves and in sharing with a lower race the Anglo-Saxon civilization that had come down to them, they did all that the will of the cause of man required of them. And the conclusive merit of their institution was in that it fitted them to accept as men their subjugation. They saw and felt their wrongs — that it was not in the compact of union that the North, becom-

ing more populous, should take the Government and deny
to their state the right to secede from it; and should invade
it for attempting to secede; and burn and plunder it; and
liberate its slaves, and put them to the government of
their masters. And to this should use the funds and
credit of the Republic in hiring troops from abroad. And
should give pensions in millions to these troops for it in
part to pay. And should turn its negroes loose upon it
to be governed without means and to be educated at its
expense, not to work for their livings but to live without, while its people should be watched to see that they
treated the negro, not as he must be treated to a tolerable
existence with him, but as they would have him treated.

They know that this was not the intention of their
fathers; that it is not in the Constitution of the Republic.
And that if it were it were there without effect; that the
madness of such a compact could not have been intended;
but if intended were to be treated as the utterances of
madmen. And, in that these things have come to pass,
there was in the men of that state a sense of wrong which
might well inspire a feeling of inseparable repugnance to
the present state. But this does not exist. In the spirit of
the wife in Ion: "That it is not the part of woman to
perplex the fortunes of a man to whom she clings," "but
to weave all that she has of fair and bright in the dark
meshes of his web inseparate from its windings," the men
of that state have accepted their fortunes as fate has cast
them, and the Republic whatever its perversities, as would
a wife her husband or parent, to be honored and sustained.
And fairly striving to accept what seemed to be the situation, they liberated their slaves, though with scarcely less
of feeling than that with which they had turned loose and
off their wives and children. And have turned from agriculture to the arts. And in the recent war with Spain
have been as prompt to the call of the republic as have
been others of her people.

And so elevated the man of that state; so elevated also was its woman. She, whether as daughter, wife or mother, was secluded by its system from the outer world. Her every want from earliest infancy was abundantly supplied. But within that system there were duties taking to their utmost her beneficent ministrations. She was in the family or state as is the soul to the body, but was in a body so transparent that her every act was visible; and so visible that she was not more incapable of a vice itself than of the impropriety that leads to it. And so secluded and enshrined she had no occasion or disposition to leave her sheltered home for contact with an outer world. She knew of her ends and offices in life but that she had learned of mothers as moral as herself. And learning that it was for her while doing all the good she could to others to contribute to the continuation of her race, she was ready of her maternal instincts, and without a sexual feeling, to discharge that duty.

And if to the man who took her to his heart and home she was not so responsive in ardent feelings as he might have wished, he had the compensation of feeling that she was "pure as the icicle" "that hangs on Dian's temple."

And such the man and woman of the ruling race in that state then, such are not the man and woman of that state now. There is not now the harmonious union of races in order to the betterment of both, but instead there is the efforts of each to preserve its existence on the same plane in opposition to the other. And in that which was the ruling race property has become the subject of legislation. Parties are forming, though not yet definitely formed, the one to keep and the other to take to individual uses the the property of the state. And in legislation, therefore, there is not the order and decorum of the olden time. The members are not so respectful of themselves and each other as they were. The most of higher offices are filled by popular elections. They are sought for their emoluments, and not by the men most fitted to fill them, but by men most fitted to secure the larger vote of those expecting to share in the patronage of such offices. And candidates for the legislature, governor, senator to congress and even for judgeships — not now for life but for a term — are instant to go upon the hustings for such vote. Nor is the man so sensible and respectful of duty to his wife or children. Nor is he so intuitively conscious that the unions for life of parents and of parents and their children are the conditions of the monogamic human state. Nor is the man sensible of his duty to shelter and support the woman to the performance of her office in continuation of his race, but is content that she shall find employments by which she may support herself. And, to his relief, is willing to share employments with her, however these may take her from her sphere and impede her in her special work of giving existence to a coming race.

Nor is he sensible of his duty to make place and office for his children and to educate and train them to the works he has for them to do, but is content and solicitous, in truth, that they be educated by the state to the nothing it has for them to do. And is even willing — and at his expense, or at the expense of those holding property — that the state shall educate the negro also to the nothing it has for him to do. And as education makes the person educated only more completely what he tends to be, he is willing that the state shall educate the negro, and at his expense to be more a negro than he is, and to become a more formidable competitor with him for existence than he is.

And so sensible of his individual existence, and so insensible of his true and necessary relations to others with him in becoming what he should be, the man of that state now is not the man of that state then.

Nor is the woman. She has been less affected by the change. She is uneasy from want of the services of slaves, and is tasked and taxed by servile services herself, but she is not yet disposed to transcend her sphere or to become independent of man or to vote or to share in public business with him or to be divorced from him. And although she has been allowed to hold separate property as a married woman, and to contract with respect to it, even with her husband, it is not clear that this has been of her seeking. Or that she would not yet prefer the state of woman as it was and as it is at the common law. But conditions changing she must change with them. The sentiment by tradition of a condition will not supply the want of the condition no longer existing, and forced of her own individual means to continue her individual existence she must ultimately comply with that condition and become as different from the woman of that state then as is the man. And such the differences in conditions, character and conduct between the whites of that state then and the whites of that state now, it must be admitted that the whites of that state then were better for all the supposable ends of man in nature than are the whites of that state now. And that they exhibited then a character and conduct they do not now and a fitness for dominition over a lower race they do not now exhibit.

CHAPTER XXXVI.

THE NEGROES WERE, ALSO, SO BETTER THEN THAN THEY ARE NOW.

They were then the beneficiaries of agricultural institutions throughout the state, into which they were not only admitted without charge, but prices were paid for them by promoters, which in effect were bonds in the precise amount of their value that they should be fed, clothed and tended in sickness properly, and in health provided with employments proper to their well-being, and instructed in the ways of such employments, and protected in them from any disturbance by themselves or others, and from every evitable injury to themselves or offspring. And that their offspring should be accepted on the same conditions. Every first slave purchased became the nucleus of a plantation and every plantation was such institution of which the negroes were better than are the people of any artificial institution established by states. And these natural institutions are better themselves to the ends of human life and to those of negro life than are such artificial institutions by states, in that they were natural and of indefinite duration, and automatic, and autonomic; and capable, therefore, of their own motions of becoming the institutions possible to the man possible.

But now they are not such beneficiaries. Nor are there such institutions. Nor are there any institutions of the whites into which they are allowed to enter without paying the prices of initiations. Nor are there any of which they can be members for life, or longer than they continue to pay their fees. Nor are they willingly admitted into any institutions of the whites. Nor are they admitted to places in any which there are whites to take.

Nor are they capable of institutions of their own. Nor if capable are there places in that state of whites for such institutions; which can exist, therefore, but as they may be able to displace and supersede the institutions of the whites. Nor of this, if capable of institutions were their institutions capable. And the whites will occupy that state to the exclusion of the negroes, who will be its outcasts as are the individuals from polygamic castes who fail of compliance with tribal rites. And the negroes of those states, therefore, are now worse than were its negroes then as are the outcasts worse than are the incasts of the polygamic tribes from which they are expelled. And to these assumptions are the experiences of its negroes before and since emancipation.

. They were then better not only in being *more*, continually, but in the way of being *better* that they might be more. They were not only protected and provisioned as they are not now; and in the conditions, therefore, to advance in numbers possible as they are not now, but they were disposed to avail themselves of their opportunities. And there was in consequence the natural increase possible, and the peace and order among them proper. And the character and conduct proper to such peace and order and to the provisions necessary to the support of themselves and whites. And, while abundantly clear that they were better as slaves here than as free in Africa, it is clear that they were better as slaves here than as free negroes here.

. In Africa they were savages in stocks at war with each other, without gods or governments, and liable to be killed, or taken and held as slaves, or sold to others as savage as themselves; while here, whether slave or free, they were in states under God and government, and not at wars or liable to be killed, or held as slaves by masters as savage as themselves. And, though it is now the fashion of monogamic peoples to commiserate them as slaves, it is to be doubted that there was ever a people so blessed as were the four hundred thousand negroes brought by slavery to this country.

The reason for this commiseration is in the fact that the commons of all the monogamic states of Europe are now in assertion of their right to patriachal power withheld from them by Lords. And that these states of America are now in exercise of that power wrested from the lords. And unwilling to admit that the right of individual liberty can be justly withheld from themselves, are commiserate of others from whom it is withheld, without the sense that this power extorted from lords must be exercised by them and upon themselves as it is now by dominant parties in this Republic, or upon a weaker race as it was by the whites upon the blacks at an earlier period. But feeling can not determine the fact of evil in slavery, nor could the fact of evil in slavery to which the negro was subject in coming here, determine that it was not the better for him that he came.

And, so better the negro here than in Africa, so better was the negro as a slave in South Carolina than he is now as a free man in that state. He was better from being in the way of being more than he is now. Of adults male and female there were the matings possible and at the earliest periods proper. And of these there were the offsprings possible, and these were fed and clothed as it was proper, and protected from the abuses of themselves or parents and from every avoidable ill or injury, with the best medical or other attention that could bestow. And as infants or adults, or as parents or offsprings, the negroes were kept in the peace, order, temperance, health and strength for the works there were for them to do in procuring provisions for their own support and well-being. And were provided with these works and were guided in the doing of them; and guided in their ways by masters whose every and only interest was that they should do the works best for themselves and so do them as that they themselves should be the better of them.

They mated from their sexual feelings and maternal instincts; and early, from these and the interests of their masters and themselves. The masters were interested that they mate — as the means to their proper offspring — and early, that they have the more abundant offspring. And they themselves were interested in that, mated, they were more considered, and still more considered from their more of offspring.

. And their offsprings were fed, clothed and tended, medically or otherwise, and protected from abuses of themselves or others, and from avoidable ills or injuries, in that every such offspring at its birth was worth one hundred dollars to the master, and more with every year of its existence.

And as infants or adults, or as parents or offspring, the negroes were kept in peace, order, temperance and health and strength for the works there were for them to do, not only for the reason that of these they could do more and better work, but for the reason that of these they were the more valuable to their masters.

Of such treatment the negroes were more abundant than they would have been without it. And they would have been without it if they had been without masters, and masters of a higher race. And without masters they are in the state considered now.

And for this reason they are not in way of being so abundant as they were before they were emancipated.

Nor for the same reason are they so fitted to become abundant, or for participation in the progress of the human race, or even for the ends of their own well-being as they were as slaves.

They were then in compound families, white and black. Every white male or female of capacity inherited or purchased slaves to supplement them in their works of being what they might be. These, in towns, were relegated to subordinate domestic offices, and in rural districts to agriculture. But whether in towns or country they were normal parts of one organic family, under presidency of the ultimate proprietor, as are children under the male parent, or one in *loco parentis* of the monogamic family. And the families, white and black, were in relation to each other as are the male and female children of such family. Male children give life, and female children the ways and means to the continuation of that life. And so did the white family give life to the black in provisions for the continuation of that life. And so does the white family give life to the black in provisions for the continuation of such life. And as male children are life, therefore, to the female the nature of that life which they accept and provision to the possibilities of an intermediate human life possible, so are white families life to the blacks, the nature of that life, which they accept and preserve to the intermediate human life of both.

Each such compound family was an organism of human life in human nature, and the blacks, as an organ of that organism, exhibited the character and conduct becoming such organ. And it is reasonably certain, that whether in town or country, or in domestic or agricultural offices, or of their own motion or the orders of masters, the negroes were in the way not only of being their most, but their best that they be their most in the way of man, however they may have been injured by the force to put and keep them in that way.

But they were not injured by that force. That force was from a master who had given bond in his ownership of the slave for his good treatment, and who had for his slave that affection for an object which its helplessness and the sense of helping it inspires. And that he was not injured was in the facts that under this rule the individuals waxed strong and the race stronger than within the time had any race before.

Nor in the slave was there the sense of injury. His sense of security from injuries was perfect. He felt assured that no one but master would be allowed to hurt him, and that his master not only would not but, to the extent of his fortune, would protect him from every evitable ill or injury from others; and that this was his feeling is seen in the facts that he was joyous, improvident, trustful and loyal, and that he venerated his master and idolized his mistress, and that he did not aspire to freedom, having made but two feeble and inconsiderable attempts in the whole course of his life in slavery; and that while inflicting violences on other slaves, he inflicted none upon his master or his master's family, and rarely any upon other white men. His master's meat-house, crib and dwelling were generally unlocked, or if locked, the slave carried the key. They guarded their master's property as they would not if it had been their own. They grieved for the loss of an implement or animal as they would if it had been their own. They were proud of their master's family and fortune. They rejoiced when a child, white or black, was born to it. They were ready for the meanest service rather than their master or his child should be unserved. They promptly risked their lives to shield their master or his family.

And when the Civil War came on, ostensibly to release them, they begged to follow their masters to the field. And when from a huge mistake they were not allowed to do so they stayed to protect and support the wives and children of their masters. And they have been known to lament in dying not the loss of life but the loss of their value to their master. They dreaded nothing so much as to be sold. And impatient of restraints as are children at school, or horses in harness, they had no disposition to be free and looked with commiseration or contempt upon the free negroes they rarely met about them. No place was so dear to them as that upon which they had been raised. And no life so dear to them as that to which they were accustomed. They freely risked their lives to shield or share the dangers of a master or a master's child.— I, myself, as a boy was left with a servant who let me fall into a well thirty-six feet deep, into which she plunged immediately after, though without permanent injury to either. And they were emulous of positions in the family and instant to retain them. They gave no notices to quit nor did they quit without notice. Nor could they be induced to quit a place secured and were always ready to assist in arresting others who had run away. Nor were any people so well and solicitously served as were their masters. Nor were any superior people so loved by their inferiors as were these masters. Nor were any inferior people so loved by their superiors as were these slaves. And no people were ever so free of responsibilities or joyous of their freedom. I have known them to begin a dance on the morning of their Christmas holiday and keep it up through every hour of every day and night to the evening of its close. And with these advantages they were comparatively free of contagious or infectious diseases. And on plantations or in towns they were altogether free from the calamities of war. And the civil war which ruined masters left them unhurt, except to the extent that they were forced to federal service. And so placed in a natural municipality; and so sheltered and protected in their places; and so without injury or the sense of it; and so sensibly and joyously accepting the situation they were further favored with a perfect education.

Education means the eduction of faculties to a fitness for the works to be accomplished. And the education of man is to a fitness for the works of man to the man possible; and of a slave to fitness for the provisions necessary to the safety and subsistence of his natural municipality. And this education he received. Such earlier municipalities were agricultural in production of provisions for their maintenance, and in every such rural municipality the every slave was given his special work and was taught to do it and was not taught to do any work beyond; and, educated perfectly to this, he was uneducated only as he was not taught to do work he did not have to do; as an organ of the human body educated to its special work were uneducated only as it shall have been untaught the duties of other organs. He had the best of educations therefore in any proper sense of that term. And he was himself the better and his municipality the better, not only of this but of his want of any other. And his want of other education can be complained of by those only who complain of such unions of unequal races. And these only can complain of this who assume that God intended of man on earth an Utopia of absolutely equal individuals under no other regulations than those imposed by their individual volitions. Such Utopia does not exist even in this Republic, when upon its emancipation from Great Britain then were the best opportunities for its existence. And the complaint of the want of education of slaves, therefore, was but the complaint that there should have been slaves or any such natural system of human life in human nature to obstruct the realization of their ideal state of individual equality.

They were also further favored by domestic discipline, and this by the most efficient means to its enforcement. In every normal human state there are rules of individual activity and conduct, for breaches of which there are punishments; and these inflicted by order of the state after judicial determination of such breach. These determinations are troublesome, expensive, sometimes wrong and always questioned as to their justice by the accused and their friends.

And the punishments by the state for breaches determined are in bodily inflictions or imprisonments, and of bodily inflictions there are mutilations or the lash. And of these it will be found that bodily inflictions are better than imprisonments and the lash than mutilations. And in monogamic states, in which the commons are encroaching on the lords in exercise of the proprietary power, it will be found that there is a constant tendency to imprisonments, even for offenses at their earlier periods considered capital. And while, therefore, in the states of this Republic at least, the better people of all are heavily charged with court expenses in determining the guilt of whites accused. This State of South Carolina is now still more heavily charged with such expenses in determining the guilt of negroes for acts unquestioned. These punishments are by imprisonment or bodily inflictions. Of these there are mutilations or the lash. Neither, in the present state of feeling, can be applied. Imprisonment, therefore, is the alternative, which, with or without labor, is further onerous. It tends also to a class of outcasts. Some become unfit for work; some can not obtain it; some become hardened, and, liberated, commit offences to get back. And it is hard to see a greater evil to that state than is in such political jurisdiction of its negroes. But all of this evil was avoided by domestic discipline, administrable before emancipation. There the master had immediate evidence of the act committed and the conditions, and was under every motive to judge it justly. The act was rarely one of insubordination, and was considered without feeling, therefore. The accused was dear to him as property and as a being at his mercy, and valuable in his ability for immediate service. Finding him guilty, therefore, the master could not mutilate him, or imprison him, and could only apply the lash, which the slave preferred, which inflicted no permanent injury, and, from his master, implied no degradation, and from which, sobered and refreshed by its counter-irritation, he returned to duty a better than he was.

And such the domestic discipline to which exclusively the negro was subject before emancipation in that state, it is hardly to be doubted that he was the better of it than he is now without it. And it is as little to be doubted that every monogamic state of man, as is the monogamic family, were the better of such discipline so enforced, if in such state there were, as there are not, the conditions of its just administration. It would do away with the onerous adjudications of ordinary offenses and with jails and penitentiaries, and the production of criminal classes and the vices and immoralities which the state can not see or reach.

But in monogamic states there are not the conditions to the just administration; there are not in any such parental functionaries; nor in any would such functionaries be permitted to exercise out of their families such discipline by the lash. In all there is the assertion of individual equality inconsistent with its exercise by one adult individual over another. And there is repugnance to its exercise by one such individual of discipline over another for the reason that we are unwilling that others be in positions we would not be in ourselves, and for the reason that if we assent to the right of such discipline over others we admit that, under like conditions, it may be rightfully exercised on us, which admission no one of us can make. And while doubtful that there ever was a people so peaceful, order-provisioned and progressive, and well within their sphere as were the negro slaves of South Carolina, it is to be doubted that they were indebted for them to anything so much as their domestic discipline, and this inflicted by the lash. Few of the men now living regret or were the worse of the whippings they got at home or at school. And few negroes regretted or were the worse of the whippings they got from their masters, while all were glad that others were whipped that committed wrong or shirked their share of work.

We may object to the system, but accepting the system, we may not object to its necessary incidents. We may object to that state that it was not an Utopia of absolutely equal individuals in the enjoyment on earth of that unconditioned beatitude hitherto expected only in heaven. But accepting that state as of normally unequal human

22

beings rightfully united in relations of inequality, we can not object to the inequalities those relations imposed, or that its slaves were under masters authorized to inflict domestic discipline, and by the lash at his discretion, or that they were not educated to duties not within their sphere, but must accept that not only were the negroes not injured by these deprivations and inflictions, but was under conditions singularly fitted to his becoming not only his most, but his best that he might be his most.

But such are not the conditions of the negro in that state now. They are not in families. They mate, and in mating simulate the monogamic family, but they are not rationally sensible of its bonds of husband and wife and parent and child. Nor are they sensible of any state of their own possible of their simulations, apart from that of the whites, in that state. Nor were they willing for a state of their own apart from that of the whites. Nor were they willing for any union of their simulations with white families. These would imply the superiority of whites, from which they have been relieved. And it would seem, therefore, that the negro is in that state now to no other end than to contest with the whites for the possession of its government. And, as the negro is essentially agamic and the white monogamic, it would seem that the negro is there but to the end of heading agamic against monogamic civilization; and, as monogamic civilization has already left the agamic far in the rear of that march of man it leads, it is to be feared that the negro is here but to be exterminated. He can not be assimilated until his every trace of color or culture has disappeared.

The Jew, who has made the laws of health religious rites, and who, in consequence of such salutary training, has become so capable as to give their theology to the better human world and to place themselves in most of the governments and enterprises of that world, are not yet entirely assimilated by it, but are detected and resisted. so that only of their common sense and their economies consequent are they able to retain their places in Teutonic states.

Such common sense, and economies consequent, the negro has not. He wants no second money until his first is spent, while Jew or Teuton wants the second as much or more than he did the first. Without conserving opportunities to ends the negro can not come to a state of his own higher than that of the agamic stock; nor can he come without this to any other relation than that of a slave to the white man of that state. This relation he would not offer, nor could the white man accept it. He can not emigrate, and would not if he could. Nor will he be miscegenated. The Latin races miscegenate the Indian, but the Teutonic races of this Republic will not the negro. He cannot be deported; it would cost more than the whites could give; the whites could not send him, and he would not go.

So situated, he is an outcast in that state. And whatever the intention with respect to him of the whites of that state, or of the Republic who have put them as freemen on that state, they must incur the fate of outcasts who, rejected for failure to comply with tribal rights, can form no tribe, nor find no state or country of their own, but as it be inhabited by agamic savages.

The test of manhood is money. That is the essence of property—the reserve of the current to the coming human life. Some, of their industries and self-denials, are able to save a fund of property for themselves, their offspring and dependents. And of these the manhood is in exact proportion to the provisions for human life they have so been able to conserve.

This truth is not accepted generally, and we are apt to place the generous before the just, and the man of good intentions before the man of better works without them. But he is not properly observant who does not see that achievements and not intentions count; that the errors of life are more fatal than its crimes, and that fools are more dangerous than rascals who will not injure us without bettering themselves, while the fools, with the best intentions, may involve us and themselves in a common ruin.

This so with individuals is so with races. And the manhood of a race is tested by its capacity for conserving money; and by this test the negro is found to be much inferior to the monogamic or polygamic man. He is incapable of the economies and self-denials necessary to the provisions for his individual safety and subsistence, and especially incapable of the provisions necessary to the safety and subsistence of the state or race. And however grateful to the plea of the natural equality of man as the ground of our emancipation from the lords of England, and disposed to make it in favor of every people to whom equality is denied; and of the negro, therefore, once held as a slave and now rejected as a free man to the monogamic whites, we are unable to make that plea effective in favor of the negro, who, however naturally the equal of the whites, is not actually their equal in the monogamic civilization they have been able to establish. Nor can our recognition of his right to that equality give it to him, more than can our recognition of his right to the color of the whites. Nor, so unequal, was he wronged in his admission to an inferior position in the civilization which gave him, in its chancery, the every right he was able to enjoy, the no one of which he could have bargained for, more than could the children of the monogamic family. And we can commiserate the negro slave but as we can commiserate the child. And the wrong of releasing these slaves from their masters was as great as were that of releasing children from their parents.

As such they are in the way of contributing nothing to the man possible of the white man of that state. Nor are they in the way of producing a man possible of themselves, or even a better or more abundant man of themselves. They are without marriage in its proper sense of an union for life; nor mating, simply, do they mate early, nor do they have the children possible, nor do they educate and train their children for the works they have for them to do. Nor have they work for them to do. They shun agriculture but as they be forced to it as their only way of obtaining subsistence, and are too improvident to acquire or hold property, and are so constituted that, obtaining a sum of money, they want no more until that be spent.

. And such the situation, character and conduct, not of every individual negro in that state, but of its negroes as a class. They are not the equals, in the way of man at least, of the slaves that were in it before emancipation.

While the object and end of slaves was to the advancement of the family, to the advancement of the state, to the advancement of the race of man, the object and end of the negro there now is not to these advancements, but to the possession of the state for what uses they can make of it. They are not conscious of their objects and ends, as are not the whites of their objects and ends, and as are not any natural beings, plant or animal. But they would individually live to their possibilities of living, and in this would substitute their natural savagery for the civilization they find existing. And they are the better to the ends of man but as their native savagery be better than the civilization acquired by the whites. Nor is there other natural reason for their being there. There is economic reason in the present want of their labor by the whites, and political reason in the want of their votes by politicians seeking nominations to the Presidency, which they can get from competitors in no other way. But beside these there are no other reasons for their being there, or natural reason in the march of man for their being at all, except as supporters of the whites. And it is quite clear that in their efforts to live into and live down the whites, and to take their states, and substitute their savagery for the civilization existing, they are not so better or so good to the ends of man as were the slaves in living into and in living up to the civizations of the whites.

Nor without this, and regarding them simply as a race of human beings to their most and best possible, are they better or so good as were the slaves. They are not so ordered, industrious, educated and trained to useful works as were the slaves. Nor have they individually the offices and employments for which they are fitted. Nor are the products of their labors so conserved and applied to their uses. Nor are they so at peace with each other and the whites. Nor are they protected and cared for by an intelligence and power superior to their own. Nor are they as contented or loyal to duty as were the slaves. Nor do they live as well and as long as did the slaves. Nor are they as free from diseases as were the slaves. Nor do they increase as did the slaves. And it is reasonably certain, therefore, that, while the slaves advanced in numbers as had no other people, the negroes are doomed to disappear from that state. And as they can not be assimilated and will not be miscegenated, and can not be deported, or take the state, or be other than its outcasts; it is as certain that they must ultimately cease to exist. And in so living and so ceasing to live, they are not so better than the slave who lived as no negro had ever lived before, and who but of forces from without had lived forever, or so long, at least, as this earth be habitable.

It may be that the negro of that state will not be entirely exterminated, for it may be that the whites in their contests of parties for possession of its government, its funds may be wasted or forced into the hands of a party leader, and that the normal state without funds of its own may cease to exist. And that the whites, without such state, may become so demoralized and dissipated as to be unable to sustain themselves against or above the negro, and that both may subside into an indistinguishable mass, in which the less artificial negro may survive. But it is

hardly possible that the negro can live to such demoralization of the whites.   And certain, therefore, that if he do
it will be as a savage, such as he was in Africa.   And
extinction or savagery his fate, it must be admitted that
the negro is not better than the slave who, at every instant
of his actual existence, was more and better than he had
been to himself.   And more and better than he had been
to his race and the race of man.

CHAPTER XXXVII.

AND THE STATE ITSELF SO BETTER THAN IT IS NOW.

It was not only so better then than it is now in its ability to sustain a larger population to the population possible, but in its ability to sustain itself as a sovereign human state and as a natural and normal human state; and to order its population, and to provision its population, and to act as a normal human state with others such in populating the earth; and as such state in a confederacy with others such in populating the territory held by the confederacy and in sustaining the integrity of such confederacy, and that to its position as a sovereign state with others of the earth. But it is not so now. It is not so able to sustain the population possible or itself as a sovereign state, or as a normal human state, or to order its population or to provision its population, or to act with others such in populating the earth, or with others such in a confederacy to populate the territory held by it and to sustain the integrity of such confederacy, and to sustain the confederacy to its position with others as a sovereign nation of the earth.

It was then so able to sustain a larger population than it can now and this to the population possible· There were in it two races, the one agamic and the other monogamic, incapable of miscegenation, and these unequal, therefore, in the way of man, but united in relations of inequality such as that the one was to order, the other to obey. And these engaged in agriculture from which there were the provisions possible and these conserved to the human life possible, of which life possible there was the population possible; and this continuing to the population ultimately possible. And it was also able to sustain itself as a sovereign human state.

It was then the member of a confederacy of states, each sovereign in that there was no higher human state to rule it. But it is not now such state but only the province of a republic which, if not itself sovereign, has yet the power to rule that state.

It may be doubted that the Republic itself is truly sovereign; in that it has no natural head but only the head which from time to time a victorious party gives it. Which itself must fall when another rises to take it off. That party for the period of its brief existence is the head to rule the body of the state. And it may be doubted that the state itself is sovereign and able to vindicate its continued existence under a head so continually subject to be taken off.

But if this Republic be sovereign it is not a normally sovereign state. The normally sovereign state must not only be able to vindicate its existence as a state, but as a state in the way of man to the man possible. And to this it must have property, and the patriarchal power of distributing that property, and of regulating its people in the use of it. Such is the agamic stocks of offspring under the orders of unmarried mothers. And such are the tribes of wives and children under the authority of polygamic male parents. And such are the states of monogamic families under governments appointed by the holders of their properties. And such were the states of unequal races under governments appointed by the higher race. But such is not the state of monogamic families whose properties and people are under the authority of a major party of adult males in no natural relation to each other or the state. And such is this Republic now, which, however it be able to vindicate its existence as a state, can not do so as a normal human state. It is not in advancement of man to the man possible, but only in advancement of the minor of two parties to a majority over the major.

No sooner does the one become established in the government than it becomes patriotism in the other to pull it down that it may take its place; the properties of the state are used by either party to advance itself. And quite clear that this is not to the man possible, it is as clear that this Republic is not a normally sovereign human state.

But such was South Carolina. She entered the union as a sovereign state, and making no renunciation of her sovran, she was as sovereign in the union as she would have been without it. And she was normally such state. Her population consisted of two races, the one black and the other white, without the possibility of their differences being obliterated. In the whites exclusively were the properties and powers of the state, and they were individually tasked to their execution. In the negroes there were the orders of masters, and they were individually tasked to their execution. Both were engaged in provisions for advancing man. There was no idleness, inefficiency or waste, and it is to be doubted that there ever was a state which, in the way of man, did so advance, or did so much to help the man of unequal races to the advancement possible.

She gave more than her share of homes to the descendants of revolutionary sires, extruded by foreign immigration from the North; she gave of her native population much to people the states of the Southwest; she gave to these states an example in the way of order, economy and progress of what a state of unequal races could do in advancement of the race of man; and this the more efficiently from the employments of her people in agriculture.

As man advances from the animal two-footed and two-handed he is inclined to shirk the drudgeries of agriculture. There is the feeling that the man of the hoe is fit for this and for nothing else, and that they are fit for a sphere above that of the man of the hoe. All would clamber to that sphere, and quit the country for the town, and agriculture for the arts, and a life of labor in support of a state for a life of dexterity in standing on such supports, or in entering an ideal Utopia without them.

But to the subsistence of any advanced people, agriculture is necessary. The agamic savage may live on reptiles, fish, or vermin, and the polygamic barbarian on game, flocks and herds. But to the caste of polygamic tribes, even, agriculture is important, and to the state of monogamic families it is the condition of existence.

No monogamic state ever started to exist but upon that basis. And the real magnitude of every such state is in proportion to such base. Of its more abundant and productive agriculture it is able to sustain a more abundant population; of its more abundant population it is able to maintain a more abundant agriculture; of the superabundant products of its agriculture it is able to support, not those only engaged in agriculture, but others beside, in furnishing conveniences and facilities for those in agriculture. So that of successful agriculture there is not only its agricultural population, but the possibility of a much more abundant population of auxiliary artisans, to whom, as to the agricultural population itself, agriculture is the condition of existence.

But while to the monogamic state of a single race agriculture is the condition of its existence at the start, there is, as I have said, in people free, the disposition to withdraw from it to arts and commerce, as it advances, with few or none left to carry it on. And there tends to be a population, therefore, not dependent on the products of the soil, but upon the products of their own inventions, for support, and to a social pie, therefore, with but an upper crust.

But such is not the tendency of a state of unequal races. The lower race is more productive of the means of subsistence wanted by both in agriculture than in any other employment. The higher race is more willingly engaged through slaves in agriculture than in any other employment. Such state of unequal races, tending of their interests to agriculture, was South Carolina; such state of a single race is South Carolina now. And the state then tending to agriculture was capable of more abundant provisions for the subsistence of its people than it is now when it turns away from it.

And it was so better in its ability to give safety to its people. It made the provisions all other peoples wanted; it wanted the fabrics of all other peoples' make. There was no cause of friction with any other human state; and without an enemy or adversary, there was no reason why its people might not be absolutely free of danger from without. But if without conceivable reason it had been attacked from without, it was abundantly able to defend itself. Its every municipality was a citadel of devoted loyalty. Its natural captain had been instant to defend it to the last, and the every slave had been a devoted soldier to sustain him. It was their home, and the only home they had ever had, or could have, or were fit for, or had conceived of, and they would have fought, suffered and died for it. And the state might have been beaten in the field and overrun by armies, but if the slaves had been armed and directed to defend their homes, they would have done it with a desperate efficiency no other people have yet exhibited. In this the state would have endured more than, from whatever motive, a foreign state could inflict, while, without conceivable motive to invasion, it was not rationally possible that it could ever be tasked to such endurance.

And so safe of danger from without, it was equally safe of danger from within. So composed and regulated were the municipalities, and so intent on the provisions for their own subsistence, and independent of each other but for the kindly offices proper to such kindred associations, there was less occasion for hostilities between them than for such between simple monogamic families adjacent to each other. Nor could hostilities between adjacent municipalities affect the safety of the state, as fueds between families do not. And the people of the state were safe, therefore, from every danger except that of subjugation by the general government. But this was not to have been apprehended. And against this the state was better able to defend itself when it had 400,000 slaves to help it than it is now with these slaves against it.

And so more and better as a sovereign human state in its self-administration of self-originated patriarchal power, and so able to order, provision and defend her people then than she is now. She then exhibited in character and conduct, not only her fitness for such state, but to be the leader of such states. She had not, perhaps, a clearer sense of the situation than had other states, or that inequality is the right of unequals, as equality is the right of equals; and that slavery was the right of the negro as the only condition upon which he could share the civilization of the white man, or existence with him.

But she had a clear sense of her existence as a state of a race of whites in charge of a race of negroes to the largest and best state possible of both; and that the Confederacy was but a copartnership through which she could have the aid of others in that work.

And such her conceptions of the situation, she acted on them with the utmost circumspection and propriety. When she saw that Congress was disposed to improve one state at the expense of another, she promptly entered her protest. When, later, she saw it disposed to put import duties on manufactured products from abroad, increasing thus the price she had to pay for them, she again protested; and when Congress persisted she assumed the power, as one of the partners forming the federal copartnership, to declare the acts *ultra vires* and void; and when troops were sent to coerce her to submission she submitted to the indignity without an outbreak. And when a compromise was effected, in an agreement that the imports should never be beyond the wants of the government, she abandoned her ordinance of nullification;

and when they did go beyond, and a surplus of revenue was found, and divided pro rata among the states, she refused her share; and when the purpose of Congress to tax imports as a policy of protecting industries at the North to the detriment of her own, she called a convention to determine whether the state should secede alone from the Republic. And when this reported that it should not alone, and that other states were not ready to concur with her in that measure for existing causes, she again subsided.

But when the Republican party of the North became powerful enough to elect a President and a majority of Congress and take the government, and under it to exercise what powers it pleased over her, and other states, she could hesitate no longer. Either she was the political entity she was when she entered the confederacy, or her vital existence had been absorbed by that body. She did not realize its absorption, and in vindication of its continued existence, she withdrew from it and resumed her sovereign powers. And with an order and solemnity becoming the occasion. She permitted no unbecoming. exhibition of popular feeling. Her secession convention was of the older, ablest and most honored men of the state. They sent commissioners to the Republican party of the North and to the states at the South, advising them of her action and the reasons for it, and expressing the hope that her sister states at the South would join her in the movement, and that the Republican party, representing the states of the North, would recognize and admit the propriety and justice of her action. And when her sister states did join her in secession, and pending negotiation the republican government consented to the preservation of the *status quo*, but a few nights after removed the garrison at Fort Moultrie to Fort Sumpter, till then unoccupied but supposed to be impregnable, and when this was condoned with the understanding that it was not to be provisioned, and when this was violated by the effort of the Star of the West to reach it with provision, she dared to fire upon it and thus break the peace of the Republic.

And when the Southern Confederacy had formed and the party still held Fort Sumpter with the expressed determination not to give it up or concur in any *modus vivendi* consistent with its occupation not as a menace; and it was determined that it should be fired on — South Carolina did the firing. And when in consequence Virginia was about to be invaded she sent 6,000 troops ordered and equipped to defend her. And during the war which followed sent largely more than her voting population to the fields of battle. And when the fate she challenged fell upon her she sunk with her ermined robes around her, unsmirched by an unbecoming act; and with her expiring breath asserting still her right to live as a state of unequal human races, and leaving a record of peace, order, propriety and progress toward the man possible not theretofore presented by any human state; and with only the one single but fatal error to mar it: that she did not realize the issue she invoked, and marshal her means to meet it.

She had millions of dollars worth of cotton which she could have placed to her credit in Europe before it was necessary to fire upon Fort Sumpter. And if she had done this the other seceding states had done the same. And there had been $250,000,000 to the credit of the Confederacy before a blow was struck.

She had also 50,000 able-bodied male slaves inured to labor, discipline and order, which she could have put at Washington before the Republican party had determined to invade the South. If she had done so the other seceding states had done the same, and there had been 500,000 trained troops in possession of the national capitol before the Republican party had had a corps to dispossess them. And it is safe to say that the Republican party had not attempted their dispossession. The Democratic party at the North had not helped them. And, as the South will have wanted but security of her right to share for her own protection in the common government, a dual government had been established such as Mr. Calhoun had died in the effort to express, or the South had been allowed to establish a government of her own.

But, if contrary to all reasonable probabilities, the Republican party had forced the Democratic party at the North to join them in a crusade against the South, and had been able to dispossess the South of the capitol and drive her armies back, and invade and overrun the South, they had not found it a state of one race fighting for the right to hold another in subjugation, but a state of both races combined to the preservation of their existences in common. And when the armies of the Confederacy had been broken there had been a guerilla warfare more inveterate than is threatened in the Philippines which would have enabled the South to endure more than the North would have been able to inflict.

But these, from an imperfect perception of the situation, she did not. And the Confederacy fell, and with it fell the state we are considering. And from its ruins rose the present state, whose first official act was more fatal to it than had been any to the antecedent state.

That had been subjugated by the Republican party assisted actively or passively by the Democratic party at the North. And to the Republican party there should have been submission. With the victorious army still in hand it could have stated and kept the terms of subjugation as could not the Democratic party at the North.

But too distracted to be passive the new state listened to overtures from that party through Mr. Johnston, President from the death of Mr. Lincoln, and hoping for another term. These were to the effect that if she with other states of the South should liberate her slaves, and do whatever else might be necessary to remove the differences between her and the states of the North, her people could come in with the Democrats of the North, outvote the Republicans and take the government, and thus participate in the administration of the victory over themselves which the Republicans had won.   And deluded by that hope she did liberate her slaves.   And thus performed a most fatal act.   The Republican party, as a war measure, had declared the negroes free.   But that was of no effect upon them in the hands of former masters without going further and actually breaking the bonds by which they had been held.   And this the Republican party had not done.   It had captured the South and that as a property was more valuable to it with its slaves than without.   With these it would have continued agricultural and to raise the raw material for the North to commerce and manufacture; and to be customers rather than competitor of the North.   And the liberation of her slaves was the last thing that party had required, or permitted, if it had the power to prevent it.

And the possession of her slaves had been of inestimable advantage to the people of that state.   They would have continued as guarantees of the peace, order, prosperity and morals of the state.   They had continued as loyal to masters as honorable as they had been.   There had been no negroes contesting with the whites the right to govern the state; or violations of white females by maddened negro males; or courts and jails replete with negro criminals; or negroes contesting with white laborers for employment; or the war of races for existence that must ultimately come.   The state had continued agricultural until some slaves could be more profitably employed in incidental arts and manufactures.   But agriculture is the normal basis of the human state.   No state has ever become great without it.   Nor would the North have been what it is without its basis of agriculture at the South.   But slavery, transcending agriculture, had entered arts.   And the liberation of her slaves, therefore, was a fatal error.

23

But, committing this, the state went on in continued submission to the dictates of the Democratic party at the North in the hope of its ultimately taking the government from the Republican;. and that she would receive a portion, however small, of the spoils.   And in this she has submitted to indignities.   Her men have not been permitted to appear prominently in Democratic councils.   When that party has been successful they have been rarely honored with unimportant offices of state.   And, while now it is apparent that the best the new state could have done was to accept the terms the Republican party saw proper to propose, it is as apparent that the worst it could have done was to attempt submission to the Democratic party.

And while so fatal was her first official act the new state has fallen off in every way from the standard of the old.   She allows her public funds to be scrambled for by politicians.   She permits the candidates for her highest offices to seek them by unbecoming means.   She gives to those who have learned and performed the duties of those offices no security that they may continue in them longer than they may be wanted by those more efficient in party service.   And she holds herself subject to the uses of the party which by whatever means is able to secure the largest popular vote.   Nor does she require her people to marry, or to marry early, or marrying to have the children possible, or to educate them for duties they may have. for them to do.   But requires them to be put upon the state to be educated.   And she allows her women to contract, and encourages them to assert themselves and to contest employment with men, and to support themselves and live single, however inconsistent that may be with the continuation of their race.   And in every way exhibits that the continuation and enlargement of her race to the man possible is not the object of her existence.   But that she exists but to the end that her people individually shall take the largest share they can of the provisions for the support of man accumulated by the antecedent state.

And of this take the largest individual employment possible. In this the present state is as different as it can be from the antecedent state. And to the ends of man in nature is not the equal of that state.

And as the negro of that state now is not the equal of the negro of that state then, and the white man of that state now is not the equal of the white of that state then, and the state now not the equal of the state then— in fitness for the ends of man on earth — it is clear that in the lights of these experiences, at least, the state of unequal races united in relations of inequality is not only possible but is the state intended by the cause of man intending that man shall be the man possible. And that if such unions be not possible again in this Republic they will be elsewhere.

CHAPTER XXXVIII.

There are now different human races. The agamic,
polygamic and monogamic; and the agamic in stocks;
and the polygamic in tribes and castes; and the monogamic in states. And the agamic in Africa, and the polygamic in Asia, and the monogamic in Europe and America.
And each of these, if it were alone, would be able to
overspread the earth but unequally. The population of
the agamic race were sparse, that of the polygamic race
were denser, and that of the monogamic race were yet
denser, while yet, as I have said, of neither were there
the population possible.

But while neither is alone upon the earth, and either
is able to expand indefinitely, their circles of expansion
must intersect. And at every such intersection there will
be the issue of existence. And every such issue must be
determined either in the extermination of the weaker by
the stronger, or in an union of the two in an intermediate
race of both. And in all their earlier intersections the
stronger will exterminate the weaker, and alone survive
to what fortunes it can individually find. But in their
later intersections it will not exterminate the weaker, but
will take it up to the subordinate offices it may be able to
fill in an economy of both, to the safety and subsistence
of both. This will be their unions, and such unions there
will be, and of the monogamic race as lords over the
agamic and polygamic races as commons. These will be
domestic in the unions of the individuals of the monogamic race exercising the patriarchal power over the

agamic and polygamic races in possession of the proletariate powers consistent with the patriarchal in their lords.

The monogamic race is strongest. More men and
women marry; of their marriages there are more children.
Of these, under the care of both parents, more attain to
maturity and usefulness in support and preservation of
the state. These, so raised, educated and trained to the
preservations of their individual existences in advancement of their families, in advancement of the states of
such families, will have more of enterprise and capacity
for successful enterprises than will individuals of the
agamic and polygamic races; of these enterprises there
will be more of provisions for peace or war than there can
be in lower races. There will thus be more and better
individuals in more and better families, in more and better
states, than there can be in any single race. And this
race, so constituted in conflict with lower races, must
supersede them.

And there must be conflicts. The monogamic state
of monogamic families of individuals, each in preservation of his own existence in families, each in preservation
of its existence in such state, must himself preserve his
existence as he can. And in this state and race must come
in contact with adjacent states and races, and in this must
expel them or absorb them if it have the power. It will
not have the power to expel or absorb adjacent monogamic states, and with these it must make the compo-
sitions necessary to their separate existences. But it
will have the power to absorb or expel the stocks and
tribes of lower races. And it will absorb them or expel
them. It can not, if it would, admit them to a limitation
of its own existence, and it would not if it could.

The proclivities of its interests in continuation of its
existence upon its moral nature are as remorseless as are
those of gravitation in its physical nature. And as it must
physically fall without props, so must it morally upon
lands in lower races unable to defend them. And such .

will be the lands of lower races adjacent to such monogamic state. Its people will migrate to such lands, practically vacant, when inconveniently crowded on their own.
And the state itself will take jurisdiction of such lands,
however occupied by lower races, when it has the motive
of interest to do so. It will have such motive. And thus
in theory of the monogamic, as the strongest human race
existing now, there will be its dominion over the lower
races of the earth, to whatever the effects of that dominion on the human race resulting.

Nor is this conclusion dependent upon theory alone,
but is as clearly indicated in inductions of phenomena.

There are monogamic states in Europe in each of
which there are classes as lords and commons, in contest
for the patriarchal power, from which the commons are
willing to retire to lands without lords, if there be such,
on which they might exercise a patriarchal power over
themselves. There were such lands in America under
agamic Indians. And there are now such lands in Africa
under agamic negroes. And as the commons of Europe
then migrated to America, so now they migrate to Africa,
for that patriarchal autonomy they can not immediately
find in their native states.

Their states also, still under lords, would move upon
other lands, and, following their commons to Africa in the
expectation of continuing their power over them, they
would take jurisdiction over the native stocks of Africa,
and also over the tribes and castes of Asia, to which their
colonizing emigrants have not yet gone. And in this latter
movement of imperial jurisdiction over foreign tribes and
castes this leading monogamic state of North America is
ready to participate. And under such conditions it is
reasonably certain that Africa, in time, will be occupied by
monogamic states, in relations of dependence or independence of European states, and to the exclusion of the
agamic races not in union with the monogamic race

invading them, and not thus becoming monogamic by induction, and thus parts of the invading race.

And it is as certain that Asia and the Pacific islands will be invaded, and thus be in states as provinces of the monogamic states of Europe.and America.

And it is as certain that these states, whether in Africa or Asia, will be of the monogamic and agamic or polygamic races united in relations of inequality, such, in effect, as were those of whites and negroes lately in this Republic.

The monogamic states of Europe will colonize Africa. The lands of Africa occupied by agamic negroes are in the same relation to the monogamic whites of Europe as were the lands of America occupied by agamic Indians. And in that the lands of America were colonized by emigrants from Europe, there is reason that so will be the lands of Africa.

There are now more men in Europe ready to migrate than there were then. In every monogamic state of Europe there are contests of lords and commons for the patriarchal power. In all the commons are more abundant and more possessed of their right to participate in that power than they ever were before. They also have the means of movement, and motives to movement they had not. They are now sustained and encouraged in emigrations by their parent states as they were not earlier. And it was to have been expected, therefore, that there would be such emigrations to Africa if the facts did not appear.

But they do appear. The leading states of Europe claim sovereignty over sections of that continent. To these their emigrants have gone, and started colonies. There is every reason that these colonies shall grow until in each there be the monogamic population possible, and in the whole of Africa such population; and that that continent, so populated and cultivated, as it may be, shall become the granary of the human world. And this contingent but upon that the colonists shall unite with natives to that end.

And they will unite with natives. Those of England may not at their start. That, the first of monogamic states now in Europe, is imperial. Its commons have so encroached upon its lords that the majority of the House of Commons is now the government. And this majority, instead of abolishing the king and lords, as they could do to the enjoyment of their power, are content to put these forward as exponents and agents to their dominion over other peoples of the earth, who are permitted to exist but as they accept that dominion and be able to sustain themselves under its exactions. The colonists of England at their start, therefore, may not unite, or be allowed to unite, with natives in human economies of both. But without this they must exterminate the natives, who, without this, will be unable to sustain themselves under such taskmasters uninterested in their preservation. Such extermination will be in every way unprofitable, while the acceptance of natives to the offices they may be able to fill in an economy of both will be every way profitable. And the emigrants of England, despite the requisitions of their home government, will ultimately unite with natives in better states of both than are possible of either race alone; or, if they do not, the colonies of England will fall before those of other monogamic states of Europe in which there will be such unions. The other monogamic states of Europe are not so imperial as is England. In all there are the same contests of lords and commons for the patriarchal power, but they are not so far advanced. In them the majorities of their Houses of Commons are not yet their governments. Nor in any of them are the powers of such houses as great as is that of the house in England. They are not so imperial, therefore, nor are their emigrants as imperious as are those of England; and, while in their contests with lords their commons have been obliged to assert the natural equality of man as the ground of their right in proportions of their numbers to participate in power, they have not advanced so far as to dominate their lords and make them their instruments in exercise of extra territorial and imperial authority. In their colonizations, therefore, the emigrating commons are less considerate of the standing and fortunes of their parent states than of their own. And less regardful of the rights of man they have been asserting in their parent states than of their own under new conditions. And so that if they can benefit themselves by uniting with natives in relations of inequality such as that, while they shall be masters, the natives shall be virtually slaves, they will not hesitate to do so.

The colonies so uniting will forge ahead of those that do not. And if the English shall persist in exclusion of natives they must fall behind and ultimately fail. They will lose the lives and labors of a lower class, and the peace and harmony of classes in natural relation to each other, and the virtues of honor and loyalty there are in such relations. And of such colonies of immigrants and natives there will be analogously such relations to each other as before the war were the whites and negroes of the slave-holding states of this Republic. But with the material difference that the slave-holding colonies will have natural heads to conserve their bodies, as the slave-holding states did not. Of these the head was the Republic, affirming the natural right of equality in man and the wrong of slavery in breach of that equality. And without such natural head they were at disadvantage. Accepting such unnatural head they could not affirm the right of their own existences, or make provisions to defend them. They could not say that they were right, but went before the world in assertion of an admitted wrong. They had $250,000,000 worth of cotton, which could have been placed in England to their credit before the firing on Fort Sumter. They had near one million able-bodied slaves, of devoted loyalty and innured to discipline and service, the half of whom they could have put under their masters on the field before the battle of Bull Run. Nor was it necessary that they should have fired upon Fort Sumter, which while quiet did no harm. Nor was it necessary that they should have seceded, by other than protest, or have withdrawn their Senators and Representatives in Congress, who, with the Democrats of the North, could have prevented any legislation injurious to their peculiar institution. Without such head there were these omissions and commissions, and the consequent fall of these states, from which is the conclusion that their systems were imperfect. But it is easy to see that if these states had had a natural and conservative head they could have stood indefinitely, in the union or out of it. Each slave-holding colony of Africa will have its head, and it is easy to see that with heads instructing them the uses to be made of natives, the every other colony will accept of natives; and that if the English do not, but persist in exterminating the natives, they will not long survive the natives exterminated, if before this they shall not have abandoned that policy from the failure of the parent state to sustain them in it; whence it will appear that in Africa, if not elsewhere, there will be unions of unequal races to a race of both.

And for reasons equally conclusive, there will be such unions also in Asia. Asia is polygamic and Africa agamic. And it will be found that the tribes and castes of Asia will offer little more effective resistance to the spread of monogamic civilization than will the agamic stocks of Africa. Accepting that man at this earth is to the man possible, we must accept that the mode of man which gives the best results will prevail over others not so efficient, and that if the monogamic mode be more efficient in production of man that mode will prevail over the polygamic or agamic mode upon every land on which their circles of expansion intersect; and that, intersecting with the polygamic mode in Asia, as with the agamic in Africa, the monogamic mode will prevail in Asia as in Africa, however in Asia there be not the domestic unions of the races in relations of inequality which are promised in Africa.

And in Asia these races will intersect. The proclivities of states to the continuations. and enlargements of their existences are as potent and persistent as are those of individuals. The states of Europe, possessed of political autonomy and superior military power, will be better able to establish and maintain jurisdictions over sections of Asia held by polygamic tribes and casts than are individual immigrants in Africa over individuals of agamic states; and for a time, at least, and that not distant, the states will assert such jurisdictions, and will become, in relation to the natives, a superior caste—such as originally were the hill tribes to the peaceful tribes they conquered in production of the castes.

It is not probable, as I have said, that any one caste has originated through evolution of a polygamic tribe. But it is more probable that tribes, all predatory, on fertile plains have become peaceful and productive to be subjugated by adjacent hill tribes still predatory, but themselves becoming peaceful to be in turn subjugated by other hill tribes still predatory, to become peaceful in their turn to be subjugated, and so on until there were series of tribes reciprocally dependent as castes, priestly, militant, industrial and servile.

And it is probable that the monogamic state, in taking authority over a district of polygamic Asia, will be as were the hill tribes to the peaceful tribes.

But, whatever the relations of the invading monogamic states of Europe to the invaded sections of polygamic Asia, it is reasonably certain that the states of Europe will invade. Such movements must follow from the fact that the monogamic states are of greater gravity than the polygamic tribes and castes, and as denser fluids must overflow and supersede the rarer. And not only is this true in theory but such movements are in fact on foot. England and France have footings on the Indias;

Holland, Portugal and Spain upon Pacific islands; Russia upon Asiatic Siberia, Manchuria and Corea.   And this Republic as a new monogamic state has taken jurisdiction of Pacific islands.   While all of these together are taking counsel of the fate of China.

It is not probable that they will agree peacefully, buc probable that they will war with each other as to their shares in that polygamic province doomed to subjugation and dismemberment by monogamic states.   But, so or not, or whatever the terms of composition, or however protracted and disastrous the conflict, it is reasonably certain that no one of the terms of composition will be the restoration of Asia to its original polygamic autonomy.

And it is as certain that the relations ultimately established between the races so in contact will be those of domestic inequality.   To this both will make resistence. And for a time the invading state will be content with imperial jurisdiction, simply, over its province contented to receive it.   But in time it will be found that this is not the way to the best and most of both.   So apart there will be hostilities active or passive; each must assert its right of individual existence at the expense of the other; the one must exact what the other can not perform, or the other perform what the one can not exact; and in these contests there will be conditions inconsistent with the continued existences of the states of both.

But as man will live as he can, and as parties can not live by fighting, but can by uniting with each other, they will unite; and in domestic relations of inequality— the only relations of unequals possible.   And there will be such unions in Asia as in Africa, and ultimately, for the same reason, in every section of the habitable earth. The only question is whether more men can live of such unions than without.   Whatever men may think about it man is here to live, and but to live to his possibility of living, as the fluid is to flow to its possibility of flowing.

And, however it is beneath the dignity of man that he crawl about the earth with as little ability to regulate his crawling as has water, it is a serious and melancholy fact that he has not more ability to regulate his movements than has water. The individual man may regulate his movements to his means of living, but he is as without ability to regulate the movements of a mass of men, each in preservation of his individual existence by such means, as is the drop the mass of water. Between men in masses there may be concert and cooperation as to its operations not apparent in the resolutions of water, but it is hard to say that the resolutions of bodies of men are less from the proclivities of their individual men in preservation of their individual existences than are the resolutions of masses of water from the proclivities of their drops. The individual man has not the power to initiate an activity without volition or a volition without motive. And the individual, therefore, is as inert as is the drop of water, without motive from the universe as had the water. And as there is water when it can be, and but as it can be, on the surface of the earth, so is there man as he can be and but as he can be on that surface. And without man have, as he has not, the power of originating his motive he will in time exist in unions of unequal races in Africa and Asia as naturally as are the seas about their shores, or as oil and water at unequal levels in the same vessel.

This truth is not admitted. And educated, able and honest-minded men are assured that while other beings come to what they can be of a life in nature of the universe, man comes to what at any time he is of a moral being in himself. And that animals two-footed and two-handed chancing to be upon the earth can of that moral being become men, and be immediately agamic, polygamic or monogamic, and in stocks, tribes, castes, and states, as it may please them.

And proof enough of this misconception is in the actions of the men of this Republic. Its independence was achieved by as able men as ever were, perhaps, in states as properly constructed as were ever states, which went at once to the formation of a general state to preserve its own existence, but in consistence with the separate equal and independent existences of the states composing it. And proof that this undertaking was ineffective is in the fact that in less than eighty years this general state subjected one section of the states composing it to the uses of another.

Further proof of incapacity is in the fact that the men of that section moving the government to subjugate the other to its uses were mainly immigrants, or the descendents of immigrants coming after the war of independence, while the men of the section subjugated were mainly the descendents of revolutionary sires.

In further proof: The men of the Revolution and their immediate descendants had imported negro slaves from Africa to help them in felling forests and cultivating lands while, from the insufficiency of these, white immigrants from Europe also came. The slaves with their masters gravitated to agriculture to the South. The immigrants and their descendants settled themselves at the North to art and commerce the agricultural products of the South. Of this both sections were equally the better. But the section of the North, from its larger voting population, was able to take the government, and took it. The section of the South, unable to submit to the wrong, seceded. The section of the North required the government to coerce them back without their slaves. Who so coerced with still their negroes, though not as slaves, obliged to live, and to work that they might live, would not have continued to raise the raw material to be manufactured and commerced by the North, but would have concluded to manufacture and commerce it themselves. And these results, not intended by the men involved of, more than average ability, are in proof of man's inability to intellectually project his fortunes.

But, beside these, there were negro slaves brought from Africa; and from savagery to civilization; and from masters who might kill and eat them to masters pledged to the extent of their fortunes that they should come to no evitable harm. And under whom the 450,000 originally imported increased in little more than one hundred years to near eight millions. Whose condition was so commiserated by those who did not own them that they were willing to take the union and risk war—not that the negroes be set free, but that the justice of their commiseration be vindicated. While to the simplest apprehension no 450,000 people were ever so blessed as were these negroes in being brought from Africa. And no 8,000,000 people were ever so cursed as were those negroes set free, who, not becoming monogamic white men by emancipation, and so, assimilable by their former masters, can have no hope of continued existences but as they may hope to subjugate their former masters, or live as outcasts at their mercy. And instead, therefore, of a state of exceptionally perfect peace and order in the Southern states there is in prospect a war of races to continue in constantly increasing barbarities until the negro or the white man, or both, shall disappear. And in this there is further proof of man's inability to project his fortunes.

There is proof also in that while the negroes can hope to live here at least but with white man and with white men but as they may take the employments white men may have to give them; and, while white men can want of the negro not instruction but manual labor merely in the works they may have for them to do, it is required that negroes be educated as are white men; and to the works of white men; and in competition with white men; and it is easy to see that such education of the negro to compete with white men instead of accepting subordinate employments were as fatal to him as were the poisons purchasable by the money his education costs.

There is proof also in that while the men of this Republic expect it to go on advancing in works by children superior to those of their parents, which were possible only as they be educated by parents to what they have for them to do, they also expect and require that children be educated by the state even against the wishes of their parents, to what it has not for them to do.

They also require that women shall vote, contract and take the employments and habiliments of men, so far as it may please them, however this may withdraw them from their maternal offices in continuation of the race. And while there is the expectation and purpose that this Republic shall be the leading state of the human world, and the belief that it is now the torch of liberty enlightening the world, they are content that its government be in majorities of adult males without the qualifications of either parentage or property, who must be in parties, therefore, the major to hold and the miner to retake the government, while the object of neither is to advance the state to what it should be, but only of the one to down the other. To this it is the policy of either to present issues the other can not accept under vigilance of the body of adult males, each of whom will have the share he can get from such administration of the state.

To either of these parties nothing is right that is of disadvantage, nothing wrong that is profitable. To either success is not only the criterion, but the test and rule of merit. And the only state possible, therefore, is that to result from the permanent establishment of the one of these parties in arbitrary authority over the other.

That is not the state which man originating himself would have. Nor is it the state he would have in regulation of himself. But it is the state into which individual men of God, in preservation of the irindividual existence and becoming monogamic without becoming masters of a

lower race, must ultimately run.   And it is to the mori-
bund state, as the decrepitude of age to the individual.

And such the results of existence to the men of this
Republic, the ablest and most favored of men, they are not
such as man self-originated and self-directed would come
to.   And, in that they are not, there is reason that man is
not of his own invention or to himself individually, or to
ends of his own appointment.   But that he is here to the
man possible by the ways possible, and these of unequal
races united in relations of inequality, as were whites and
negroes in these Southern states.   And that these relations having come before their time, but necessary to the
course of man on earth, will be renewed at their proper
times in other states.

24

CHAPTER XXXIX.

These, I have assumed, will occur through colonizations in Africa or imperialisms becoming colonizations in
Asia. And so established on either continent they will
not be again dissolved. To their dissolutions it will be
necessary that these states be under governments of adult
males. That of these the majority shall be monogamic
whites. And that of these the majority shall be without
such unions with the lower races. And these states will
not be under such governments. Nor of the higher race
will the majority be without unions with the lower.

These states, wherever formed, will not be under governments of adult males. Such males are in governments
only of mongamic states, and in these only after the commons shall have become possessed of the patriarchal
power originally in lords. They will have become possessed of that power by prescriptions or revolutions;
these will have been effected through such males who
thus becoming possessed of that power will hold it. But
through prescriptions or revolutions effected by adult
males there will not be the patriarchal power in the whites
of a state of whites and negroes formed in Africa, or of
whites and yellow races formed in Asia. The monogamic
whites will be the natural lords of the agamic blacks or
polygamic yellow races, with whom, as commons, they
may unite as lords. And as there will not be the agency
of adult males to establish that power, there will not be
the males to claim its exercise. Every such union of
these unequal races will be a natural municipality of which
the male parent of the white family will be chief magistrate, as is the male parent of the monogamic family, and

the state will be but the aggregate of these municipalities, the government of which will be by appointment, not of adult males as in the adult monogamic states, but of the male parents of the white families.

The whites, therefore, were not under governments of such males. Nor were there in any such state a majority of whites. Every monogamic male parent of that race able to take and hold in service one individual of the lower race will take him if he is to be had; and he were to be had. The European immigrant to Africa, for instance, will meet millions of the negro race in stocks at wars with each other, in which those only will be taken alive who can be sold or held as slaves. These the immigrant will take for what he may be pleased to give for them. And, taking one, he were the better able to take more. He were moved by every consideration of interest and humanity to do so. And it can not happen, therefore, that in any such state there will be more whites than negroes.

And, unreasonable that in any such state there should be a majority of whites, it were the more unreasonable that there should be a majority of whites without negro slaves; and without such unions, therefore, with the lower race.

This so in Africa will be so in Asia. Monogamic civilization in Europe and America in turning back upon the polygamic civilization of Asia will do so, not by colonizations or emigrants as it will in Africa, but by proconsular establishments. The states of Europe and America in such movements will be imperial. Each will take possession of its section as a conquered province to be ruled by emissaries, military and political. But in time the province will not be able to endure what such rulers may inflict, or such rulers be able to inflict what the province can endure. And in either case these monogamic and polygamic peoples will be face to face as individuals merely to adopt the *modus vivendi* possible, or perish without it. This will consist in their acceptance of the domestic relations of inequality proper to the well being of both. This will be their union such as will have been adopted by the immigrants and natives in Africa. There will have been no miscegenation of the races; the individuals of which, respectively, will be as distinct at the end as at the beginning of any one such imperial process. In such unions there will not be governments of adult males, but only of monogamic men as lords over polygamic men as their commons. Nor in such will there be more of the monogamic than of the polygamic race. Nor of the monogamic race will there be a majority, at any time or place, not in union with individuals of the polygamic race. And without these conditions the unions formed, whether in Africa or Asia, will not be dissolved. These were as natural and persistent of reciprocal wants of these races for each other as are the unions of adult male and female in the monogamic family, or as are those of parents and their children in such family, or as were those of whites and negroes lately in this Republic.

The states of whites and negroes, though nominally so, were not really under governments of adult males. The states without slaves were so, but so were not the states with slaves, which were really under governments of proprietary male parents. The adult male without parentage or property, in the sense of their participations in the state, was as without political value as if he did not exist.

Nor in states with slaves were the whites in the majority from any natural cause. Here the foreign slave trade had been arrested. Whites not able to procure slaves were forced to do without them. And there were more whites than negroes therefore in these states. And for the same reason there was a majority of whites not in unions with the negro. But this would not be the case with whites and lower races in Africa and Asia. Here the negroes had to be brought from Africa, and that importation was prohibited. There they were at hand in vast numbers, and to be had for the taking, and they would be taken in numbers possible by every capable white man. There were thus in either Africa or Asia unequal races in states not under governments of adult males, of which the stronger race were the most numerous. Nor of this were the majority without the union with the lower race. And as without these conditions the union had not been dissolved in this Republic; they will not be dissolved without them in Africa or Asia.

And the unions here were not dissolved without these conditions. If these states had not been under governments by appointments of adult males the immigrants and their descendents, of whom there was a majority of such males, would not have taken the government of the Republic. Without this there had been no secessions. And without this there had not been the liberation of the slaves; or if the whites had not been more numerous than the blacks there had not been whites without slaves. Or any whites therefore to desire their liberations, or, if of the whites constituting the majority of the adult males the greater number had not been without slaves, and without unions, therefore, with the lower race, there had not been the dissolutions of the unions that did occur.

And as in the states of unequal races to be formed in Africa or Asia there will not be either governments of adult males or majorities of whites, or majorities of these without unions with lower races, it is reasonably certain that the unions there or elsewhere will not be again dissolved.

And this becomes the more certain when we consider that to the dissolution of such unions, once formed, there must be the aversions to them of both the races involved, or of the states of these races united, or of other human states in which there are not such unions. And there were not such aversions to them.

The higher race will have no such aversion, since with liberty of action they will have entered into them only as they shall have been agreeable; and for the further reason that, in supporting itself upon such foreign territory, it will want the help of natives. And for the yet further reason that if it do not have the help it will have the hostility of natives. And to its own establishment and continued existence upon the lands of natives, it must absorb or expel them; absorption will be profitable, expulsion expensive. There were absorption in such unions, expulsion ending in extermination without. And, from both interest and humanity, it will favor unions.

When America was colonized it was under Indians, whose unions with the whites might have helped them greatly. It is not clear, perhaps, that they could have united with the whites, but it is clear that, not uniting with the Teutonic whites, at least, they have been exterminated by them. And so must be other natives under like conditions; and the wars with Indians, and the waste of life and means, and the terrors of frontier life, attest the costs of exterminating a native race. And interest, without the help of humanity, will persuade an invading to spare a native race. And as the one can spare the other but in uniting with it, it will unite with it, and will not be averse to that union to which, by such considerations, it will have been impelled.

Nor will the lower races be averse to such unions with the higher. They may be singularly savage, as were the Indians, and so be able to resist absorption, as have the Indians, so that of them and whites there may be no such unions. And to such hypothetical unions — not facts accomplished — they may be unalterably averse. But the races already in such unions will not be averse to them. Nor will the weaker race be so averse, as might be the stronger. The weaker were to the stronger as were the woman to the man, or the offspring to the parent, in the monogamic family. And as, before they were sensible of their reciprocal fitnesses for each other, the woman might be averse to marriage with men, and children to the discipline of parents, and to the family requiring it, so the inexperienced, weaker race may be averse to an union for life with the stronger, and to the disciplines that union may require. But, experienced and sensible of its reciprocal attachment to such race, and of the fact that it can continue to exist but of its relation to such race, it will not only not be averse to that relation, but will be as true to it and conservative of it as is the wife to that of marriage or children of the family. And of this truth there is proof in the experiences of this Republic.

While the Indians, inexperienced of the advantages of unions with Teutonic immigrants, continued hostile, and have been exterminated, or are in the way of being exterminated, negroes, as savage, accepted such unions, became submissive, peaceful, loyal, and prospered and progressed in numbers and capacities as few peoples had ever done before.

They were submissive. Those were the best contented that were the most considerately and strictly ruled. And they were peaceful, though of native stocks that had never been at peace; they rarely assaulted each other, and more rarely a white man; and the instances were phenomenally rare in which a negro ever raised his hand against his master. And they were loyal. They guarded their master's home and property, lamented that they could not follow him to the field of battle, and staid behind to support and protect his family; and they prospered and progressed in a brief period from 450,000 to 8,000,000, and from savagery the darkest to a civilization more perfect than a negro had ever known before.

This might not have been so with the Indian, though it is not clear it would not. But there is ground for the belief that it will be so with the natives of Africa and Asia; that there will be no more aversions of the weaker race to unions formed than there were of negroes here.

There is nothing to suggest that the negro here would ever have made a serious effort to his liberation; there is much to show that an effort, however serious, would not have been successful. And, instructed by these experiences, we are warranted in assuming that states of unions of unequal races established elsewhere will not be subverted by the aversions to such unions of the races involved.

Nor will these unions be dissolved by the aversions to them of these states themselves. The states themselves will be to the unions of races in them, as were lately the slave states of this Republic to slavery. And while it may be doubted that any being, inanimate or animate, can be averse to the conditions of its own existence, it is quite certain that these states were not averse to that slavery of which they existed, and that if they had lived until of their own motions they had abolished slavery they would have lived indefinitely.

They did not avow slavery. While using it as a prostitute they did not venture to espouse it. The constitutional convention of the confederacy, existing and acting of that institution, adopted the clause in their ordinance that no foreign slaves should ever be imported. And the convention of South Carolina, considering that clause and admitting that it was wrong and that if the trade in slaves be piracy the slaves they held were plunder, accepted it as policy. Assuming a sentiment of the civilized world against slavery they proposed to propitiate that sentiment by the declaration that the wrong should go no further. The policy was denied. It was affirmed that if it were wrong to take slaves it were wrong to hold them; that this wrong could never become right by proscription; and that, acting in the cause of slavery, we could not hope to succeed in the establishment of a cause we had not the manhood to avow. But this mistaken sense of policy prevailed and slavery fell in all the states, but not from their aversions to it. Nor of this alone had there been the abolition of it in a single state.

Nor will they be abolished by the aversions of foreign states to their unions of unequal races. The feelings of foreign states as to such unions will be as are the feelings of other peoples as to unions of adults male and female. Themselves of such unions they will see no wrong in them. But if when such states are formed in Africa or Asia there be other states not of such unions they will be as are the monarchies of Europe to the democracy of this Republic. And, as of the aversions of monarchies to this democracy it has not fallen, so will not fall the future states of unequal races.

It is probable that when future states of unequal races begin to form at one place they will begin to form at others. And that when they shall be completely formed in Africa and Asia they will have been formed at all other places possible. And that there will be none but states of unequal races to object to unions of races in Africa or Asia. But if there be they will be in agamic stocks and polygamic tribes and castes. And these will be as impotent, whatever their aversions to such states, as are the Indian tribes to this democratic state.

The conservative feeling of the monogamic world has been averse to this Republic, and the radical in favor of it. In all the European states there being contests of classes as lords and commons for the patriarchal power, there is the feeling of lords, exercising that power over commons, against this Republic, in which the commons are victorious. But for the same reason there is the feeling of all commons in its favor. And there was the feeling of lords in favor of its institution of slavery, and of commons against it. And, as the governments of European states are yet in lords, the governments of Europe have been in favor of it, and their subjects generally against it. But no state of Europe, whatever its feeling, has ventured to attack this Republic for reason of its democracy; and the less has any one thought of attacking it for reason of its slavery. And as this Republic, while protecting slavery, was in relation to the states of Europe and the world as were the states of Africa and Asia to the outer world. And as this was not assailed by such states of Europe so will not be these in Africa and Asia.

But if they should be assailed they will be able to sustain themselves. If all the states of the earth had combined against this Republic for reason of its holding slaves they would not have suppressed it, or detached from it a single state. And the less chance were there that the outer world, combining against states in Africa or Asia for holding lower races in subjection, would suppress them.

It is thus clear that states of unequal races again forming will not be again suppressed as were the states of the confederacy. And the question of what mode of man will ultimately rule the coming human world is but the question whether states of unequal human races will again be formed, and for the reasons given they will be formed.

If not, the monogamic man is sufficient for the man possible. There is to be the man possible. And monogamic man, attaining to his maturity in any state from the possession by its commons of the patriarchal power, may put that power in adult males to be exercised by majorities to which there must be parties, major and minor, the major of which for the time of its majority will hold the government; which the minor by the means possible will take from them, in itself becoming major. And in this way of parties struggling for supremacy in states there is to be the man possible and the best man possible that he may be his most, if of the monogamic man there is to be the man possible. And it is quite clear that of parties so struggling against each other there is not to be such man. It is not clear that a state of such parties can long con-

tinue to exist. While it is clear that of parties so contesting for existence there will not be the most man possible. And equally clear that there will not be the best
man possible that he may be his most. And if, of monogamic man, self-differentiated, there be not such man,
there can and will be such man of unequal human races
united in a race of both. And these, necessary to the
man possible, when united again their unions will not be
again dissolved.

CHAPTER XL.

Such the theory of an essential being of this universe, in which is life, of which is nàture, of which is man to the man possible, it suggests two questions — the one as to the race of man, and the other as to the races, white and black, in this Republic. And as to the race, whether it be better ruled by its humanities or its inhumanities? And as to the races, white and black, in this Republic, whether they can continually coexist, or whether, if not, the one can long survive the other?

And first, whether the race of man shall be ruled by its humanities or its inhumanities? Its humanities are exhibited in its assertion of its individuals against the state and race, and its inhumanities in its assertions of its state and race against its individuals. It is of its humanities that no one race is allowed to enslave another, and that in monogamic states capital and other corporal punishments are being abated or abolished, and that convicts are cared for as they were not without their crimes; and that women are encouraged to assert themselves to independence of men, and children to independence of their parents; and that the indolent and improvident are to be provided for at the expense of the provident; and that the morally and mentally infirm are supported to an offspring so afflicted; and that insurgents are applauded and helped; and that operatives are enabled to dictate the terms of their employment; and that adult males without parentage or property are admitted to administer the property of parents to the uses of their dominant party in the state.

Such are the dictates of man's humanities, while of his inhumanities the dictates are that a superior may enslave an inferior human race to the betterment of both; and that punishments adequate to crimes be inflicted; and that the treatment of convicts be punishments rather than rewards for their crimes; and that women shall not assert their independence of men, or children their independence of their parents; or that the indolent and improvident be provided for at the expense of the industrious and provident; or the morally or mentally infirm be supported to an offspring in like affliction, to the weakening of the race; or that all insurgents be applauded and helped, or that operatives dictate the terms of their employment; or that adult males without parentage or property be admitted to administer the property of parents to the uses of a party.

. And, such the differences of man's humanities and inhumanities, it is clearly a question whether he be the better of the one than of the other, and this to be answered only by the answer to the further question, whether he be here to himself or to his race.

If men be here as individuals merely, and to the enjoyments of their current lives without obligations to do other than what may be agreeable, even in continuation of their race on earth, they were evidently the better of their humanities—allowing them, without detriment, the harmonious indulgence of their human sympathies.

But if they be not here as individuals merely, but as factors of a race of man possible, they are not so evidently better of their humanities. Such man possible were the most man at any one time possibly able to subsist in safety upon the garnered products of the cultured earth. And to this he were the man, in character and conduct, best fitted to cultivate the earth to its utmost products, and to garner these and conserve and share them to the most men able to subsist upon them. And without such inhumanities there were not such races of man.

Without the domestic enslavement of a weaker by a stronger race, there were not the peace, discipline and order between races possible; or, without these, the provisions for the safety and subsistence of either race possible; or, without these, the man of either race possible. And the less were there the man possible of all the human races in relation. Nor were there such in any state of punishments inadequate to crimes; or of convicts the better of their punishments; or of women in the places of men; or of children independent of their parents; or of indolents supported by the industrious; or of the morally or mentally infirm supported to offspring by the state. And if men on earth, therefore, be to themselves merely — who at any one time may happen to exist upon it, and who are without end or obligation, even to continue their race — and but to the pleasurable enjoyment of their individual lives, they were clearly the better of their humanities. But if they be here not to themselves merely at any time existing, but to the race of man possibly able to exist under the conditions, and under obligation to continue the race of man to the man possible, and to comply with the conditions of such continuation, they are as clearly not the better of their humanities, but of their inhumanities, so called, the every one of which were necessary to the discharge of such obligation to such end. And as man, for the reasons given earlier, is to his race and not to himself, he is the better of his inhumanities, as the individual is the better of his pains and labors in discharge of duty, however they be irksome. And mindful that the errors of life are more fatal than its crimes, we are bound to suppress our feelings of humanity, in derogation of the state and race, however proper they may seem to be, and however sincere our sense of their propriety.

And such the questions as to the race of man suggested by this theory, there is a question as to the races white and black of more immediate interest to the men of this Republic. The whites are monogamic and the blacks agamic naturally. And these are to each other in the Republic as were two fishes of different orders within a single shell. Without they be able to unite in a fish intermediate of both, able to form a single shell for both, each must grow and evolve into a shell of its own. And in this the one must exclude the other, or both must perish in the conflict for their individual existences. And so must it be with the whites and blacks of this Republic without they be able to unite in a race intermediate of both, as they did in the states of the South, each must grow and evolve into a civilization of its own; exclusive of the other one, or both must perish in such conflict for their individual existences.

Of the many simplicities exhibited by the men of this Republic of adult males, not the least is that of assuming that they, of their intentions simply, can so assimilate these races as that both can live under the civilization of the one, without the sense in either of its differences from the other, and without the assertion by each of a civilization of its own.

The first simplicity was in supposing that majorities of adult males, without the qualifications of parentage or property, could give to the monogamic state of proprietary male parents a constitutional government, or other government than that consisting in the volitions of a victorious party.

The next was in supposing that the constitution adopted would sustain the states as equal and independent sovereignties, while in a little less than eighty years one section of the states has remorselessly subjugated the other.

The next was in supposing that by attracting immigrants from Europe, they, the founders of the Republic and their descendants, would be helped, while a careful investigation will reveal that the descendants of Revolutionary sires were mainly at the South, and the descendants of immigrants were mainly at the North. And that the patriots of the Republic had procured from the pauper populations of Europe the masters of their posterity, which they intended to be free.

The next is in supposing that this Republic can exist continually in greatness and glory under no other government than that consisting in the volitions of a victorious party, the only reason and principle of whose existence is that it shall take for its partisans the largest share it can of the funds and fortunes of the state.

And the next, and not the least, is in supposing that the state at the instance of such party can so assimilate the races white and black, and monogamic and agamic, as that they shall form one consistent, homogeneous and normal human state — a supposition as reasonable as that at the instance of such party the two shell fishes in the single shell shall so assimilate each other into one of both.

It is not clear, perhaps, that the sensible men of the Republic really indulge' in this illusion.

When, from continual immigration, the states of the North acquired the population of adult males to take the government, they took it, as they were bound to do, and when the states of the South would not submit to this they were invaded and subjugated, as they were bound to be.

And when, at the instance of Mr. Johnson — then President, by the death of Mr. Lincoln — the subjugated whites of the South proposed to join with the Democrats of the North and out-vote the Republicans and take the government from them, that party disfranchised whites and gave the elective franchise to their negroes. And doing this, and so assisting the right of negroes to participate in the government equally with whites, some sensible men of that party, to be consistent in assisting the political equality of negroes, have been obliged to affirm their natural equality also. And from that affirmation, and not from real belief in the fact, they assume it to be true, and act upon it as if it were. Others, dazed by the glittering generalities of our declaration of independence, and mistaking them for the gateway to a new career of human being, are more sincere in the belief that the individuals of all races are naturally equal, and differ but from differences of education, and that all can be trained by proper discipline into one homogeneous and consistent state.

But whether sincere or simulated, this belief, it is illusive. The political party, in government of this state, can not of its intentions cause the races, white and black, now in it to renounce their specific differences and become one more than they can the two different fishes in the single shell to renounce their specific differences and become one.

Nor without such renunciation can it cause these races to concur in a natural state of both more than it can cause the fishes, without such renunciation, to concur in a natural fish of both.

At no such dictation will the whites become the blacks. Nor will they miscegenate the blacks, under any order, into an intermediate race of both. Nor without this will they admit them to their families, fraternities, or governments, nor will they share with them employments, nor will the whites allow to negroes any employments they themselves may want from which they can exclude them. And the more numerous and more capable, and holding the governments of states, the whites can exclude the negroes from any employments they may want, and they will ultimately want every employment that can give to an individual the means of subsistence.

At present, with vast areas of land uncultivated — and capable, when cultivated, of supporting a population many times larger than that of the Republic now — there are many employments not wanted by white men, and in consequence the negroes yet live almost as well as do the

25

whites.   But this will not continue indefinitely; the negro, now helping the white, will come to be in his way, and when in his way will be removed.

It is only in admitting his inequality with whites, and respecting their sensibilities, and accepting the servile employments they may have to give him, that the negro can hope to share a state with whites, and for these courses of conduct he is every way unfitted.   He can not acknowledge an inequality he does not realize, or realize what they do not see, and what the whites themselves insist does not exist.   Nor, in natural assertion of himself as a negro, can he respect the sensibilities of whites in asserting themselves as such.   But, beside this, he is a lower animal, and in the males of lower animals at times there is a madness from sexual excitement, which, in the male negro, at such times, is resistlessly attracted by the white female, and there are those shocks to the finer sensibilities of the whites — enough to antagonize the races, if there were nothing more.   Nor will he accept the servile offices the whites may have to give him, nor will he fit himself for such acceptance, but, instead, will be educated as white men are, and to do what white men will have to do, and not those things which they will have to do in subordination to the whites.   And necessary, therefore, to the continuing coexistence of these races in this Republic that to the negro there be courses of conduct to supplement the white man, they are in every way unfitted for such courses.   And the expectation that, at the instance of a party possessed of the government, these races will so assimilate as that neither will be sensible of its separate existence, and so concur in a natural and normal state of both, is utterly illusive.

Antagonisms must occur, and become more intense as they approach.   The civilization of one will not accommodate them both, and as it has been with the Indian, so must it be with the negro — that in contest for existence with a superior race he must give way if that involve his existence.

And such the fate of the negro, not greatly better will be that of the white man. He will be able to suppress the negro as he has the Indian, and for a time, during which, from his great advantages, he will be able to impress and oppress other peoples of the earth. But under government of a party of adult males that party and the state it governs must come under dominion of its leader, becoming a tyrant, who will defend it as he can from aspirants to take it from him, until such state shall be too wasted to preserve its separate existence. And to the question, therefore, as to what, in the lights of this theory, will be the fate of races white and black in this Republic, the answer is that the white must extinguish the black, itself to be extinguished in the war of tyrants, actual or would-be, for its government.

Nor is this pictured prediction one of unwarranted gloom. States must grow old, as do individuals, and such eruptions, necessary to the ending of a state, are analogous to the eruptive ailments that close the lives of individuals, while to the present whites and blacks in this Republic, there are prospects of more pleasant lives than are open to many other peoples of the earth.

The negroes, more elevated in the scale of humanity by the discipline of slavery, are in situations to give themselves, with little labor, the means to satisfy their every want. They are safe from ills and injuries and from the consequences of their own superstitions, passions and imprudences, by the superior civilization of the whites — into the equal of which no negroes have ever entered before. It will be long, and not perhaps within the lives of any now living, before the inevitable war of races will begin, and when it does it will be long before it will exhibit the barbarities of wars between negroes in Africa, or agamic peoples elsewhere. And as the pleasurable enjoyment of their individual lives without consideration of their state or race possible is all the negroes ask for, it may be safely said that no generation of negroes, or other agamic peoples, had ever such prospects as have these.

Nor are those of the whites less fair. They are coming to be scarcely more considerate of their state or race than are the negroes, and are scarcely less eager in the enjoyment of their individual lives. They have more abundant means for the satisfaction of their wants; their civilization and position in the human world secure them against injuries until the war of races shall really begin. And in that they will not be apt to suffer more than they have from their war with Indians. And pending, or after that, they will have nothing more to dread until there shall be the usurpation of the state by a victorious party leader, when prominent men will suffer. These will doubtless be advised, as were such men at Rome, that it would be agreeable to the Emperor that they dispose of themselves, and they will doubtless be as reluctant to follow such advice. But the common people, not prominent, will be apt to have as pleasant and peaceful lives as they ever had before, and as did the people of Italy, who prospered as much, or more, in the earlier ages of the Empire than they had done in those of the Republic.

The prospect, therefore, of a war of races, ending in the extinction of the negro and the establishment of an empire, in extinction of the present democratic state, is not insufferably gloomy to the whites and negroes of the Republic now. They and their immediate descendants will have died long before either event, while, in the meantime, they and their immediate offspring will have had more pleasant lives than have had other peoples of the earth. And with this they are apt to be, and seem to be, content, though neither may hope to leave on earth an indefinitely existing state or race.

And thus it is that while the theory of an essential being of the universe, in which is life, of which is nature, of which is man to the man possible, is in disaffirmance of the individual as against the race, and of the humanities, so-called, by indulgence in which the individual may hope to sustain himself as such against his race, and in disaffirmance also of the proposition of a victorious party in this Republic to so assimilate its races, white and black, as that they will form into but one natural and normal state, there is nothing to show, or suggest, that the theory is not true, or that man, accepting its truth in his every act to the continuance of his existence and as the condition to such continuation, should not admit it to be true.

CHAPTER XLI

BUT ANOTHER QUESTION OF MORE IMPORTANCE TO THE MEN OF THIS REPUBLIC.

And that the question whether the Republic shall end in contests of adult males for its spoils, or, surviving these, shall assert itself to continued existence as a natural patriarchal and normal monogamic state.

The natural and normal monogamic state is of monogamic families, each under the authority actual, or traditional, of its proprietary male parent, in whom is the patriarchal power of government, consistent with the proprietary powers of liberty and property, in his family. And in the male parents of such families together, there is the patriarchal power of government, consistent with the proprietary powers of liberty and property in the individuals of the families composing the state. And the normal monogamic state, therefore, is under the patriarchal power of its male parents, in which each has rightfully an equal voice as to the rights and liberties of its individuals.

But of parents some are male and some female. And of these parents some have acquired, or inherited, properties for the support of their families, and some have not, and of these those only holding these properties can rightfully say in what proportions and manner they be applied to the uses of the state, whose fully qualified patriarchs, therefore, are its proprietary parents in office, whether the families be of parents living or of parents dead. And the normal monogamic state, therefore, is not a democracy, but an aristocracy of proprietary parents. And such states were the colonies when emancipated from Great Britain. In the colonists there were the proprietary rights of monogamic families, and in Great Britain there had been the patriarchal powers of the male parents. But the emancipation had been achieved by adult males, without the qualifications of either parentage or property. And these, thus taking the patriarchal power, retained it together with their inherent proprietary powers; and of these proceeded to form themselves into states, and these into the Republic, through parties of themselves, the major of which, during the time of its majority, should exercise the patriarchal power of government over the minor party, whose constituents, during its minority, should enjoy only their proprietary powers consistent with the patriarchal in the major.

This provisional state of adult males was necessary under the conditions. The proprietary male parents, actual or traditional, of the colonies, were not ready to assert themselves to the patriarchal power of a normal monogamic state. They were not sensible of such state, or of their ability to form it, or sustain it, and that there be states at all it was necessary that adult males, without the conditions of parentage or property, should form them.

But this provisional state was clearly in occlusion of an antecedent monogamic state of monogamic families. Without these there could not have been the adult monogamic males to form such state. And the question is whether that real monogamic state underlying the provisional Republic shall share its impending fate, or, surviving the Republic of adult males, shall assert itself to a continuing existence as such monogamic state among the states and races of the earth.

The fate of the Republic, as a state of adult males, is impending. Its parties are in mortal combat for its spoils. Neither, as the member of a democratic state, can survive the other; nor can the democratic state survive its members, when the occluded monogamic state must perish with it, or must survive it as a patriarchal state in which there are unequal races the one of which shall rule the other, or in which the Republic shall be the patriarch over foreign states.

The combat of parties for the spoils of the present state is mortal. They are the one in assertion of the power of the state to control its people, and the other of the power of the people. to control the state. And in this contest the party of the people must prevail. That of the state can offer little more to its active partisans than a continuation of the honors and rewards of the offices they already hold. That of the people can offer to its partisans without offices not only the offices. held by the others, but shares of such other plunder of the state as they may be pleased to take. And such offer the majority of adult males must accept. They are the people, each egoistic, and moved only by a sense of his individual interests. These prompting him to his share of the public fund, with nothing to counteract them but the powers of the state to protect it, that power must be insufficient. The people's party, therefore, must ultimately take the fund upon which the state subsists, and with it the state, to the extinction of the party of the state defending it. And the people's party, therefore, must prevail over that of the state, if under no other motive than that of its spoils.

But as further inducements to its majority, that party can offer to support labor against capital, and operatives against employers, and to tolerate strikes and condemn trusts, and to sustain the demands of strikers that no others take their vacant places, and that the state be not allowed to protect itself by injunctions against evils threatened, and to approve combinations of laborers and condemn those of capitalists, and to require that the state shall educate the people, and that criminals be treated kindly, and that convicts be cared for as they were not before their crimes, and that majorities of such adult males without property shall put bonds upon their states and municipalities for propertied minorities, resisting them, to pay.

And it is not possible that the people can resist such offers, or fail of a party to accept them in dissolution of the state, and of the party of the state, and in such acceptance become other, ultimately, than an unarticulated mass of unrelated individuals, without other government than that of their individual volitions.

Or this, or the party of the state must assert itself under a party leader to its government, who thus becomes an arbitrary monarch, to the extinguishment of the people's party. And thus the combat is mortal. And to this are the experiences of this Republic.

Of these parties — of the state and people — the first were Whigs and Tories, the Whigs affirming the right of the colonists to govern themselves, and the Tories the right of England to govern them. The next were Democrats and Whigs, the Democrats affirming the right of the people forming the state to control it, and the Whigs the right of the state, so formed, to control its people. The next were Republicans and Democrats, the Republicans affirming the rights of the people, and the Democrats the powers of the state. And the next and present parties are Democrats and Republicans, the Democrats now affirming the rights of the people and the Republicans the powers of the state. In each of these contests, up to that now pending between the Democrats as the party of the people and the Republicans as the party of the state, that of the people has prevailed. And if it do not now prevail, it will be for the reason that the people do not accept the Democratic party as their exponent, but will have determined that the Republican party will do more for them in partitioning the state they now hold than can the Democratic, seeking it. Nor is it quite clear that, if the Democratic party shall secure a popular majority, the Republican party will admit the legality of the election and surrender the state.

At the end of the Civil War, when it was proposed
that the men of the South should join the Democrats of
the North and take the state from the Republicans, that
party disfranchised whites and gave the electoral vote to
negroes.   When Tilden was elected, but by a questionable
majority, over Hayes, President Grant was required to
withhold from him the office.

And now, when the Republic has taken jurisdiction
over Atlantic and Pacific islands, and has vested its President with an army of an hundred thousand men to sustain
it — all of whom hope for promotion — and has many thousands more of citizens hoping to share the profits of their
administration, and has near one million pensioners, whose
pensions might be taken from them by the adversary party
coming into power, and many thousand civil officers who
might lose their places upon such event, it is not clear
that the people will not regard the Republican as their
party, and sustain that party in its possession of the state
by force.   So sustained and organized, it were invincible
by any force the victorious but unorganized Democratic
party could bring against it.

That party were less efficient than were the confederated Southern states; it were less inspired by a sense
of right than was the Confederacy; and that falling before
the Republic in the hands of the Republicans, so would
the Democratic party in assertion of its right to the state
by such election.

But if the Democratic party shall take the state from
the Republican, it will be but to take its place as the party
of the state against the Republican, or some other party
of the people.   And taking the place of the Republican
party as that of the state, it will take all its patriarchal
powers, and with them the jurisdictions asserted over
foreign islands, with its soldiers and citizens expecting
offices abroad, and pensioners and civil officers at home.
And then, if a people's party shall form against it, as it
must, and secure a majority against it, that party will be

apt to repudiate the election and withhold the state. But if it shall not, still another people's party will take the state, who will not, and can not, give it up to another party of the people.

Upon the $1,000,000,000 expended yearly by the party of the state so many will come to live, with nothing else to live on, as to constitute an invincible army to defend it. This army will form under a party leader, who will at once become the monarch; or, without this, it will fritter itself in factions to a mob of unordered individuals, who, to exist, must have their tyrant.

The people's party, therefore, now or at some future time, must take the state by force, itself to become subject to an arbitrary monarch, when the Republic of adult males, as a democracy, will cease to exist. And then the question will arise whether this monogamic state of proprietary male parents shall cease with it, or survive it.

It can survive, if, before the extinction of the present state of adult males, it shall form into functionaries of its patriarchal and proprietary powers in supplement and support of each other to a state of both, in which there will not be these functionaries warring on each other to the destruction of the monogamic state, but in which there will be these reinforcing each other in support of this monogamic state to tutelary jurisdiction over the stocks, tribes and castes of agamic and polygamic races.

To this it must withdraw from the negroes of the Republic the elective franchise, and require them to be represented in assertion of their civil rights, as are infants by their guardians. It must also apply the same rule to the lower races in Cuba, Porto Rico, Hawaii, and the Philippine and Samoan Islands, of which it has taken jurisdiction. And if this monogamic state were not too much demoralized by the state of adult males it carries, it were capable of such assertion of itself. It has the power. In such union of its functionaries it has made one section of its states, originally sovereign, to subjugate another, and it has

disfranchised white masters and enfranchised negro slaves
and put them over masters. And doing so much of evil
to its own monogamic race, it easily has power to do so
much of good to lower races as would consist in forcing
them to live as may be best for them and the race of man.

But it has been much demoralized. To its integrity
as a normal monogamic state, it must affirm the rite of
marriage, and that this be indissoluble and for the lives of
parties, and that adults marry early and that they have the
children possible, and that they educate their children to
the works they have for them to do in support of the
family, to the support of the state; and to this that the
male parent, or the one in *loco parentis*, have the legal
estate in the property of the family or ward; and that of
this he make application personally to the uses of the
family or ward, and through legislators to the uses of the
state; and that while every such actual or appointed parent
be an elector of representatives, to declare the rights and
liberties of individuals, only those holding such property
shall be an elector of representatives to the disposition of
such property. And such its integrity that, under the
state of adult males, it has been much perverted.

It is not considered the duty of adults, male and female,
to marry, or to marry early, or that their marriages be indissoluble and for life, or that of these there be the children
possible, or that these be educated by their parents to
what they have for them to do in support of the family, in
support of the state, but that the state shall educate them
to the nothing it has for them to do — and to their unfit-
ness, therefore, for duties to the family and state. Nor
is it considered that the propertied parent alone should
have exclusive disposition of his property, but that majorities of states and municipalities without properties may
put it under bonds and assessments, opposed by such
parents, of the proceeds of which the unpropertied majorities will have the use. Nor is it considered that such
parents, whether with or without property, shall have

exclusively the power to appoint the legislators to determine the rights and liberties of individuals.

And such the breaches of integrity in this real monogamic state from the intrusion of the state of adult males, it is not certain that it can emerge from the fragments of that state and assert itself to a tutelary jurisdiction of the lower races with which it may come in contact. But if it should it would much advance the human race.

It would present to monogamic peoples coming after to their patriarchal, with their proprietary powers, an instance and example of how these powers can be exercised in concert to a normal monogamic state. It would show them that while they can not be exercised apart and through parties of adult males in contest for the state, but only through parties of proprietary parents, both affirming their proprietary and patriarchal powers, not in opposition to each other, but in supplement and support of each other, in sustaining the monogamic state to its tutelary jurisdiction over the states of lower races that they also become monogamic by induction, and so concur in the advancement of the human race through the monogamic race. It seems to be assumed that every generation of human individuals may act as though it were the last, and with no obligation but to provide for themselves. But the human race advances. The monogamic leads; and, in leading, can take with it the lower races as it did the negroes in the Southern states. And to such leadership the monogamic state may survive the state of adult males. But to this they must assert themselves as lords over such lower races as their commons to intermediate states of both, in which the monogamic peoples will have the patriarchal power, and those of the lower races the proprietary powers in subjection to that patriarchal in the monogamic race.

But it is to be feared that the people of this Republic, discharged of the state of adult males, would not be capable of such jurisdiction. They accept that all men are equal, and that, among equals, equality is right, and that no one race, therefore, can rightfully take jurisdiction over another. To such assertion of themselves it were necessary, as I have said, that they withdraw the elective franchise from the negroes of. the Republic, and that, to their enjoyment of civil rights they, as infants, be represented by their guardians. And that to the lower races ·in Cuba, Porto Rico, Hawaii, and the Philippine and ·Samoan Islands, they apply the same rule, and this to the ˙betterment of them, and to the support of the monogamic race. But it is to be doubted that any large portion of our people would favor this policy, or that any party of the government will adopt it; or that, adopted by the government, it could be carried to effect with the party of the people necessarily against it.

And it is to be doubted in fact, that any monogamic commons, so coming to their patriarchal and proprietary powers can directly so exercise them together in assert-·ing the supremacy of the monogamic race. But it is ·rather to be expected that, though the monogamic race be destined to lead the other races of the earth, and this through combination of its powers, this continuation will ·occur incidentally and unconsciously, as did that through which the whites became masters of the blacks in the earlier years of the Republic.

In that the patriarchal and proprietary powers of the monogamic whites were combined to their exercise upon the agamic blacks, who were singularly benefited by such exercises. But it is to be doubted if any white was conscious of the significance of his act; or that any state of these whites, denying civil and political rights to the blacks, was conscious of inaugurating a new era in human history, or that in placing unequal races in natural relations of inequality to each other it was giving to the monogamic race its proper position as the leader of the human race, or that it was combining the powers patri-˙archal and proprietary of the monogamic race to their proper office of tutelary jurisdiction over lower races, but there is reason that it thought then, as it seems to think now, that the only office of these powers is in sustaining the state and people of that state of males in relation to each other, so that alone, if necessary, or with the other states of the Republic, it might continue its existence to the ends it might appoint. And it is to be expected, therefore, that, while the monogamic race must lead the human world, it must come to that leadership without the conscious intention of its states or individuals. And it is to be doubted that this Republic, so discharged of its government by adult males, can so assert itself.

But it were of advantage to itself and the human race if it should. It were better for itself that it live in peaceable superiority to lower races under it and contributing to its support, than die from the contests of parties for its spoils. And it were better for such races that they have such ruler to order their activities and restrain them from their vices, as would this Republic in such superiority. And it were of advantage to other monogamic states, not yet at their majorities, to have such example of how a monogamic state, emancipated, can start on its career as such, without such parties of adult males, or the wars of parties for its spoils.

Of its powers to exercise such jurisdiction, as I have said, there can be no question. It has subjugated one section of its own states admitted to be sovereign, and taken the lives and liberties of its people without due process of law, and their properties without just compensation, and has inflicted upon them cruel and unusual punishments in separating slaves and masters, and have made other than gold and silver a currency for the payment of debts, all but the last of which were averse to natural right, and all to the constitutional compact of these sovereign states under which the Republic exists. And doing these things against its own people, having every claim on its forbearance, and to their irreparable injury, it could easily exercise such benignant power over lower races, with no such claims upon its forbearance, as would consist in forcing them to live as they can to the betterment of themselves and of the human race, and so advance rather than obstruct the course of Providence in man.

But for the reasons stated it is to be doubted that it can so assert itself, and to be feared, therefore, that it must await its not distant end in the war of parties for its spoils, and the question of whether it shall so assert itself, or perish of its parties, is of importance to the men of the Republic.

They may not be able to act upon it, but the sense of it may moderate the zeal of parties, or cause an intermediate party to arise and assert the existence and interests of the real state. There is no such party now, but such party might arise, and, if not able to assert the real state, might hold the balance between the parties now at issue, and so protract the existence of the artificial state. From this have come advantages no people have ever known before. These may be continued so long as the present state may last. In considering the question they may find the way by which, if this real monogamic state can not assert itself, others coming after may; and, in every one of its aspects, therefore, the question of whether this Republic shall end in the contests of parties for its spoils, or shall assert itself to a continued existence as a monogamic state, is of importance to the men of this Republic.

It is important to them as individuals that this Republic of adult males shall last for the lives of them and their immediate descendants. It is important to them as members of this monogamic state that it assert itself to a continued existence as such state. So doing it may live to indefinitely distant ages in benefits and blessings to the human race. Without this even its name may be forgotten. And as they may not live for themselves alone, as the boon of life to them is upon the condition that they continue human life in the ways possible to the man possible, it is important to them that they comply with this condition. It were virtue to do so, and vice not to do so, and as the practice of virtue is its own reward, and the practice of vice its own punishment, however we be unable to figure out their values, the men of this Republic will be the better or the worse as they consider or refuse to consider the question of whether this monogamic state shall or shall not continue its existence, and, when the state of adult males shall fall (as fall it must) from the contests of its state and people, whether the real monogamic state shall fall with it or survive it.

And though it may make little difference to the present generation, who will have ended their pleasurable lives before the fall, it will be of importance to that providence, of which is man, that this generation shall do the work of which it may be capable. This will consist in its taking patriarchal jurisdiction over weaker states. Through the Republican party, it has now imperial jurisdiction over Atlantic and Pacific islands. But that must become patriarchal and exact that these foreign states shall execute the orders of this Republic in the relations of their races; and that the stronger rule the weaker. But it is to be doubted that these orders can be issued.

The Republican party exists from the denial of the right of any one people to rule another, and it can not, therefore, assert directly even its imperial jurisdiction over these states. And leading men, under whatever name, opposed to the Republican party, were as unable as is that party to assert such jurisdiction. A party affirming the right and power of this Republic to such jurisdiction over weaker foreign states to be benefited by it might be formed; there were offices and emoluments to attract a larger party than the Republican. But there is an indisposition in men opposed to the Republican party to assert such power as there is among the Republicans themselves.

Apprehensive of this, I lately addressed many distinguished men not in that party proposing a party to the end that this Republic take jurisdiction over the foreign states within its power, that there be the peace and order in them possible only of their peoples in natural relations to each other. But, as might have been expected, from no one of them have I had reply. And from their utterances on other occasions, I gather that, in their belief, or in their acceptance at least, the right of self-government is in every individual of every state, and at any age, is inalienable. And there is reason to believe, therefore, that however desirable it be that this Republic emancipate itself and inaugurate a patriarchal age, there is ground to doubt of that achievement.

CHAPTER XLII.

I thus complete the work of a tolerably extended life. More than fifty years ago I ventured to propose the legitimation of the foreign slave trade. There were states at the South of the Republic with slaves, and states at the North without them. Those of the South had grown upon a laboring population of slaves and their increase, imported from Africa, and those of the North upon a laboring population of immigrants from Europe. But importations had been prohibited and immigration promoted. And while the states at the South could advance but upon the natural increase of its laboring population, those of the North could advance not only upon the natural increase of its immigrants already there, but upon the hundreds of thousands coming yearly. These all went to the North and soon acquired, individually, the elective franchise, while the slaves at the South were individually without it.

And as the government of the Republic had been made dependent upon the volitions of a majority of its voting population it seemed certain that the states at the North in virtue of their larger voting population, merely, would be able to take the government as soon as a party should be formed to that issue. And it seemed certain that to that issue a party would be formed; that when formed it would be forced by the proclivities of individual interest, as absolute as those of physical gravitations, to take the government through the election of a sectional President and a majority of Congress; that to that the states of the South would not submit, but would secede from the Union. That to this the states of the North would not submit, but would take what steps they could to hold them. And that a collision would result, the consequences of which could not then be éstimated. But it also assumed that if the foreign slave trade were reopened so that the states of the South could get what slaves they wanted at importers prices they would take them and advance *pari passu* with the North. That men of the North would take them at such prices in place of pauper immigrants, even then becoming troublesome. That the States of the. South would see in this security to their institution, and would not be more concerned about the election of a President and Congress by the vote of a party at the North than about any previous election by a party opposed to that favored by themselves. .

And it seemed also that if the South were to demand the reopening of the foreign slave trade as the alternative of secession the North would accept that alternative. The leading interests at the North were dependent upon slavery at the South. From having slaves the South was agricultural. From not having slaves the North was mechanical and commercial. The South raised the raw material which the North manufactured and commerced; and was richer of the plantations of the South in the hands of masters over slaves than if she owned them.

But these without slaves had been without products. Without the products of plantations the factories and ships of the North had been without value. And interest, the. declivity down which human action goes, would have moved the North to favor the enlargements of slavery at greater losses than she would incur in the reopening of the foreign slave trade.

And, seeing these things, I did what I could to bring the South to a sense of the situation and to make that demand. But she would not make it. And I then believed and now believe that if she had made it, it would have been granted. That the election of Mr. Lincoln and a majority of Congress would have been without significance. That there had been no secession consequent; and no firing on Fort Sumpter; and no invasion of the South; and no loss of a million lives; or the liberation of slaves, or their elective franchise through which to dominate their former masters; or the million pensionaries; or the war of classes threatened at the North; or the war of races threatened at the South; or the charge upon this government to exercise over the inhabitants of other states the discipline for the exercise of which it subjugated the South.

But for no reasons then presented could the South be induced to make the demand. She was content to practice it as a wrong but not to affirm it as a right—if the trade be piracy the slave is plunder—and she preferred the holding of the slave as plunder to the task of removing from the act the brand of piracy, and to prostitute the institution rather than espouse it. And, the demand not made, the consequences came, and for a time it seemed that the union of unequal races, so full of promise to the race of man, was ended here without the prospect of its beginning elsewhere; and that with it must end the labors of my earlier life.

But, after a short time to my private fortunes, I concluded to resume the subject. Regarding nature as the will of God in power and purpose from the axis of the universe; and believing that of this there was man; and that in man the power was in parents, and purpose in their offspring. And that in monogamic man advancing to the man possible there had come to be classes of families unequally able to provide the means for the safety and support of the state—the capable class termed lords and the incapable commons—and that in the lords there was power and in the commons purpose. And that of these there was ultimately to be the man possible.

But seeing that in every progressive monogamic state the commons, of the same race as the lords, must encroach upon them and take from them the patriarchal power and use it unilaterally on themselves and lords, or upon a lower race of commons (under them), as lords. And believing that the colonists of this Republic were the first commons that had ever come by ordered evolution to such power over their lords; and that they were the first, therefore, in the position to determine whether they should go alone in exercise of that power through parties major and minor, of themselves, upon themselves, or exercise it as patriarchs on a race of agamic or polygamic peoples as their proletariate—and believing, also, that they had made their election to exercise it on themselves, and not upon a lower race; and that in this they were not acting of the nature of the word of God from the axis of the universe, but were departing from it to an artificial state of their own invention in which the motive principle was not the word of God in nature, but the resolution of their own individual volitions. And believing that they were not capable of such substitution, and that their state must perish in the attempt; and that in the attempt to perpetuate the existence of their artificial state they must take jurisdiction over foreign states in which there are unequal races; that over these they can efficiently exercise their foreign jurisdiction only by putting the superior races in their dependencies over the inferior, that in this way they will induce foreign states to unions of unequal races, of which they will have been themselves incapable; and will have put them in the perpetuity of progress and well-being necessary to kindred natures in relation.

And believing this, and that this Republic is at the point at which human nature, accomplishing the man possible of a single race, is ready to turn unto states of unequal races to a yet better and more abundant man. And that it is the hinge, therefore, on which human nature turns from states of single races to states of different races united. And that, though it has not itself been able to make that turn, I have come to realize that its experiences in what it has done and in what it has not done, are most important. And that to this cause of man on earth there can be no work so profitable as that which truly tells what those experiences have been.

This I have tried to do; and show, not what men think they are, but what they are in fact. And that the experiences of this Republic are of more importance than those of any other human state that has yet existed is in the fact that they give examples of a natural and an artificial human state. The state of this Republic, through the agamic, polygamic and monogamic stages of its existence, and through the earlier periods of the monogamic stage until the commons had become possessed of its patriarchal power, exhibits a perfect example of a natural human state from exercise of patriarchal and proletariate powers. And after its commons had become possessed of those powers and had put them in parties of adult males — the major party to exercise the patriarchal powers and the minor the proletariate, it exhibits as perfect an example of an artificial state. And that the natural is in every way as superior to the artificial state as is the living to the extirpated plant.

While the colonists held slaves, and forced them to the monogamic mode of life and to the industries and economies necessary to their well-being, there was a continuation of the natural human state and a state without its equal in the moral and physical elevation of its people. But when it rose above its proletariate of slaves to take a proletariate of its own people, in no other way different from its patriarchs than in being on the opposite side to them — it ceased to be natural, and became the artificial product of man's invention in constructing a state not of his nature but of his intelligence. And while this state is lauded and its men are exultant at the thought of their having superseded nature, there is ground for the conclusion in the mind of every rational man that it is destined to a ruinous end, with but the hope that, if it may not itself continue in the race of man to the man possible through unions of unequal races, it may yet initiate such unions in its foreign dependencies or may enable them to continue the march of man to the man possible.

But the more conclusive reason for the continuation of this work was in the facts—*first*, that in this Republic there are, or were, two moving dioramas, the one of human life in human nature, and the other of human life not in human nature; and, *next*, that in these dioramas there are the decisive evidences of an universe of infinite being finite.

The more obvious instances of human life in human nature are the human families in which the individuals — male and female parents and male and female offspring — represent life, and the families, agamic, polygamic or monogamic, the nature of that life. Each such family is the unit being possible of the individuals living under the conditions to their best and most. And the forces by which the individuals are drawn into the relations of the family are as real as those by which the constituents of the individuals are drawn into the relations of which there is the individual. The forming forces of the individual are insensible, while the individual is sensible. And so the forming forces of the family are insensible, while the individuals of the family are sensible. And the forces that form the individual, or the family, are as real, though invisible, as are the individual and the family.

There are scarcely less obvious instances of human life in human nature in the states of monogamic families.

In every such state the families are charged with their individual existences, which charge they can execute in no other way than each in being to its most and best under the conditions. This requires that it shall produce and conserve provisions for its safety and subsistence possible. Of this some are capable and some are not. . And the families holding such provisions prescribe the conditions upon which they shall be shared by those not holding them. And are in relation to such incapables as are parents to their children. And of the laws declared by the capables and accepted by the incapables there is the nascent monogamic state, as of the laws of parents charged with off-spring there is the nascent monogamic family.

Such was the human life in human nature of this Republic when it consisted, as it did at first, of masters and slaves. And such were the states of the South after slavery had been abolished at the North.

But after its abolition at the North, and since its abolition by the Republic, there is no such human life in human nature here, but only a human life striving to live without nature.

The human nature of human life is an insensible moral being accepting sensible and physical lives to the positions in relation to each other, in which they can be best and most themselves to the family and state the best and most. And, as such, it is the tutelary genius of such of such life. But in Northern states before the Civil War there was no such nature, nor is there such nature in this Republic now. That nature was of the word of God to human life at this earth, delivered through universal nature, from the axis of the universe. But the human lives of this Republic do not accept it; the individuals possessed of their lives prefer a nature of their own invention, such as may result to them from parties of themselves battling with each other for the patriarchal power. This is not of nature, or of the nature of the word of God, more than are the parties of such nature. And in this, therefore, this Republic is now a moving diorama of life without nature, as originally it was such of life in nature. And I was instant that states of after ages should have the record of these facts, however they be repudiated or ignored by this and other states existing now.

And a yet more potent reason for the continuation of this work was in the fact that in this Republic there are conclusive evidences of an universe of infinite being finite.

The Republic itself is a being finite, since it is not infinite, but is of beings infinite. There can be no being finite but of beings infinite in reciprocal limitations of each other. And the Republic, therefore, is not only being finite, but is the finite of beings infinite. Of the finite of infinites there is necessarily an universe, and this as necessarily exclusive of all but infinite beings finite.

It is thus plain that this Republic is of the finite universe, and that this is of infinite being finite is further apparent in the fact that there is no being infinite seen by us. Our axioms, geometrical and trigonometrical, are not true, nor are the problems they establish truths. It is not true that the included angles of a triangle are actually equal to two right angles, or that the exterior angles are equal to four right angles, or that the points of any two straight lines are at the same distances from each other, or that there are straight lines, or that these can be parallel. If this were so, then these lines and angles were infinite. And the axioms are in assertion of an infinite universe which does not exist, but only a finite universe, where lines and angles, however they be without sensible limits, diverge from one point to meet at another, however distant, within the finite universe. With these facts our observations and experiences are consistent. And from their importance I would give them further treatment, but the infirmities of extreme age prevent me. And I must submit the work as it stands, with but this further remark: that this state of being in which we are is an universe of universes; that there is a whole universe of atomic infinites, the one dynamic and the other static, and the one life and the other nature, and the one in eccentric radiations of dynamic life from the axis of the universe and the other in concentric radiations of nature, meeting and coercing life in its radiations from such axis. But that this universe of infinites in reciprocal limitations of each other on that axis is of infinitessimal units, each an universe of infinitessimal infinites in limitations of each other. That these units occur at the every possible point of contact between the radiations, eccentric and concentric, of life and nature, and these develop and evolve, as, under the conditions of continued coincidences, becomes possible. Each, thus an original unit and universe of infinites in limitations of each other, becomes an unit and universe of the being possible at every such point. And such the unit and universe of every infinitessimal being finite, of which the one infinite is dynamic and the other static, and the one life and the other nature; such is the moment of electric force, of which the minus is life and the plus nature; and such the spark, of which the heat is life and the light nature; and such the molecule of elemental matter, of which the negative atom is life and the positive nature; and such the compound matter molecule, of which the acid is life and the base nature; and such the sun, whose explosive space center is life to its constrictive crust, and atmosphere nature; and such the earth, whose space center is its life and its crust, and atmosphere its nature; and such the plant, whose staminate principle is its life to its pistillate its nature; and such the animal, whose male is its life and its female its nature; and such the man, whose man is his life and whose woman is his nature; and such the family of man, whose parents are life to their offspring nature; and such the states of man, in which the capables are life to the incapables nature. Each is an universe of that being possible at, from and about the point of its existence in the general universe of infinite being finite. So it is, within itself, an universe of that peculiar being of which it is, and so it is the exclusive being of that universe. And such is the being finite, and such the moment of force, and such the spark, and such the molecule of elemental matter and of compound matter, and of the sun and earth, and the plant, animal and family and state of man.

But such is not this Republic now, and such is not the state of any individual men, who have agreed to divide its powers, vital and natural, between them, so that the major party shall have the vital powers and the minor the natural. These parties are in no sense to each other as are. the parents and offspring of the family, or as are. the competent and incompetent families of the state. And of their volitional activities they can no more make a normal human state than they can make a vital man, animal or plant. There are two processes of man at this earth's surface — the one of human life into the human nature of it possible, and the other of human life, not into the human nature of it possible, but into the contrivances of the individuals at any time existing, by which each individual may get the better of others in using the properties of the state, accumulated by antecedent individuals. Of these powers the one is conservative and the other destructive of the state; and the one to the most and best man possible and the other to the least and worst. And to determine whether man at this earth is to the man possible of an essential being of the universe as announced in the title-page of this work, it is only necessary to determine whether he is here to the nature possible of his life, or only to the nature of his own invention. And as for the reasons given he is not here to a nature of his own invention, but is here to the human nature possible of his human life, we must conclude that he is here to the man possible of such being of the universe; and, as is declared in the title-page, that man at this earth is to the man possible of an essential being of the universe.

Lightning Source UK Ltd.
Milton Keynes UK
UKHW011429010219
336574UK00009B/654/P